Traditions, Lies from Birth

Volume #1

Mark Stroderd

2nd Edition

October 5, 2024

Traditions

Lies from Birth

Volume 1 – 2nd edition

Getting older and wiser is a wonderful thing. That said, what is wisdom? Or maybe a better question, what is wisdom today? Is wisdom the pursuit of an eternal relationship? Is wisdom the pursuit of financial independence? We could continue.

Life's paths of pursuit all end whether they are accomplished or not. Many reach the end of life's paths and learn they followed lies from birth, traditions of men. Enjoy the journey of **Christian** Hebrew Research of the divine and inspired Word of God from the original Hebrew text. Everything else is a translation.

Personal apologies to those who endured the 1st edition while I learn how to be a better writer.

No, this book was not an effort of one person. There were many who tolerated hours at restaurants and coffee shops. That said, there was one person that enjoyed my company, and was able to tolerate me more than the rest (smile). We shared a common passion to research the original Hebrew text. This book could not have been written without the influences, revelations of understanding, and thousands of hours of research provided by my friend Micah Coop. Thank you, Micah, only eternity can repay you for the love and joy you shared with me in this effort. It's amazing that the human body can survived the 55-gallon barrels of coffee that was consumed in this effort. Praying this book will represent our efforts to further reveal our Salvation in Jesus whose Hebrew name is Yeshua. Blessings to you and all you love.

Thank you to the most angelic wife a man could ever marry. With loving tears, I express my gratitude to My Sweet Lisa who loved me through this adventure. Thank you for enduring and loving me more each day. I have no idea how you do it. You are the most amazing wife on the planet. Blessings to you and all you love.

Table of Contents

Chapter 1 Uiitzr – Formed

<u>A Personal Note:</u>

First! You do not have to know Hebrew or the Hebrew alphabet to read this book! Everything you need to know about the original Hebrew text and the Hebrew letters will be provided with simple clarity throughout the book! By the time we get to the end of the book, your understanding of the original text will be enlightened (smile).

Many people experience life changing circumstances. Is it possible to share a near death experience that someone hasn't already told? That said, the percentage of people that experience these stories is small. Even fewer people experience more than one. Those experiences and a "~~little~~ lot of help from a friend" inspired the efforts to publish the *"Traditions – Lies from Birth"* series.

It's May 6, 2005, and I am in the Hospital ER. The doctor has just advised me that I have experienced a subarachnoid brain hemorrhage, and my brain has been reduced to half its size. She is short with her words and advises that the morphine has eliminated the pain, but my body is in shock, and she estimates it can only handle another fifteen minutes at my current blood pressure and heart rate. There is nothing more that medicine can do, and my only hope is prayer. The detailed life story of this event is in my book *"It's That Same Story Again"*. Yes, I prayed and literally within a minute my heart rate and blood pressure returned to normal.

It's May 7, 2005, and there are eleven of us prepared for surgery today. The surgeon announces to all of us that at least seven of us will not survive the surgery and since my scenario was the gravest that I would be first. He hands me a phone and tells me that I have five minutes to speak with my children.

An hour later I am sitting in my hospital room while my doctor from surgery advises me that subarachnoid brain hemorrhage was healed before the surgery procedure began. Literally, my head wasn't shaved, and nothing was done *by the doctors*. He expressed that they do not use the word "miracles" in medicine and then told me that since the hemorrhaging stopped that my body continue to heal itself and remove the blood from around my brain. And he continued…

It's May 20, 2005, and I am already back to work. I'm a software engineer and was sent to a new assignment for a company named Million Air at

Hobby Airport in Houston, Tx. After a few days I learned that the man leading their technology was the husband of the research nurse that documented my miraculous healing in the surgery room just two weeks prior.

I experienced four undeniable miraculous experiences within that two-week period. My search for why I am still alive continues to this day. That's what a near death experience did to me.

It's September 19, 2021, and I just visited another Bible Study. I've attended church and community Bible studies for more than four decades. At this time of my life, I rarely leave a community Bible study with anything to write home about. But this one was different. There were at least five Christians in the room that could understand the original Hebrew writing. Everybody in the room was Christian and openly believed in the Salvation Gospel. For the first time in my life, I am having a Bible study with Christians that know how to read and study Biblical Hebrew.

Everybody in the room reflected how the original Hebrew text of these verses being discussed applied to their Lord and Savior. Nobody in the room was anything but Christian. Everybody in the room was believers of our Savior! Nobody in the room could speak Hebrew but several knew the Hebrew alphabet and how to translate any Hebrew word from the original Hebrew scriptures. Without question they had a depth of understanding about scriptures that I was not familiar with. I had a lot to write home about! I didn't realize that I subliminally thought the phrase "Christian Hebrew" was an oxymoron. It was a four-hour Bible Study and still everyone there that day remembers my interruptive and obnoxious first visit (smile)!

My wife was not with me for that Bible study experience but when I returned home, she knew within a day that something was different, and life would never be the same. This book is not a life drama story, again, that is in my book series "It's That Same Story Again" and I promise not to mention it again.

It's November 1, 2021, and I can read Hebrew. That's correct. I learned how to read and study Biblical Hebrew in forty-five days. I wish you could hear me scream that this is not related to my intelligence! Biblical Hebrew is arguably the first language on earth and it's a heart language. Sure, smart people can learn it, but it only takes the desire of the heart to understand it. I am convinced that ANYBODY can learn Biblical Hebrew within a couple months. Recently I taught how to read and study Hebrew in a one-day, 8-hour class. It is truly that easy to get started. I have also witnessed a man that required only 17 days to learn what took me 45 days. It's truly that easy!

I continued diligently researching the original Hebrew scriptures until January 21, 2023, when I suddenly experienced a massive heart attack. The doctor told my wife that the severity of a heart attack is measured by the concentration of a particular protein in the blood and my protein level was the highest he had ever witnessed by a survivor. Five days later I leave the hospital and I am taking baby steps. I felt like it was my last day to live. Thankfully they did not do open heart surgery but did install four stents. There were complications.

From the moment I returned to my chair at home, my commitment to Hebrew research is a matter of life and death. I must document what I already know before my last day in this world. I learned Hebrew late in life and must document it for when my kids are old and will take the time to read it. That said, I will not write five paragraphs of preparations to say one sentence. I will not "sugar coat" what I have learned. I am trying to balance how to share information without being perceived as an "informant". Just know that I am a Christian and nothing I learned in my Hebrew research changed my Salvation. Biblical Hebrew validates the Gospel of Jesus is salvation. That said, prepare yourself for an amazing journey of Biblical understanding. When you cry, simply take a break, and talk to your Savior. When you get mad, simply put the book down for a couple days and pray. Despite the implied confidence portrayed in my words, this is my best effort to share what I have learned, and it is still incomplete. Despite my comments about the English translations, understand that I view them as simply being incomplete as well.

It's April 1, 2024, and I just taught my first 8-hour Learn Hebrew seminar. Yes, I practiced teaching this class with one student and it worked. The goal is to teach it well enough that the student loves the language and leaves with tools to exercise all the efforts of research discussed in this book. Yes, Hebrew is so simple that you can be introduced to it in one day and learn it in as little as three weeks! I proved it is easy to learn and plan to prove it again and again!

I pray that God will bless you in this journey.
Glory to the King.

Before explaining how easy it is to include the original Hebrew text in your Bible Study efforts, let's review a simple example of the results and consider how old you were when you learned what you are about to see. For some, this may be that day.

Jonah 1:1 KJV: Now the word of the LORD came unto Jonah the son of Amittai, saying,

Jonah's name translated to English is Dove. Yes, Dove! From Jesus's baptism we know that the dove is a symbol of the Holy Spirit.

Jonah's father's name Amittai translated to English means "My Truth". So, Dove, a symbol of the Holy Spirit, is the son of My Truth. My Truth is a great name for the Holy Spirit's father (smile). Also, the name of the father of Peter, the Apostle Peter whose name was changed to Rock, is Jonah. Our Savior is the Rock of our Salvation. Peter, whose name is changed to Rock, is the son of Dove.

Matthew 16:17 KJV: And Jesus answered and said unto him, Blessed art thou, Simon **Barjona**: for flesh and blood hath not revealed it unto thee, but my Father which is in heaven.

Can you remember how old you were when you learned that "Barjona" in the KJV means "Son of Jonah"? This is not an endorsement of any translation, but the NKJV translates it as "Bar-Jonah" and the NIV translates it as "Son of Jonah". Imagine a ten-year-old is inspired to the read the Bible in a year. Then does it again at age eleven and yet again at age twelve but doesn't learn that "Barjona" meant son of Jonah until age twenty. That kid was sixty years old when he learned that the name Jonah translates to Dove.

After two near-death experiences and decades of loyal church attendance I decided to learn Hebrew. I was 61 years old. I am a Christian that knows how to read and study Hebrew words. I am not unique; my research leads me to believe there are millions of Christians that know how to read and study Hebrew today.

I dedicate this book to my children and the many people that I hurt on life's path. This book is the first of a series that will declare what I didn't know then, but now I do.

Again, I pray that God will bless you in this journey.
Glory to the King.

Let's begin with a fictitious story to assist in establishing a spirit of sharing information.

Bob, a former Christian, and now outspoken atheist was talking to Jiff, a Christian brother from his past, "*Let me make sure I understand and don't interrupt. You still believe that if Adam and Eve would not have eaten from the tree, that they would still be alive in the garden. You claim that death is the penalty of sin, so if you don't eat the tree then you have no sin and live forever. But you also believe in a Savior that died that never sinned. You can't have it both ways. If the penalty of sin is death, then how can you claim that your Savior, who died, was without sin? I never understood it. Those two stories contradict each other and it's ridiculous for the churches to think they can have it both ways. You must pick a side, either the penalty of sin is death, or it isn't. How can you explain it?*"

Jiff replies, "*Bob, I love the question. Please don't interrupt because I think I have an answer for you. The Book of Matthew 26:53-54 tells of the situation in the Garden of Gethsemane where Peter cuts off the ear of a man trying to arrest Jesus. Jesus miraculously heals the man's ear then declares to Peter that He could pray to His Father and He would immediately send more than twelve legions of Angels. Then Jesus asked Peter that if He did that then how would the scriptures be fulfilled?*

Jesus didn't die because of any sin committed. He willfully stayed on the cross until His death to fulfill the scriptures. He literally chose not to come off the cross. If He had committed one sin, then He would have justly died on the cross for His own sin. His willingness to stay on the cross, and His choice to accept the penalty of sin, all resulted in His death. His willful <u>death</u> is the sole act of Him becoming sin. His only participation in the sin story is His death, the penalty of sin. His death is synonymous with Him becoming sin. This is what he was explaining to Peter in the garden."

Hopefully, this fictitious story is an example of our ability to join Jiff and see Bob as opposition to our beliefs and faith. What's even more amazing is that many of us have this unexplainable desire to want Jiff to answer Bob with our words. Though we don't disagree with Jiff; we would simply say it differently. There are words that Jiff used that we wouldn't. We want to answer Bob's accusations our own way even though we might agree that Jiff got it right.

We could continue that thought of critiquing Jiff. There are so many sermons and Bible studies from our past that are at total recall that we could use to answer Bob. Bottom line is that though Jiff answered the question, it is nearly impossible to get 100% approval from all believers of the Gospel of Jiff's choice of words. As fellow believers we reserve the right to answer questions with our own understanding and many times hold our Christian brothers accountable if they use what we will call a "reserved word" improperly.

Something as simple as calling new understanding of scripture "knowledge" rather than "revelation" can be a struggle for some Christians. For some, years of study and Church has developed a list of "reserved words".

There are moments when we find it difficult to categorize what we learn as knowledge attained from our own efforts or a gift of revelation from our Savior. We won't share our internal battle to simply pick a category and begin writing. Let's pray we find the use of these words interchangeable and not offensive. For certain it would be awesome if everyone, especially my own kids, would search out what is shared for yourself.

This book does not imply that what is shared is only available in this book. Most of what is shared has been attained from others and everything shared has been "searched out". Neither a prophet nor an oracle participated in writing this book, rather a mere Christian that has been saved by the Gospel and love our Savior. A Christian that can only wish to be as weird as my kids believe him to be (smile).

Let's start simple and then we will take bigger bites as we go.

Imagine one of your friends declaring that they have decided to study the Bible one word at a time. Craziness, right? It's near impossible to confirm, but it has been reported that there are approximately 31,000 words in the original Hebrew text that are only used one time. Researching will confirm that there are thousands of unique words, it's just difficult to confirm the count. Can you think of one English word in the KJV that is used only once in the Bible? Yes, after much research we found that the word "direction" is in the KJV one time. More amazing is that the word "directions" is not in the KJV. Congratulations, you have just completed your first "one word at a time" study of the Bible.

Proverbs 25:2 KJV: It is the glory of God to conceal a thing: but the *honour of kings* is to search out a matter.

Matthew 4:4 KJV: But he answered and said, It is written, Man shall not live by bread alone, but by every word that proceedeth out of the mouth of God.

Let's *choose* to understand what Jesus says in Matthew 4:4 to mean exactly what He says. Jesus didn't say "every verse", "every chapter", or "every book". He said *EVERY WORD! By the end of this book, you will know why!*

Let's combine what God tells us in Proverbs 25:2 with what Jesus tells us in Matthew 4:4 and exercise the *Honor of Kings* and *search out* ONE SINGLE WORD from the original Hebrew text to reveal what God finds glory in concealing.

We will begin with a few words that bring amazing new understanding but also do not create conflict or confrontation with what we already know.

Learning the depth of a Hebrew word does not change salvation. Many Christians that reveal the original Hebrew text are often interrupted by other Christians and repeatedly asked, "Are you still a Christian?" or "Do you think if people don't know this that they will go to hell?" Though it's necessary to respect their concern, *they are experiencing that very familiar unspoken subliminal understanding that* "Christian Hebrew" *is an oxymoron.* That said, we will repeatedly address this topic.

Before we search out our first noun, know that by the end of this book we will search out entire chapters. Yes, contrary to what you have been told, it's that easy! Like riding a bike, the expertise of this effort only requires we spend more time practicing. Glory to the King!

The first Hebrew word we will search out is the Hebrew word translated as "formed" in Genesis 2:7. The word "formed" is in the KJV thirty-one times, but the Hebrew word Uiitzr (וייצר) translated as "formed" in Genesis 2:7 is a unique Hebrew word only spoken by our Creator one time in the original Hebrew text. That said, if you were to do a KJV Biblical study on the word "formed" then you would include all thirty-one instances of how it is used in the KJV. But if we do what Jesus said in "Matthew 4:4", we will experience researching the beauty of a single Hebrew word spoken by our Creator one time.

Before writing this book, many Christians that know how to read and research Hebrew shared in the effort to "search out" thousands of Hebrew words. This word was chosen as the first to be shared only because it is so interesting and provides clarity of how we will pursue *searching out* and applying this unique method of study that was introduced to by our Savior in Matthew 4:4.

Now that we know that this word (וייצר) translated as "formed" is unique, how are we going to define or translate it in English? Well, before we researched Hebrew words, we learned the Hebrew alphabet. Doesn't that sound familiar? Yes, just like going to first grade and learning the ABC's before learning to read. See, this isn't difficult and simply makes common sense.

The Hebrew alphabet is far different than the English ABC's. Each letter of the Hebrew Alphabet has 1) its own definition, 2) a numerical value 3) a word that is normally three letters in length that further enhances the definition, 4) a depth of mystery and practical application but both of those are never to contradict the literal meaning of the word.

Many times, the definition of a Hebrew word can be gleaned from the combined definitions of the letters that spell the word, especially nouns. That said, ***almost none of the Hebrew nouns were translated but rather they were transliterated. They were transliterated into English based on sound and not translated from the Hebrew definition.*** For example, the Hebrew town named Bet-lechem is transliterated into English as Bethlehem but the English translation of Bet-lechem is "House of Bread". That said, the translation of Bethlehem is not provided in the translations. Though the phrase *"house of bread"* may be familiar in some churches, it does not exist in the KJV.

There are twenty-two letters in the Hebrew alphabet and five of those are spelled differently when they are the last letter of a word. There are very talented teachers on many internet sites that have published videos teaching the Hebrew alphabet. John Kostik is one of those teachers, and his videos are on Rumble. Go to http:rumble.com, and search for "DutchUncleJohn". Dutch Uncle John is a friend, and you will love him.

Is defining a Hebrew word the same as translating a Hebrew word into English? Well, it would be difficult to deny that this is what we are doing. ***We are attempting to translate a noun that was not translated but rather it was transliterated***. That said, we are about to learn how easy it is to define one Hebrew word and how the beauty of the definition makes it difficult to translate into a single English word. It's easy to translate the nouns, but it's difficult to include the depth of understanding into the English translation. This is a common problem for anyone that translates one language into another. Many times, the languages do not share a one-word translation, and the translator must provide the definition of the word to be translated.

We are ready to define (Search Out) our first Hebrew word. The definition of the letters for the word translated as Formed (Uiitzr וייצר) in Genesis 2:7 is a bit different. Visually the first thing we notice about the Hebrew spelling of this word is the First and Last letters are both letters that represent Jesus, whose Hebrew name is Yeshua. Hebrew is read from right to left so the first letter is the Vav (ו). The Hebrew letter Vav is defined as the Straight Up Man with the Nail. For those that have learned the Hebrew alphabet, can you recall that moment of pondering the idea that there is a Hebrew letter that means the life of a "Straight Up Man with the Nail"?

All Hebrew letters have a definition that is easy to apply. Many view the letter Vav (ו) to be referring to our Savior's sinless life and His Crucifixion. If you don't know Hebrew, congratulations, you just learned the 6th letter of the Hebrew alphabet. The added mystery about this letter is that it is the 6th letter of the Hebrew alphabet and the number six in the Bible refers to man. The 6th letter of the alphabet is referencing Christ walking in the flesh, and this is the first letter of the word translated as "Formed". That provides a lot of added understanding to this word, and we still have four letters to go.

So, the first letter of the word references Yeshua/Jesus, now let's look at the last letter of the word which is the 20th letter of the Hebrew alphabet, Resh (ר). The letter Resh (ר) means either Prince or Head. So, Jesus is the Son of God, the Prince, and He is also the Head of the House of God. So, both the First and the Last letters of this Hebrew word reference our Savior.

There is a very simple trick to learn Hebrew really, really, really fast. Don't use your brain! Seriously, the quicker you accept that Hebrew is our Father's language then the quicker you will realize that it has to be simple or else only the "intellectuals" will learn it. It's not a brain language, it's a heart language.

Personal Note: When most of us began studying the Hebrew alphabet nobody told us to put our brain in our pocket and learn it with our heart. My wife watched as I cried in joyful disbelief of what I was learning. From the beginning of my learning experience, I would pray and tell my Creator how amazing His language is. I repeatedly told Him each time it amazed me. I honestly believe that because I included Him in my research, that He enjoyed showing me the next revelation which greatly shortened my time to learn. Oh, how I wish I had learned this when I was much younger.

Learning the Hebrew alphabet is not an effort of acquiring intelligence, it's an effort of growing a relationship. Put your brain in your pocket and learn the Hebrew alphabet with your emotions, your spirit, and your heart. Don't memorize and don't take notes. Simply enjoy each moment and continue to the next letter. Don't listen to the same video because you didn't understand! Initially simply enjoy hearing the depth of understanding of each letter while doing your best to enjoy what you hear.

You won't realize this until we "search out" a few more words but the phrase "First and Last" is going to reveal itself repeatedly. There are four scriptures that literally reference Jesus as *"The First and the Last"*. They are Isaiah 44:6, Revelation 1:17, Revelation 22:12, and Revelation 22:13. This book will reveal that our Savior is concealed as *"The First and the Last"* more than twenty-thousand times throughout the Old and New Testament (smile).

So, the first letter, Vav (ו), of the Hebrew word (וייצר) translated as "formed" represents Jesus's sinless life and him crucified with a nail. The last letter, Resh (ר), represents a Prince. Our Savior is the Prince, the Son of God. The first and last letters of this word represent Jesus.

The remaining three letters (ייצ) in the middle include two Yods (יי). The Yod (י) is the 10th letter of the Hebrew alphabet, and it means "The Hand That Does Might Deeds". The greatest deed of the hand was staying on the cross. He could have come down, but He *chose* to leave His two hands on the cross until He died. This word has two Yods (יי) which suggest that whatever God did, it included Him using both hands. Is that significant?

There are very few Hebrew words that have two Yods (יי) within their spelling and even fewer where the Yods (יי) are side by side. In the Creation story there are three things "created" that references God using both hands. Yes, he created everything else using one hand. The trees, land, plants, animals, sun, and moon were all created using one hand. But, to make man and *two other things* that we will save for later, took both hands. No surprise, right? He's the potter, we are the clay.

When we think of using both hands it reminds us of Jeremiah Chapter 18:1-4 and the amazing story of the potter at the wheel. It takes two hands for a potter to form a clay vessel. There is a lot to unpack in those four verses. Much later in this book we will share understanding of *one of the other things* created with both hands that is concealed in these four verses.

Using both hands also reminds us of Matthew 27:6-10 where they used the silver that betrayed Christ to purchase the potter's field and fulfill the prophecies told by Jeremiah. The money that was used to "break" our Savior's "clay" body purchased the field of broken clay vessels.

The last letter in the three middle letters of the word (ייצ) is the letter Tsadi (צ) which means Righteousness. Well, of course, right?

The definition of the letters that spell the Hebrew word (וייצר) translated as "Formed" in Genesis 2:7 hints to the idea that it was done by the life of Jesus (ו), The Resurrected Christ (ר), Both Hands of the Father (יי), and their Righteousness (צ). No, we won't attempt to make doctrine out of it, but we sure can love it and magnify our Savior and Creator. Does anybody have a clue of what God was doing when He formed man? Surely, we are 100% certain that if we were to witness it, we wouldn't call it "forming". Because we have no idea of how to properly translate this word, we would likely write an entire paragraph explaining what we don't know. If we did this with every word, our Bible translation would be too big to carry to church. Maybe that's how it was supposed to be (smile).

Genesis 2:7 KJV: And the Lord God *formed* (וייצר) man of the dust of the ground, and breathed into his nostrils the breath of life; and man became a living soul.

Also, the word "Nostrils" is in the KJV fourteen times, but the Hebrew word translated as "Nostrils" in this verse is only found twice in the original Hebrew text. The other verse is Genesis 7:22 where everything with the breath of life in their nostrils died from the flood.

Glory to the King!

Chapter 2 eshe – Lamb

In 2015 a free software application enabling the ability to search Hebrew text was made public. The program is called ISA Basic Beta3, Copyright Scripture4All Publishing. The analytics and details provided in this book are attained from the use of this application. It's amazing that the ability to electronically research the original Hebrew text is less than ten years old. We are the first generation to have access to this technology and method of research. That said, Surprise! We are human and rarely go a day without making a mistake. Enjoy this effort, check this effort, let us know if you find an error. We are dedicated to this effort because of our love for our children. That's the best warranty we can provide to those that read this book.

The remainder of this book will not provide the background journey of what it's like to find differences in the original Hebrew text and the translations. We chose not to include the many conversations trying to relate to a day in the life of the KJV translators. We will be more forthcoming in Volume 2 of this series.

We have heard the word "Lamb" at almost every church service ever attended. Could there possibly be anything concealed in the Hebrew root word for Lamb that is new? What could we have missed in four decades of church and Biblical study?

The Hebrew root word for lamb is "שה - eshe". Remember, Hebrew is read from right to left so the first letter that spells lamb is the 21st letter of the Hebrew alphabet Shin (ש) and it means destruction. The second letter is the 5th letter of the Hebrew alphabet Hey (ה) and it means revelation. If the letter Hey (ה) is at the beginning of a word, then it means "Behold" and at the end of a word it means "To Be Revealed". So, the two letters combined give us the definition of Lamb **"Destruction to be Revealed"**.

Are the wires in your head firing off and thinking of several ways this description could be applied in scripture. Could it be referring to the cross where the destruction of Jesus's body was clearly revealed? Revealed means that it could be physically seen. Prior to the cross, His destruction could be read in prophecy, but it was not yet "revealed". "Destruction to be Revealed" could also be any sighting after His Resurrection. It could be when He visited the disciples and revealed that the destruction couldn't keep Him in the grave. Or it could be referring to His second coming for the same reason. Though all those scenarios fit the definition of Lamb, let's look at another example of the word Lamb, destruction to be revealed, the amazing name and story of Moses.

Moses was sent by God to draw out His people from Egypt and escort them to the promised land. We also remember that Moses was not allowed to enter the promised land. Do you recall many sermons that compared Moses's story to the second coming of our Savior who can take us to the promised land? Let's do *The Honor of Kings* and search out these two stories to reveal what God has gloriously concealed.

The phrase "Lamb of God" is another commonly known phrase included almost weekly in church sermons. Many of us have experienced how this phrase is used during a church sermon, though each of our opinions vary a bit. Though the words "Lamb of God" applies to every story and moment of Jesus's life, this phrase is mostly used while telling the story of His beaten and battered body and His death on the cross. The phrase is rarely included in the story of His burial or resurrection. When we share the story of "doubting" Thomas we don't usually reference the phrase "Lamb of God". Likewise, we don't commonly include the phrase when telling the story of His burial. That said, let's search out whether the phrase "Lamb of God" is concealed in a story that is linked to any time of Jesus's life other than His beating and crucifixion.

Most are familiar with the lamb as a sacrifice and the lamb sacrificed during the Passover in Egypt. Both of those stories have obvious links to the cross. Again, is there a COMPELLING concealed link of the word "lamb" referenced to any other time of Jesus's story other than His beatings and the cross.

The last word of the Old Testament in the KJV is curse. The Hebrew word that was translated as curse is Chrm (חרם). The last letter of that word, which is also the last letter of the Old Testament is the Mem (ם). Because it is the last letter of the word it is the Sofit form of the letter, and it is referred to as the Closed Womb (ם). If the letter Mem (מ) is not the last letter of a word, then it is not the Sofit form of the letter and referred to as the Open Womb (מ). So, the last Hebrew letter of the Old Testament is a Closed Womb (ם) and if you turn the last page of the Old Testament, you will read the genealogy of Yeshua (Jesus) who was born of a Virgin, a Closed Womb and broke the curse (חרם).

Yeshua (Jesus), the lamb of God, was born of a Closed Womb and is returning to take us *into* the promised land.

The Hebrew name of Moses is Moshe (מֹשֶׁה). Do you see it? Yes, the last two letters of Moses's name (שׁה) spell the word lamb. The first letter of Moses's name is the Hebrew letter Mem (מ). Because it is not the last letter of his name, the letter means an Open Womb. Moses was not born of a Virgin. Moses led the people out of Egypt which represents The World, but he could not take them into the promised land.

Yeshua (Jesus), the lamb of God, was born of a Closed Womb and is returning to *take us into* the promised land. Moses, whose name also means The Lamb born of an Open Womb could take the people *to the promised* land but *could not take them into the promised land*. With this understanding, we could conclude that the lamb, "Destruction to be Revealed", also represents Yeshua's (Jesus's) second coming, another visual of the resurrected Christ from His destruction during His first visit.

There is more! From the story of Moses, we know that Joshua took God's people into the promised land. The Hebrew name Joshua means "God is Salvation". Yeshua, the Hebrew name of Jesus, means "Salvation". Joshua, God is Salvation, took the people into the promised land and Yeshua, whose name translated means Salvation, is returning to take us to the promised land.

Glory to the King

Chapter 3 Gal (גל) – Revealed

Let's continue taking small steps to understanding how the original Hebrew text provides additional depth of understanding.

Just a reminder that every time we use the phrase "search out" we are referring to the *Honor of Kings* in Psalm 25:2.

Proverbs 25:2 KJV: It is the glory of God to conceal a thing: but the ***honour of kings*** is to <u>search out</u> a matter.

It is awesome that our God refers to our efforts of research as the "Honor of Kings". According to God, we are doing something that he calls "Honor of Kings".

Ok, so the next two words we will <u>*SEARCH OUT*</u> are ***VERY INTERESTING***. Let's reveal what is concealed in the root Hebrew word Gal (גל) which means Reveal. Wow, read that slow (smile).

It's necessary for you to know that in the next chapter we will be searching out the word Gilgal (גלגל) which is spelled as though duplicating the letters that spell Gal (גל). It's as though Gilgal means "Reveal (גל) Reveal (גל)". It reminds us of when Jesus says "Verily, verily".

One of the common phrases many of us have heard for many years is that the Old Testament is the New Testament concealed and the New Testament is the Old Testament revealed. Many have learned from Hebrew research that it is true to an extreme. We have also learned how our God conceals revelation within the words and letters of His language.

The research of Gal (גל) and Gilgal (גלגל) does not invoke any contention with any church traditions. Nonetheless, it is crucial that we understand what is revealed of these two words because that understanding will be used throughout the remainder of the book. Yes, this is a *BIG ONE*.

Because of the amount of research, the documentation of the research is provided in the last chapter of this book and includes additional revelations.

The root Hebrew word for "Reveal" is Gal (גל) and is found *ten* times in the original Hebrew Old Testament called the Tanakh. In Hebrew the number ten represents completion, the number five represents revelation, and the number four represents a door or repentance. The number **ONE** is the God number. Knowing that, let's review how this word is used in those ten scriptures.

The first five occurrences of the word Gal (גל) are translated in the KJV as HEAP and references a Heap of Stones. The Hebrew word for stone is Abin (אבן) and means "The Father and the Son". The Father and the Son are like a stone that cannot be separated. Does that also lend understanding to the phrase "The Cleft of the Rock"?

The next four occurrences of the word Gal (גל) in the KJV are translated as a verb and refer to something being Rolled or removed to expose. Yes, the exact same word is translated as a verb rather than a noun. There are many words in the English language that are both nouns and verbs. One of them is the word "Salvation" (smile). Our Savior is Salvation, and our Savior brought Salvation.

Even the translators could discern that these two letters meant something different these four times than the previous five times. So, we have five occurrences that reveal a heap of stones, then we have four occurrences that reveal something being rolled away to expose. Five represents revelation and/or grace and four is a door or repentance. Do you see it?

The tenth occurrence in the KJV of the word Gal (גל) relates to His darling bride in a private garden. OH MY! First, know that this is SO BIG that the research to reveal (Gal - גל) it takes more than four pages. The tenth occurrence is a single instance, and God has prepared a PRIVATE GARDEN for His DARLING BRIDE. What else can we say except, "Let's go prove it!"

Combining the revelations of those ten occurrences reveals that the glory of God concealed by the single word Gal is:

> ***Roll away the stones and reveal (expose)***
> ***our Savior has resurrected to create a private garden***
> ***for His darling bride to share eternity!***

Isn't that beautiful? The concealed revelation of the word REVEAL in the Old Testament tells us about the resurrection story of our Savior. Wow! Is that life? Enjoy the last chapter of documentation.

Honor of Kings – The Documentation, Research, Searching Out of Gal is the last chapter of this book.

Glory to the King!

Chapter 4 Gilgal (גלגל) – To Roll

There is a path of life that must be traveled before the desire for revelation occurs. For some that path is a short smooth road acquiring revelation at a safe speed. While others travel the roughest terrain for most of their available lifetime before finding that smooth road going the correct direction and are constantly getting speeding tickets. Oddly enough, years later these two very different roads experience a detour requiring them to share a mile. How does that work out?

After traveling for miles, it's those "moments on the porch" where we encounter *a revealing* experience. God bless those who detour from the interstate and share time on our porch.

Just like when Jesus says, "Verily, verily", Gilgal (גלגל) repeats the spelling of Gal (גל). Gilgal is a verb and in Hebrew it means "to roll away". Yes, the place named Gilgal in scripture is like naming a town with a verb. A similar name in English would be Running, Tx. Enjoy as we exercise our privilege of the *Honor of Kings* and search out the meaning of the verb Gilgal that is converted to a noun.

Many have witnessed that lack of poetry of mathematicians. Math and poetry seldom are the talents of a single person. Yet, the Words of God seem to require poetry for analysis. That said, let's be committed to sharing what has been revealed (Gal גל) about Gilgal (גלגל). Unlike Gal (גל), the understanding of Gilgal (גלגל) literally flows like sitting on a porch in a well-manicured backyard. So, relax, no memorizing.

The definition of the letters that spell Gilgal is, "One Revelation (גל) Reveals Another Revelation (גל)" or "The wealth (ג) of authority (ל) leads to more wealth (ג) of authority (ל)." Consider your understanding of Gal (גל) and now convert that to a verb. A revealing is something you see, it's a noun. Gilgal is something you do so that you can see a revealing. Gilgal is like the act of unwrapping a present. Understanding that a present can only be unwrapped once is why there is only *ONE GILGAL*.

The Hebrew root word for Gilgal is only used twice in the Old Testament, but variations of the word Gilgal is in our KJV 39 times, and *SUPPOSEDLY* it is not used in the New Testament. Don't get mad! They simply used its definition rather than the word, which we will reveal was a

PERFECT TRANSLATION. Remember, you can only roll-away something once! Then you give it a name and talk about it. There was already a "rolling away" in the Old Testament and it was named Gilgal which means to roll away. The rolling away of the stone to reveal the tomb was empty is a *New Present* with a new name. We call it *The Resurrection or First Fruits*, it's not the same unwrapping as *Gilgal*.

Did you know that "First Fruits" is concealed in the first word God ever spoke? In Hebrew "In the Beginning" is also "In First Fruits". Oops, no hijacking, we will search that out later.

The story of Gilgal is in Joshua Chapters 4-5. Gilgal is the name given to the place on the other side of the Jordan River where Israel crossed from the wilderness. Just like the Red Sea story, the waters of the Jordan were parted, and the people crossed on dry land. Now let's review Joshua 5:9 and the significance of Gilgal.

Joshua 5:9 KJV: And the Lord (יהוה) said unto Joshua, This day have I *rolled away* (גלותי) the reproach (את- חרפת) of Egypt from off you. Wherefore the name of the place is called Gilgal (גלגל) unto this day.

The Hebrew word (גלותי) translated as "rolled away" *is a unique word* only in the Hebrew Old Testament one time. Note that the root word (גל) for Reveal is the first two letters of this word (גַלּותי). The definition of this word attained from the Hebrew letters that spell the word is, "Reveal (גַל) the Straight Up Man with the Nail (ו) whose Covenant (ת) was By His Hand that does Mighty Deeds (י)".

To understand the significance of Gilgal requires us to undertake the near impossible exercise of forgetting our past understanding. The most difficult part of our past teaching on Gilgal is the fact that it just wasn't a memorialized story. It never made our "top ten list". Let's fix that.

Below is a list of a few events from the Gilgal story that might remind us of a similar New Testament story.

- Joshua 4:19 tells us that this is where they entered the promised land.
- Joshua 4 tells us that the waters of the river Jordan were parted, and they crossed on dry land just like when they left Egypt. Since Egypt represents the World, it's as though the waters are like a chasm between God's people and the World.

- The Hebrew word (גלותי) meaning "Rolled Away" *only occurs one time in the original text*.
- This Hebrew word (את-חרפת) for "reproach" is in the Old Testament sixteen times and this is the only instance that has the prefix "את" which is the stamp of "The First and The Last", our Savior. We will search out the meaning of "את" later.
- God rolled away the reproach of Egypt (The World) after they crossed Jordan.
- God rolled away the Stone at the tomb of Jesus. That stone represented the reproach of Rome (The World).
- Joshua 4:19 tells us they entered the Promised Land on the 10th Day of the 1st Month – This is the same date of the Triumphal Entry of Jesus into Jerusalem.
- Joshua 5:9 tells us that at Gilgal God rolled away the reproach (filth) of Egypt from off His people. At the Resurrection God will roll away the filth of sin from His people.

The Roman Empire's role in the crucifixion resembles the role of Egypt during the Exodus. Rome judged, sentenced, and crucified Jesus. Then they placed guards to ensure the stone that covered the exit of the tomb would not be rolled away. Just like when Joshua led Israel into the promised land and God rolled away the reproach of Egypt at Gilgal, He also rolled the stone at Jesus's tomb revealing that He was no longer under the reproach of Rome. The story of Gilgal is the concealed Old Testament shadow of the resurrection.

Deuteronomy 11:30 KJV: Are they not on the other side Jordan, by the way where the sun goeth down, in the land of the Canaanites, which dwell in the champaign over against Gilgal (הגלגל), beside the plains of Moreh (מרה)?

The first mentioning of Gilgal is Deuteronomy 11:30 where Moses prophesies in that chapter about the crossing of Jordan. There is so much to unpack in this verse. The definition of the Hebrew letters that spell Moreh is, "The Womb (מ) of the Prince (ר) to be Revealed (ה)". Concealed in this verse is another reference to the virgin birth of our Savior and it's in the same verse that conceals the resurrection, "Behold (ה) Gilgal (גלגל)".

Revelation 6:14 KJV: And the heaven departed as a scroll when it is rolled together; and every mountain and island were moved out of their places.

Revelation 6:14 provides another moment where something is "rolled back". When the "roll back (Gilgal)" happens this time, it will be at His second coming. Could each instance of the letters that spell reveal (Gal גל) in the word Gilgal (גלגל) possibly be related to the revealing of the 1st and 2nd coming where something is rolled back? The first time was a stone, and the second time will be the heavens.

We have an amazing journey of revelations to search out. Continue while praying as we roll back (גלגל) to witness what's revealed (גל). I pray the Authority (ל) of Wealth (ג) pours out His riches.

The Hebrew spelling of twenty-three of the thirty-nine occurrences of Gilgal is הגלגל. This is the same spelling used in Deuteronomy 11:30 which has the Hebrew letter Hey (ה) preceding it. When this letter is before a noun it is translated as the word "The". Yes, pretty unremarkable. Hebrew scholars will confirm that this "*unremarkableness*" is exactly that, it is simply the word "The". That said, many Christians that know Hebrew have a problem with this.

The letter Hey (ה) is the "Revelation and/or Grace" letter of Hebrew. It literally means revelation (behold) and/or grace. The pictograph paleo-Hebrew of this letter is a man with his arms raised and apparently jumping up and down from excitement. That's more like it! Behold, God has rolled the stone away. Behold, God has rolled away the reproach of Egypt from you. Behold, your Savior has risen. Most Christians that know Hebrew prefer "***BEHOLD***"! Gilgal (הגלגל) - Behold (ה), One Revelation (גל) Reveals Another Revelation (גל).

GilGal means "Rolled Away" and in Gilgal God rolled away the reproach (sin) of Egypt. Galilee means "to roll". Coincidence? We will reveal more about ***rolling away reproach*** later.

Glory to the King!

Chapter 5 Cedar

Otz (עץ) – Tree, Arz (ארז) – Cedar,
u qutz (וקוץ) – Thorn, and u drdr (ודרדר) – Weed/Thistle

Like most common Bible stories, the garden of Eden has points of interest that are almost never shared in a Church or Biblical Study session. One of those points of interest is focused on the fact that the land was cursed because of man's sin. The land didn't do anything wrong. The trees did not sin, yet they were cursed along with the land.

The Hebrew word (עץ) for tree is Otz (עץ), and it is spelled (from right to left) Ayin (ע), which means eye, and Tsadi (ץ) which means righteousness. The definition of the letters that spell the word (עץ) is, "See Righteousness". Knowing this changes our view when we step outside.

Romans 8:22 KJV: For we know that the whole creation groaneth and travaileth in pain together until now.

Romans 8:22 tells us that the whole creation groans and travails. Is it because it is waiting for the curse to be removed? Is the phrase "the whole creation" referring to everything that lives other than humans? If so, then it is implying that all living creation can communicate in some manner with its Creator. Though we can't explain it, that is what it seems. We're not going to *get tangled around the axle* and neither will *we die on this hill*; (laughing) it's just something that this word brings into our view.

Personal Note: Contrary to traditional understanding, Hebrew is a very simple language to learn. This book was written after tenaciously studying Hebrew words for nearly three years. Having attended college, I believe my interest, dedication, and continued investment to study is beyond the requirements of any college student that has graduated in the study of Biblical Hebrew. That is not a declaration to reveal my confessed issues with arrogance, but rather to express how disappointing it was that I lived nearly the entire allotted time to live before being introduced to this beautiful language. I want so badly to blame that on somebody other than me. He knows that I love His language. Now that I know, is loving His language in any way related to loving His Word or Words? I don't know, but I do know that studying Hebrew isn't a burden but rather a privilege. Try it! I have witnessed people learning how to read and research Hebrew in less than thirty days.

Because most of the common nouns were translated, the names of many trees are included in scripture. Now that we know that a tree (עץ) means "See (ע) Righteousness (ץ)", hopefully we share the anxiety to search out the spelling of types of trees. That said, we will only search out Cedar (ארז).

The Hebrew word (ארז) for Cedar is Arz ארז. The first letter of the word is Alef (א) which is the God letter. The second letter is Resh (ר) which means Prince or Head. The last letter is Zayin (ז) which means Perfection or Sword. The Zayin (ז) looks very similar to the Vav (ו). The definition of the Word derived from the letters is, "The Father (God א) and His Son (ר) are Perfect (ז)."

And then there was silence! Imagine if the greatest story ever told included providing us with the understanding that trees are a visual image of righteousness and that the Hebrew word for Cedar translates into English as "The Father and His Son are Perfect" or "The Father and the Son are a Sword". Ok, let's admit it, telling anyone that Jesus was nailed to a cedar tree is conjecture. That said, wouldn't we bet the farm that He was. Similar to the blood of Abel crying out from the ground, if that uprooted and sawed Cedar Tree could talk, it would say, "He is righteous and perfect!"

There is one more proof that our Savior gave Himself on a Cedar tree. We are all familiar that numbers represent purpose in the Hebrew language. In fact, the Hebrew alphabet is alpha-numeric. The first letter Alef (א), commonly referred to as "The God Letter" has a value of one. In Hebrew the number eleven represents a covering, and it is also referenced as being "one short" of the number twelve which means "a government". The word (ארז) Cedar occurs eleven times in the original Hebrew text. Is it possible that the 12th occurrence is our Savior on the Cross giving Himself to establish His government?

How is that possible? Does each occurrence of a word and the number of occurrences of a word provide additional revelation to God's word? NO WAY, RIGHT? If that were true, then it would be impossible to translate the omniscience of the original language into any other language. Ok, if this is true then it's always true, so, what is the significance of the occurrences of the word (עץ) translated as tree?

The occurrences of the word (עץ) translated as tree require us to learn an additional depth of understanding of the Hebrew alphabet. Each letter of the alphabet includes a word that spells the pronunciation of the letter. For example, the word Alef (אלף) is the word of the first letter Alef (א), the God letter. Again, each letter also has a numeric value, and the Alef (א) has a value of one. Hebrew is read right-to-left, so the second letter of the word Alef (אלף) is the Lamed (ל) at its value is thirty. Likewise, the third letter is the letter Pey (ף) and its value is eighty. The sum of the letters that spell Alef is 111.

The word (עץ) that means tree occurs in the original text 109 times. Is it possible that the tree of the cross was telling us that the Father (110) and the Son (111) are righteous? Coincidence?

Let's continue this study by searching out the Hebrew words for Thorn and Thistle. First, we will reveal that the original Hebrew of thorns and thistles in Genesis 3:18 are singular and not plural. Then we will review the revelation from that understanding.

Genesis 3:18 KJV: Thorns (וקוץ) also and thistles (ודרדר) shall it bring forth to thee; and thou shalt eat the herb of the field.

In Hebrew, all plural forms of a noun have the Hebrew letters Yod and Mem (ים) at the end of the noun. Research for yourself and confirm that Genesis 3:18 refers to a single thorn and a single thistle. Also, the Hebrew root word for Thorn is (קוץ). The word (וקוץ) means "And (ו) Thorn (קוץ)".

Now we will search out two verses that use thorns and thistles. One provides the plural forms and the other the singular. Psalm 118:12 is the example of the plural and Hosea 10:8 is the singular form of these two words.

Psalm 118:12 KJV: They compassed me about like bees: they are quenched as the fire of thorns (קוצים): for in the name of the LORD I will destroy them.

One of the three times that the plural form of thorns is in scripture occurs in Psalm 118:12. The reason the plural form (קוצים) is not similar to the singular form (קוץ) is because the Hebrew letter Tsadi (צ) is one of five Hebrew letters that are written differently when it is the last letter of the word. So, ץ and צ are the same letter.

Hosea 10:8 KJV: The high places also of Aven (און), the sin of Israel, shall be destroyed: the thorn (קוץ) and the thistle (ודרדר) shall come up on their altars; and they shall say to the mountains, Cover us; and to the hills, Fall on us.

A quick diversion. The word (און) translated as "Aven" occurs seventy-seven times in the original text and means "lawlessness". However, the word "lawlessness" is not in the KJV, it's in the NKJV nine times but only in the New Testament, and it is in the NIV four times but only the New Testament. Lawlessness is violating God's Law. Do you think reading the word "lawlessness" seventy-seven times rather than idolatry, witchcraft, evil doers, and other words that define sin rather than the word "lawlessness" would have an impact on the rhetoric of our culture concerning the law? At first glance, when we read Hosea 10:8, it seems to hint that Aven is a city and we would never know that it had anything to do with lawlessness. Coincidence? Also, the Hebrew word translated as "shall be destroyed" is unique, only in the original text one time. The phrase "shall be destroyed" occurs thirteen times in the KJV Old Testament.

Back to our topic of Thorns and Thistles.

Hosea 10:8 uses the same form of the words for thorn and thistle as Genesis 3:18 and it translates both words as singular. To reveal the impact that Genesis 3:18 is singular rather than plural let's consider a few questions. Do you think Adam knew that the thorn and the thistle were singular instead of plural? Do you think Moses who wrote these words knew he was writing the singular instead of the plural? What changes in the story of Genesis Chapter 3 if the thorn and thistle are singular rather than plural?

Surely, the patriarchs of old knew the thorn and thistle in Genesis 3:18 were singular. Surely, Moses knew it when he scribed it. The big question is, what does that reveal, and did they know what it revealed?

Most of us have been correctly taught that the seed of the woman in Genesis 3:15 is prophecy concerning the 1st coming of Jesus. Without providing additional evidence it would be fairly easy to agree that Hosea 10:8 is referring to Jesus's second coming. If Genesis 3:18 is singular, then is it reasonable to consider that this single thorn and single thistle is the same referenced in Hosea 10:8? If so, do the judgments of the fall of man in Genesis 3 include prophecy of both the 1st and 2nd coming? Knowing that Genesis 3:18 references the 2nd coming of Christ is equally as priceless as knowing Genesis 3:15 references His first coming. Do you believe the patriarchs of old knew and believed this revelation?

The definition of the letters of the Hebrew words translated as Thorns and Thistles in Genesis 3:18 is equally amazing. For thorns (וקוץ) the definition is, "The Straight up Man with the Nail (ו) is Holy (ק), and the Straight up Man with the Nail (ו) is Righteous (ק)." What makes that interesting is to understand that there are people in scripture that are Holy but not Righteous. The definition of the letters for Thistles (ודרדר) is, "The Straight up Man with the Nail (ו) is the Door (ד) to the Prince (ר) is the Door (ד) to the Prince(ר)." Yes, another example of the letters within a word repeating. What's more interesting is that the word (דר) occurs seven times in the original text and is translated as "generations". So, Thistles could mean that Jesus (ו) is for generation (דר) after generation (דר) which is another way to say, "Jesus is the same yesterday, today, and forever." Is that significant?

Glory to the King!

Chapter 6 Donkey

Many of us have impressive educational resumes. That said, nearly every character trait utilized to attain an impressive educational resume contributes to making it difficult to learn Hebrew. Correct, that doesn't make sense but as we continue it will make perfect sense.

The next Hebrew word we will search out is Donkey. Oh, we will love this word and all its references in scripture. You would have never guessed that the word Donkey would make it this high on the priority list, right? Well, by the time this chapter is finished, hopefully you will begin seeing the consistent increase of revelation in stories you already knew, and it will build a passion to invest a month and learn the Hebrew letters.

If you ever owned a donkey then you know that in addition to possessing distinctive personality qualities, they also possess the instinctive nature to protect. This is why many farmers with herd animals usually have at least one donkey in the herd to protect the herd from predators. What is also very common is that the predator will generally attack the weakest animal in the herd, which is usually the goat's kid or the cow's calf or the pregnant mother. Rarely will the predator attack the ram or bull. The instinctive nature of the donkey is to protect the herd, especially the womb with a child or the young of the herd. Farmers know that a female donkey has more instinctive protective character than a male. There are several internet videos that reveal this instinctive nature.

Once again, let's recall what Jesus told us in Matthew 4:4.

Matthew 4:4 KJV: But he answered and said, It is written, Man shall not live by bread alone, but by every word that proceedeth out of the mouth of God (יהוה).

Notice that He didn't say by every verse, chapter, or book but by every word.

The Hebrew word Chmor (חמור) means female donkey and occurs *30 times* in the original text. The definition of the letters that spell Chmor (חמור) is, "The Protection (ח) of the Womb (מ), of the Straight-up man with the Nail (ו), and the Prince (ר)." So, the noun of a female donkey in Hebrew tells us that it will protect the womb of our Savior's birth, our Savior during His time in the flesh (including the triumphal entry), and the Prince (Son of God).

First, realize that these animals were named by Adam, right? Do you think Adam spoke Hebrew? Do you think he spent time learning the behavior of these animals before they were named? Surely, he did, right? So, Mary is riding the animal that God ordained from creation to be the protector of the womb of our Savior into Bethlehem.

A couple of the most common stories where a donkey is included are when Mary, the mother of Jesus rode a donkey to Bethlehem and the other is when Jesus rode a donkey into Jerusalem which is commonly referred to as the triumphal entry. There are more occurrences but let's limit our research to these two occurrences.

Picture your Savior riding into Jerusalem on a colt while we search out Matthew 21:2 and Zechariah 9:9.

Matthew 21:2 KJV: Saying unto them, Go into the village over against you, and straightway ye shall find an ass tied, and a colt with her: loose **them**, and bring **them** unto me.

Zechariah 9:9 KJV: Rejoice greatly, O daughter of Zion; shout, O daughter of Jerusalem: behold, thy King cometh unto thee: he is just, and having salvation; lowly, and **riding upon an ass** (חמור), **and upon a colt** (אתנות) **the foal** of an ass.

This ***role of the donkey*** in the story of Jesus entering Jerusalem the week of the crucifixion is referred to as the "The Triumphal Entry" and has been retold with pictures and movies with many variations. Isn't it clear from Matthew 21:2 and Zechariah 9:9 that there are ***two*** donkeys entering Jerusalem. One is the mother, and the other is a colt (male, a female foal is called a filly), her foal following her which Jesus is riding. Most Christians are unaware that there were two donkeys entering Jerusalem during the triumphal entry.

Now, let's research the two stories of Mary's journey to Bethlehem and Jesus's Triumphal entry journey to reveal what's concealed in the translation of the nouns of these two stories.

A chiasm is the repetition of similar ideas in the reverse sequence. To understand this chiasmic relationship requires understanding the Hebrew meanings of the names of the departure and arrival towns in these two stories. Enjoy the beauty of the Gospel that will be revealed in the translation of the names of these towns.

Story #1 Mary Riding a Donkey from Nazareth to Bethlehem – Do you agree that it is interesting to learn that the town of Nazareth is not mentioned in the Old Testament? But there is a reference to the word Netzer in Isaiah 11:1.

Isaiah 11:1 KJV: And there shall come forth a **rod** (חטר) out of the stem of Jesse, and a Branch (Netzer or Natzer - ונצר) shall grow out of his roots:

It is interesting that the word "Branch" in Isaiah 11:1 is spelled with a capital "B". The Hebrew word for Branch in this verse is Natzer, and it means to watch or guard something that will bear fruit. The only other verse where Natzer is found is Proverbs 24:12.

Proverbs 24:12 KJV: If thou sayest, Behold, we knew it not; doth not he that pondereth the heart consider it? and he that keepeth (Netzer or Natzer - ונצר) thy soul, doth not he know it? and shall not he render to every man according to his works?

In Proverbs 24:12 Netzer is translated in the KJV as "keepeth" while other translations (NIV, NLT, EXB, etc) translate it as "guards" or "protects". Nonetheless, these two instances have a link to Jesus. Could this "Branch" from Netzar that "keepeth" my soul be a Nazarene?

We already know that Bethlehem translated means "The House of Bread". What many don't know is that the prior to being name Bethlehem, the Bible referred to it as Ephratah which means "Fruitfulness".

Conclusion – Mary and Joseph are traveling from a place that guards or protects to the fruitful house of bread.

Story #2 Jesus Riding a Donkey from Bethphage, then Bethany to Jerusalem.

Mark 11:1 KJV: And when they came nigh to Jerusalem, unto Bethphage and Bethany, at the mount of Olives, he sendeth forth two of his disciples,

The Hebrew translation for Bethphage is "House of Unripe Figs", and for Bethany is "House of Figs", and for Jerusalem is "Foundation of Peace".

Conclusion – Jesus traveled from fruitfulness to a place of peace.

From the translation of the names of the cities it would appear they went in opposite directions. Glory to the King!

Isn't it interesting to learn that Jesus was in Bethany, the House of Figs, seeking fruit from a fig tree that had no fruitfulness, so He cursed it. We are familiar with the symbolism of Israel and figs, but in this story, let's focus on the names of the cities. Learning Hebrew, revealed that the name Bethany translates to "The House of Figs". Add that knowledge to all the fig tree symbolism of your past and glean new revelations.

***

I pray the following exercise of the *Honor of Kings* is as life changing. Enjoy the reward of **AMAZING REVELATION** of scripture.

***

First, since we will be referencing these two stories so often, let's abbreviate the Joseph and Mary travels from Nazareth to Bethlehem by calling it the Mary story and likewise the triumphal entry as the Jesus story.

The Mary and Jesus stories are the first chiasmic stories we will research. It is very likely that a chiasmic relationship is something new for most. By the end of this book series, you will see that this is a common method where our Creator conceals incredible revelation. Know that all chiasmic stories often have many chiasmic comparisons. Let's identify other chiasmic relationships of these two stories.

- Mary story leaves a guarded place for a fruitful place.
  - Mary story is a journey to his birth.
    - Mary story has a mother and her son riding.
      - Mary Story has a father figure walking.
      - *Jesus Story does not have a father riding.*
    - Jesus story has the mother (donkey) and her son walking.
  - Jesus story is a journey to his death.
- Jesus story leaves a fruitful place for a guarded place.

Isn't it ironic that we don't have a chiasmic relationship because in the Jesus story the Father is missing? Okay, so you see the task, we are looking for scriptural evidence that the Father is clearly present with His son at the triumphal entry. ***Impossible to exaggerate the privilege*** to be made aware of the need to search out the *Honor of Kings* of this matter. We are searching out information that we never considered to investigate. Just imagine the impact if we find this.

To find this concealed story we must approach the scriptures with complete bias. Ignore nothing as potential evidence. We are looking for evidence of something never found or even considered as necessary to be found. One could argue this isn't a pressing matter but consider all that changes in this story if we find that the Father entered Jerusalem with His Son while riding the mother donkey. Just the thought of it makes sense. What father wouldn't let his son enter that environment without being by his side.

So first, let's pray and rejoice that the desire for this effort is revealed to us. We already expressed that this isn't something we find but rather something He must reveal. If He wants us to know, He must reveal it. We also know from personal experience and many experiences shared by friends, that when He reveals something, it is beautiful and magnificent.

Again, from my personal experience I have learned that few people were aware that there were two donkeys in the triumphal entry. When I learned of these two donkeys many years ago, I had never heard of a Biblical chiasmic story. Also, I didn't know Hebrew, so I didn't know the depth of the Father's language. Tasks like this were never on my radar. But now, when I re-read the triumphal entry, then research the original Hebrew, revelations are *SCREAMING* something that has been concealed from me my entire life. Now you get to search out what has been revealed to decide for yourself.

What is the scripture *SCREAMING*? It is screaming for us to correct the disparity of reverence between the role of the fathers in these two stories. While Joseph is perceived to have an unblemished participation, the Father bears the role of one that forsakes His Son.

In the story of Mary and Joseph traveling to Bethlehem for His birth, the role of Joseph as a father is without blemish. We won't fill this chapter with examples of highest praise and righteous character that are told and inferred about Joseph. We know the story well; almost all that know the Bethlehem story are aware of the beautiful fatherly role of Joseph during the birth of Christ. Like all stories of a childbirth, the birth of Christ story is a time of celebration. But wait! We are researching these two stories to find any evidence of participation of Jesus's Father in Heaven. Well, His role is not absent in the birth story. Without His participation, this story wouldn't exist.

Because Joseph did not live to witness the crucifixion, we are granted the privilege of providing our own conjecture of how we feel he would have handled it. Surely, we agree that we have never heard any negative conjecture of what Joseph would have done if he had lived to witness the crucifixion. Joseph rightfully gets positive press.

On the contrary, Jesus's real Father, our Father, did not get the privilege of being unavailable during His Son's crucifixion. Though our Father's participation in the story is described with a minimal number of scriptures, there is no lack of rhetoric and conjecture of those verses. What is the scripture *SCREAMING*? How does the understanding of scripture, and the rhetoric (conjecture) change if there is scriptural evidence that He physically entered Jerusalem with His son?

Did Jesus's real Father experience and participate in the story of Jesus's death with as much respect that is given to Joseph in the story of His birth? Does the original Hebrew text provide untold revelation of this story? If we find clear evidence that the Father is riding into Jerusalem with His son, then how does that impact the traditional passed-down teachings and scriptures of the triumphal entry and the events of the crucifixion story? Can the mere understanding that there are two donkeys make this big of a splash? Before reviewing the impact of these two donkeys in answering these questions, we must prepare by gleaning insight into Matthew 27:46.

Matthew 27:46 KJV: And about the ninth hour Jesus cried with a loud voice, saying, Eli, Eli, lama sabachthani? that is to say, *My God, my God, why hast thou forsaken me?*

Anyone who has attended church for a decade has heard multiple sermons of this verse. Certainly, almost every year during the week of the crucifixion. Many of us have attended church for decades and heard many sermons of the triumphal entry and the crucifixion. That said, most likely every sermon explains and consistently reveals that Jesus was forsaken by His Father on the cross. Let's reveal scripture that has been concealed from most of us for generations. Scripture that might have been spoken publicly but it just never made it on our radar and never changed the rhetoric the son being forsaken by the Father.

It seems that many times authors of books are burdened with sharing what cannot and should not be shared from behind a pulpit. Churches cannot schedule a risky sermon with potential that less than 100% of the congregation will agree. The pulpit is not for correcting passed down interpretations that we inherited from birth.

From birth we have always been taught that Christ was forsaken by His Father because He chose to become sin while on the cross and sin is not allowed in the presence of the Father. So, even if we prove that the Father was with His son at the triumphal entry, it does not change that He is a father that forsakes his son, and we still deny Him the accolades we give to Joseph. Well, under those conditions, we don't want to find Him riding into Jerusalem as a loving Father only to reveal Him as a forsaking Father a few days later. Is there any ABSOLUTE SCRIPTURAL evidence to prove that He has never forsaken His son? We will deal with the ramifications of that understanding after it is proven, but first, is there SCRIPTURAL evidence that would prove His innocence?

The verse where Jesus expresses His Father has forsaken Him is Matthew 24:46. Let's review the event of verse 48 to determine if there is any concealed evidence to prove otherwise. Verse 48 is crucial evidence that provides details of an event that took place after the supposed forsaking in Matthew 27:46. To be clear, prior to what is about to be revealed, the Father has supposedly already forsaken His son.

Matthew 27:48 KJV: And straightway one of them ran, and took a spunge, and filled it with vinegar, and put it on a reed, and gave him to drink.

Jesus is given a drink two verses after He is supposedly forsaken. Two verses after He takes this drink, He "yielded up the ghost". Now let's read that same incident as shared by the Gospel of John. (John 19:28-29)

John 19:28-29 KJV: [28] After this, Jesus knowing that all things were now accomplished, *that the scripture might be fulfilled*, saith, I thirst.
[29] Now there was set a vessel full of vinegar: and they filled a spunge with vinegar, and put it upon hyssop, and put it to his mouth.

Verse 29 reveals that this is the same event mentioned in Matthew 27:48 though it does include the use of hyssop which we will search out later. Now let's look at verse 28 and notice the part of the scripture emphasized *"that the scripture might be fulfilled"*. So, just before His death He declares He is thirsty to *FULFILL SCRIPTURE.* What scripture did he fulfill by saying, "I thirst"?

How old were you when you learned what your Savior was referencing when He spoke these words? Traditions, Lies from Birth, also includes postponement of truth. Yes, we will answer this question later in this book. Yes, *it is beautiful.*

At the moment, FAR MORE IMPORTANT is to realize that He is still trying to make it clear that He is the Messiah. So, He went from being forsaken by His Father two verses ago and is once again fulfilling the Will of the Father. He is still working to leave evidence that can be found after His death of who He is. Hmm? Note: later we will prove that this event is all about the hyssop.

Now that we know He is still trying to provide evidence that He is the Messiah, let's consider if there is any evidence that would hint or prove that He is doing the same thing two verses prior in Matthew 27:46 where we claim He is forsaken. Can we find any proof that would lend understanding that every word He spoke while on the cross fulfilled the Will of His Father and did not bring shame to His Father. Is there proof that would reveal 27:46 as simply another act of Jesus to prove He is the Messiah just as He did in verse 48? Is there clear scriptural proof that the same Father in *Matthew 26:53-54* that Jesus proclaims would send more than twelve legions of Angels, is a Father that would NEVER FORSAKE HIS SON? Let's review Psalm 22:1 and Matthew 27:46 together.

Psalm 22:1 KJV: *My God, my God, why hast thou forsaken me?* why art thou so far from helping me, and from the words of my roaring?

Matthew 27:46 KJV: And about the ninth hour Jesus cried with a loud voice, saying, Eli, Eli, lama sabachthani? that is to say, *My God, my God, why hast thou forsaken me?*

Psalm 22 is Holy Ground. It's a Psalm of David and is certainly one of the most powerful. A Psalm quoted by Christ while on the cross. There are many public videos of sermons available that provide a view of why Christ quoted this Psalm. That said, we have yet to find a video teaching of Psalm 22 that defends the Good, Good, Father by proving He would never forsake His Son. How old were you when you were introduced to the idea that your Savior might have been quoting Psalm 22:1?

Think about it. Why would David and Jesus quote the same words? Is Jesus agreeing with David about His Father? Is Jesus saying, "Yea David, you were right. He has forsaken you at your hour of need and now He's forsaking me." No way, right! Jesus didn't quote this verse to reinforce any bad character of the Father! Jesus quoted this verse to prove the prophecies of King Beloved in Psalm 22. The Father is a Good, Good, Father. HE WOULD NEVER FORSAKE HIS SON!

We can't estimate the percentage of Christians that are unaware that Jesus is called the Son of David (Luke 18:38-39). There are many scriptures confirming that the Lord loved David. There is a common phrase "David the beloved" that is almost always quoted when preaching about David. That said, the phrase "David, the beloved" is not in the Bible. The Hebrew translation of the word David is "beloved". Yes, just like Oz means goat, David means Beloved. Knowing his name is Beloved adds to the stories of his life and once again makes us ponder past understanding. David is not just called by the title "Beloved", but his name is "Beloved". Everywhere you see the word David, you can substitute it with Beloved.

Eight times in the New Testament God refers to Jesus as "beloved son". It seems appropriate that Jesus, the beloved son, would quote King Beloved's words from Psalm 22:1?

Surely, we agree that John was aware of King Beloved's Psalm that Jesus quoted and obviously he was aware of the scripture that was fulfilled. Most importantly, is this enough evidence to consider that Matthew 27:46 was for the same purpose as Matthew 27:48? Is Psalm 22:1 enough to render the Good, Good, Father NOT GUILTY of forsaking His Son? Is there more evidence? Yes, almost every verse of Psalm Chapter 22 has more evidence. Let's search out verses 16-18.

Psalm 22:16-18 KJV: [16] For dogs have compassed me: the assembly of the wicked have inclosed me: they pierced my hands and my feet.
[17] I may tell all my bones: they look and stare upon me.
[18] They part my garments among them, and cast lots upon my vesture.

King Beloved (David) plays many roles in the scriptures. He is the only appointed King, a priest, a prophet, and a Psalmist. Psalm 22 can be viewed as another effort of the Messiah to reveal Himself to those that did not recognize Him. Let's review Psalm 22:1 from the NIV.

Psalm 22:1 NIV:
Psalm 22**[a]** **For the director of music. To the tune of "The Doe of the Morning." A psalm of David.**

[1] My God, my God, why have you forsaken me?
  Why are you so far from saving me,
    so far from my cries of anguish?

Notice the footnote "[a]" underlined on what appears to be the header of Psalm 22. This header is not included in the KJV. Below is the footnote copied from an online Bible app.

Psalm 22:1 In Hebrew texts 22:1-31 is numbered 22:2-32.

Yes, the headers of all Psalm are included in the original Hebrew text. In fact, the header in the original text is labeled as "Verse 1". This header is provided in the NKJV, NIV, and likely several other translations but it is not provided in the KJV. Why didn't the translators include the headers of 55 Psalms that were provided in the original text? Is there anything significant in the header that was omitted by the 17th Century translators? Yes! And it will be revealed later in the book.

Let's look at Psalm 22:8.

Psalm 22:8 KJV: He **_trusted_** (גל) **_on the LORD_** (יהוה) *that he would deliver him* (יפלטהו)[1]: *let him deliver him* (יצילהו)[1], seeing he delighted in him.

Earlier we revealed that several translations have a footnote showing that the first Hebrew word of Psalm 22:8 literally means "**_Roll_**". So, the first three words in the original Hebrew text are "*Roll to Yahweh*". Also, there are two Hebrew words in this verse that are only used once in the Bible. My understanding of the Hebrew in this verse is "*The Father Reveals Himself by Rolling Away the Stone and Delivers His Son and Rescues His Son Because He Delights in Him*".

Doesn't it make sense that both original Hebrew words translated as "*that he would deliver him*" and "*let him deliver him*" are unique. The Father delivered and rescued His son in a unique manner never done before. He rolled away the reproach of Rome just like He rolled away the reproach of Egypt at Gilgal. I believe that if this evidence were provided in a trial by jury, the Father would be found **NOT GUILTY OF FORSAKING HIS SON**. The Good, Good, Father of our Savior is Righteous and Holy.

Personal Note:

Before continuing and resolving the other problems this causes, let's reveal some of the problems this fixes that are never discussed. The second letter of the Hebrew alphabet is the Bet (ב) which means house. The first letter is the Alef (א) which is the God letter. Those two letters combined (אב) spell Father which can be defined as God's (א) House (ב). Can God's house ever be seen as anything other than Righteous and Holy. Can His house participate in our 21st century version of dysfunctionality? Does the thought of suggesting that the Father could forsake His son violate the 3rd Commandment which means "to make His name insignificant"? Is it conceivable that the Father planned this forsaking event from the foundations of the Earth? After what we just learned, is it still possible that to believe that He would do something to His Son that we would never do to ours, especially if we only have one? If the Father can forsake His son, then the apple doesn't fall far from the tree, right? Like Father, like Son. Jesus says that He and His Father are one. Is our Savior capable of forsaking us because of our sins like His Father supposedly did to Him? Can Jesus possibly be better than His Father, especially after He repeatedly declares He isn't? If this new explanation where the Father does not forsake His son was your understanding from birth, could you be convinced to change and see the Father as a forsaking Father? Of course not! Let's **NAIL** this understanding of the Straight Up Man with the Nail by resolving the last few issues that were also passed down before our birth, and embrace our Father as the Good, Good, Father that He is. Let's rid ourselves of the rhetoric passed down that teaches otherwise. Our Father is a Good Father!

Now that our Father is not one that will forsake, we have a new problem. Many have traveled the road of attending various denominations. Isn't it concerning that the passed down story is told the same by almost all churches? The denominations teach that the Father forsook His son in verse 46 because their application (explanation) of Paul's writing in 2 Corinthians 5:21, Jesus became sin. Though there is no doubt that Jesus became sin while on the cross, this teaching is so indoctrinated that it seems sinful to consider or pursue an alternative explanation.

Many of us have witnessed this story from "the Church". Again, we are taught that Jesus is forsaken by His Father in verse 46 because of "this moment" when Jesus quotes Psalm 22:1. At that "specific moment", He became sin and His Father forsook Him. We are taught that verse 46 fulfills Paul's writings in 2 Corinthians 5:21 and our Savior is forsaken because His Father will not allow sin in His presence. This is passed down interpretation, application, and understanding of scripture that existed before we were born. This teaching is the "bedrock of doctrine" taught by almost all churches. Is there an alternative explanation of Paul's writing that will explain how our Savior became sin that does not require us to view our Good, Good, Father this way?

2 Corinthians 5:21 KJV: For he hath made him to be sin for us, who knew no sin; that we might be made the righteousness of God in him.

There is no doubt that Jesus became sin while on the cross. The question is when? We have searched out clear evidence that He didn't become sin in verse 46 and there is clear evidence that the Father didn't forsake Him. When did Jesus who knew no sin become sin? How is it possible for Him to become sin and not be forsaken by His Father? ***What is the exact moment that 2 Corinthians 5:21 was fulfilled and our Savior became sin?*** This question becomes easier to answer if you participate in a silly exercise. This is not joke; you must go with me on this. This silly exercise will hopefully help us see what we are not accustomed to seeing. Let's reveal that you have already read the answer to this question but didn't see it.

Here we go. (smile) Ask yourself or anyone you know if they have ever eaten a Jiffy peanut butter sandwich and almost everyone will answer yes. We can prove that nobody has ever eaten a Jiffy peanut butter sandwich because Jiffy doesn't exist, it's actually called **Jiff**. Well, our mind has been conditioned to hear and accept what we have perceived for so long. The exercise is to simply make us aware that it is human nature to overlook what we read and see and replace it with what has been repeatedly viewed and heard. Now we are ready to hear the alternative explanation. *At which **exact moment** did Jesus become sin on the cross?*

In the first chapter of this book, we shared a fictitious story about an atheist named Bob asking a question to his Christian friend Jiff (smile). This time read Bob's argument and question, then read Jiff's answer which explains clearly when Jesus became sin.

Bob, a former Christian, and now outspoken atheist was talking to Jiff, a Christian brother from his past, "*Let me make sure I understand and don't interrupt. You still believe that if Adam and Eve would not have eaten from the tree, that they would still be alive in the garden. You claim that death is the penalty of sin, so if you don't eat the tree then you have no sin and live forever. But you also believe in a Savior that died that never sinned. You can't have it both ways. If the penalty of sin is death, then how can you claim that your Savior, who died, was without sin? I never understood it. Those two stories contradict each other and it's ridiculous for the churches to think they can have it both ways. You must pick a side, either the penalty of sin is death, or it isn't. How can you explain it?"*

Jiff replies, *"Bob, I love the question. Please don't interrupt because I think I have an answer for you. The Book of Matthew 26:53-54 tells of the situation in the Garden of Gethsemane where Peter cuts off the ear of a man trying to arrest Jesus. Jesus miraculously heals the man's ear then declares to Peter that He could pray to His Father and He would immediately send more than twelve legions of Angels. Then Jesus asked Peter that if He did that then how would the scriptures be fulfilled?*

Jesus didn't die because of any sin committed. He willfully stayed on the cross until His death to fulfill the scriptures. He literally chose not to come off the cross. If He had committed one sin, then He would have justly died on the cross for His own sin. His willingness to stay on the cross, and His choice to accept the penalty of sin, all resulted in His death. <u>His willful death</u> is the sole act of Him becoming sin. His only participation in the sin story is His death, the penalty of sin. His death is synonymous with Him becoming sin."

Yes, this book took a big risk that many people would read that conversation and totally discard the rest of the book. A risk that had to be taken to over-rule a lifetime of doctrine embedded in passed down teaching. A doctrine most of us were taught and passed down to our kids. That said, this is an amazing moment for those that understand the path we just took. No, we aren't nearly done.

After decades of believing the passed down traditional story, let's take some time to **soak** in this new understanding for one more paragraph. We have heard "the forsaken story" our whole life, let's repeat this new understanding in one more paragraph. Isn't it awesome to have a valid explanation of 2 Corinthians 5:21 that does not require us to view the Father as one that forsakes His Son? Isn't Psalm 22 amazing? Likewise, isn't it refreshing to know that Jesus said those words in verse 46 and there was no strife in the Father's house. Surely the Father knew what His son was speaking of, right? Can you imagine Jesus telling His bride to come and visit His Father and then the bride says, "You are such an awesome Son. You stayed on that cross even when your dad forsook you, yet you still claim your Father is better than you. No way." Or "I don't want to meet your dad that has forsaken you, my dad never did that to me?" Or even worse, "I had a horrible dad that did me wrong at my greatest time of need just like your dad did to you. I have no desire to visit your ugly father. I lived my life as a Christian for you, not him."

Personal Note:

The "Forsaking Father Doctrine" is so indoctrinated that many will still cleave to it. I can't and won't go back to that. I have repented and will never entertain that doctrine again. I will tell the story in a book and publish it for the whole world to see. I have joyously endured the wrath of Christians that oppose this view. *I cannot wait for Salvation, the translation of Yeshua's name, to escort me to meet His Good, Good, Father that is incapable of forsaking anyone.*

Glory to the King!

Personal Note to my kids:

Hey kids! Sadly, your dad isn't as weird as you think!

I could end this lesson right here, right? Why can't I just say that there were two donkeys entering Jerusalem and Jesus was on the colt and His Father on the colt's mother? Boom! The lesson is done and let's move on. I just can't! I feel that would resemble a style of learning that I inherited from birth.

I have passion to continue providing more proof that my loving Father was with His Son for the entire week of the triumphal entry. I must also provide a rebuttal to Proverbs 22:8 which so many declare was the moment of forsaking in that chapter.

I am convinced that the evidence that proves the Father was with Jesus during the Triumphal entry is concealed in these two donkeys. I am **<u>DETERMINED</u>** to prove that not only is my Father not one that forsakes but He is also one that will carry your burden. I must prove that Salvation's (Jesus) loving Father was with Him the entire way.

Just the day before his crucifixion, Jesus declared that His Father would dispatch more than 12 legions of Angels. We know that never changed, right? Do we have a new vision that the entire crucifixion story took place with His loving Father by His side? This would be 100% contrary to the passed down traditions that existed before our birth.

Matthew 21:2 KJV: Saying unto them, Go into the village over against you, and straightway ye shall find an ass tied, and a colt with her: loose ***them***, and bring ***them*** unto me.

Once again, there are many variations of this story but as you can see, in Matthew 21:2 Jesus says to bring **THEM** (both donkeys).

Now let's look at Zechariah 9:9 one more time and see that it also prophecies of two donkeys.

Zechariah 9:9 KJV: Rejoice greatly, O daughter of Zion; shout, O daughter of Jerusalem: behold, thy King cometh unto thee: he is just, and having salvation; lowly, and **riding upon an ass (חמור)[30], and upon a colt (עיר) the foal of an ass (אתנות)**[2].

Notice that the two Hebrew words translated as donkey are not spelled the same. Jesus is riding on her colt (a male foal) of a female donkey (אתנות). This verse provides the spelling of a *male donkey* (חמור) which occurs 30 times in the original text and a *female donkey* (אתנות) which occurs twice in the original text. That said, understand that both of these words are referencing the colt's mother. Let's search out the spelling of each donkey to determine what is concealed within the original Hebrew. First, let's search out the female donkey.

There are many ways to apply the definition of the Hebrew letters that spell the female donkey (אתנות). My favorite is:

"The Father's (א) Covenant (ת) is the life (נ)
of the straight-up man with the nail (ו) and the cross (ת)."

The definition of the Hebrew letters for this Word adds revelation to Jesus's many references that He does the will of His Father. The definition makes it clear that His Father's covenant lives, and that Jesus's life and crucifixion fulfilled that covenant.

What is also interesting about this word is that the first two letters spell the word Et (את). These are the ***FIRST*** letter and the ***LAST*** letter of the Hebrew alphabet. This is another reference for ***First and Last*** that is not available in the translations. Later we will search out the word Et (את) but for now know that in The Book of the Revelation, Jesus refers to Himself as The Alpha and the Omega. Alpha and Omega are the first and last letters of the Greek alphabet, the Hebrew equivalent is the Alef (א) and the Tav (ת). The word Et (את) is like

Jesus's signet ring, His stamp. Also, know that the letter Tav (ת) can mean either Covenant or Cross. Now, let's add this understanding to our definition.

"Jesus (את) is the Father's (א) Covenant (ת),
His life (ב) as straight-up man with the nail (ו)
and on the cross (ת) is the Covenant."

The definition of the Hebrew letters that spell "female donkey" confirms that our Savior was riding her colt. I am confident that we will find the Father on the colt's mother.

Now let's search out the definition of the Hebrew letters that spell the first word (חמור) translated as donkey in this verse. Let's search it out with the intent of finding our Loving Father. The definition of the Hebrew letters that spell donkey (חמור) is:

"The Protection (ח) of the Womb (מ)[1],
the Straight-up man with the Nail (ו)[2],
and the Prince (ר)[3]".

So, the definition of the letters that spell donkey (חמור) protects three things 1) Jesus's birth, 2) His life as a straight up man and on the cross with the nail, and 3) and His resurrection proving that He is the Prince, the Son of God.

Is it coincidence that Zechariah 9:9 is the 30th occurrence of the word (חמור) translated as donkey and it's the verse that prophecies about the triumphal entry? The number thirty represents betrayal. How could this possibly be a coincidence?

Is it also coincidence that the word (אתנות) translated as female donkey occurs twice in the original text and the second time is found in the same verse as the "30th – betrayal" occurrence of the word (חמור) that means donkey? The number two represents a witness. Two donkeys entered Jerusalem during the triumphal entry. The Father and the Son are witnesses of the Good, Good, Father's Will for the redemption of man.

Are we convinced? Our Savior openly declares that His Father can Love even greater than Him. A humble Loving Father that protected His son. He never left His side. The last letter (ר - *Prince*) of this word (חמור) proves that ***He Protected Knowing He Would Resurrect His Son.***

Our Savior willfully suffered the shame and sin's penalty of death. By His Own Hand He willfully suffered the mockery and shame of a Roman cross because He loved the World. His Father **willfully suffered** the pain of watching the innocent blood of His murdered Son on the same Earth that He created.

<u>**Spoiler alert!**</u> Later we will search out *the first word ever spoken by the Father*. That word means "IN THE RESURRECTION".

Are we convinced that the ***Good, Good, Father*** is sitting on that Donkey and leading the way for His Son to be victorious over Sin and Death? Later we will search out the signs that Jesus revealed on the cross of conquering both sin and death. ***Yes, there was a unique sign for each.***

Many have only recently seen the story in this light. How many times do we re-read this chapter? This is beautiful and all of it is scripture-based! No conjecture!

While we are seeing the Father in a renewed reverence, this is an awesome time to reveal understanding of the 3rd Commandment.

Exodus 20:7 KJV: Thou shalt not take the name of the LORD thy God in vain (לשוא); for the LORD will not hold him guiltless that taketh his name in vain.

The Hebrew word translated as vain is Lashua (לשוא) and would be better translated as futility, the act of making His name pointless, useless, small, and insignificant. The definition of the Hebrew letters is "The Authority (ל) of the Destruction (ש) of The Straight Up Man With the Nail (ו) and His Father (א).

Nobody does a better job of making the Father insignificant than His enemy. We are guilty and forgiven for making His name small. The origin of our ability to make His name small originated in the garden. Realizing that the enemy had nearly 2,000 years of influence since the resurrection and our birth, we are certain that he is the source of the passed down deception that our Father was absent during the triumphal entry. He is the deceiver that hid the protecting mother of the colt. He is the deceiver that portrayed our Father as one that would forsake His Son.

Hey kids, I prefer you search out everything shared in this chapter until it is your story. Oh, how I wish I had known this when you were young.

Glory to the King!

Chapter 7 Stone, Rock

Believers are creationist and very aware of the phrase "intelligent design". So far, we have only performed the *Honor of Kings* for about ten words. We have an entire Bible to get done! Your first week of studying the Hebrew letters you will likely find yourself amidst a maze of understanding. Every time you turned a corner there will be more new revelation. It's like exploring a hiking trail through the DNA helix. You will confirm that it wasn't a brain effort. There is life in each Word. In our past we memorized verses with very little understanding of each word. Now we are learning words that bring life to each verse.

The next two Hebrew words we will research are Stone and Rock. You will love searching out these two words. The Hebrew word Abn (אבן) means Stone and the word Tzur (צור) means Rock.

The definition of the letters that spell Abn (אבן) is, "God's (א) House (ב) is Life (ן)." What's even more interesting is that the 1st two letters (אב) of Stone (אבן) spell Aba (אב) which means Father and the last two letters (בן) spell the word Ben (בן) which means Son. Abn (אבן) is the Father and the Son!

Acts 4:11 KJV: This is the stone (אבן) which was set at nought of you builders, which is become the head of the corner.

The stone that the builders rejected is both the Father and the Son. Enjoy rewiring all the other stone-related scriptures of your past.

The definition of the letters that of the word Tzur(צור) translated as "Rock" is, "Righteous (צ) is the Straight-up Man with the Nail (ו) and the Prince (ר)." This literally means that while Salvation walked on the Earth and dwelling in Heaven are both representations of Righteousness. Glory to the King!

A stone (abn אבן) is the Father (aba אב) and the Son (ben בן), and a Rock (tzur צור) is just the Son (ben בן).

So, Jesus tells Peter that upon this rock (tzur צור) I will build My church. Add to this that Peter's father's name is Jonah. Remember, "Simon bar Jonah"? Let's review the translation of the Greek "Simon Bar Jonah" in the KJV, NKJV, and NIV.

Matthew 16:17 <u>KJV</u>: And Jesus answered and said unto him, Blessed art thou, Simon ***Barjona***: for flesh and blood hath not revealed it unto thee, but my Father which is in heaven.

Matthew 16:17 <u>NKJV</u>: Jesus answered and said to him, "Blessed are you, Simon ***Bar-Jonah***, for flesh and blood has not revealed this to you, but My Father who is in heaven.

Matthew 16:17 <u>NIV</u>: Jesus replied, "Blessed are you, ***Simon son of Jonah***, for this was not revealed to you by flesh and blood, but by my Father in heaven.

Together, the three translations reveal that the word "Bar" is another spelling of the word Son. Sure, most Bible studiers know that Bar means son and they know that "Simon Barjona" means "Simon son of Jonah". Kids in before the early 70's only had one English translation, the KJV. How many kids, whose Granddad gave them a Bible for their birthday, understood that "Barjona" is "son of Jonah"? Some kids read the entire KJV Bible in a year without knowing the meaning of the nouns that were transliterated. Some kids read their Bible year, after year, not knowing. How old were those kids before they knew "Barjona" was "son of Jonah"? What's the point of the translators concealing information via transliteration?

Today, many teachers of children's church inform kids of truths not learned by kids in the past. Today, some kids know that Peter's father was named Jonah, and it means Dove. In some cases, these children learned it fifty years earlier in life than their teacher. Glory to the King!

The Hebrew name Jonah means Dove and the son of Dove is the Rock of the Church. Just ponder on that. Can you imagine how Biblical study and revelation would be different if the noun Jonah were translated, and The Book of Jonah was named The Book of Dove? As we continue, we will keep a list of the TRANSLATED names of the books of the Bible.

- Book of Friend (Ruth)
- Book of Dove (Jonah)

How appropriate for Yeshua (ישוע) to build His church on the son of Dove (the symbol of the spirit). Thank you, Father, we love Your Word in Your language!

Glory to the King?

Chapter 8 Atonement

It is such a treat to share the *Honor of Kings (Psalm 25:2)* effort to reveal hidden revelations about the Hebrew <u>words</u> translated as Atonement. The word Atonement is in the KJV 70 times, 69 times in the Old Testament and only once in the New Testament. That's a statistic that is a bit shocking. From all the sermons we have heard, wouldn't you "bet the farm" that the word atonement was in the New Testament more than once. Hebrew research reveals <u>seventeen different Hebrew words translated as Atonement</u>. Several of those Hebrew words are in the original Hebrew scriptures one time. It's also fair to *estimate* those seventeen Hebrew words have been translated as something other than Atonement nearly one hundred times. What do we do with those stats?

Once again, we have Hebrew words in scripture one time that are not translated as a unique English word. And now, we are talking about the word Atonement! That said, before continuing, understand we are searching out the word Atonement and not the word "Remission".

Hebrews 9:22 KJV: And <u>almost all things are by the law</u> purged with blood; and without shedding of blood is no remission.

It is **crucial** to not confuse the following research of Atonement with Remission. Our research is going to focus on the passed down traditions based on the Hebrew words translated as Atonement. Nothing in this chapter is related to searching out the word remission. We have heard many sermons where both words atonement and remission are preached, and we leave the service with the idea that these two terms were somehow related. Again, nothing in this chapter applies to remission.

Let's review the use of the word Atonement in Exodus Chapter 30 where we find that Israel is taking a census ordered by God.

Exodus 30:12 KJV: When thou takest the sum of the children of Israel after their number, then shall they give every man a ransom (כפר) for his soul unto the Lord, when thou numberest them; that there be no plague among them, when thou numberest them.

They are taking a census, and it appears each man is going to pay something as a ransom for his soul to prevent a plague among the people. So, if they don't pay the ransom then there will be a plague. Yep, that pretty much is the definition of a ransom. How is this related to the word Atonement?

The Hebrew word translated as ransom is (כפר) and it is in the Old Testament Hebrew (Tanakh) fourteen times. The issue is that in Exodus 29:33 KJV this Hebrew word (כפר) is translated as Atonement.

Let's continue this ransom story.

Exodus 30:15 KJV: The rich shall not give more, and the poor shall not give less than half a shekel, when they give an offering unto the LORD, to make an atonement (לכפר) for your souls.

The Hebrew word translated as Atonement (לכפר) in this verse is in the Old Testament (Tanakh) twenty-five times. You can see that the root Hebrew noun (לכפר) of ransom in the verse 30:12 is the same as atonement. Look at this verse carefully and confirm that you agree that it says they are using money to make an atonement. Surely, each person could have been handed a grain of rice at the door so that everyone could be counted, right? Money is being used and it is being referred to as an atonement.

The key point here is that atonement is being made by something besides blood. This is why I declared from the beginning that we are searching out Atonement and not Remission. We are already finding scriptural evidence that they are not the same.

Another key point in this verse is that each person is making an atonement for themselves. Is that correct? Is that what you see? Are there many ways and purposes to atone?

Hebrew research reveals that Atonement is a covering or a shelter which is consistent with what most of us are taught in church and hopefully you agree. That said, we have documented eleven occurrences in the KJV Old Testament where these same Hebrew words are translated as something other than Atonement. Most of those occurrences are translated as forms of reconciliation rather than a covering.

Okay, what's the point? There are _unexplained_ variations of purposes of atonement that appear to be identified by variations of Hebrew spelling. That said, rather than searching out more examples of the multiple Hebrew words translated as atonement, let's look at Jonah 4:6, am amazing story that includes a physical covering (atonement?).

Jonah 4:6 KJV: And the Lord God *prepared* (וַיְמַן) a *gourd* (קִיקָיוֹן), and made it to come up over Jonah, that it might be a shadow over his head, to deliver him from his grief (מֵרָעָתוֹ). So Jonah was exceeding (גְדוֹלָה) *glad* (שִׂמְחָה) of the gourd.

Let's make a list of what is concealed that provides critical understanding of this verse and atonement? What is NOT TOLD in this verse or story that would bring depth of understanding about atonement?

1) Jonah's name translated to English is Dove. Yes, DOVE!
2) From Noah's story, the Dove returned with a broken Olive Branch, which is why we view it as a symbol of the Holy Spirit.
3) From Jesus's baptism we know the Dove is a symbol of the Holy Spirit.
4) The spelling of the Hebrew word for gourd (קִיקָיוֹן) is unique, only once in the Old Testament.
5) The Hebrew word for "prepared" (וַיְמַן) is also translated as <u>appointed</u>, provided, and arranged.
6) The Hebrew word translated as "glad" is in the Hebrew Old Testament thirty-five times and is translated as "rejoicing" *every time* except here.
7) The Hebrew word translated as "exceeding" is in the Hebrew Old Testament seventy-two times and is almost always translated as "great". So instead of Jonah being "exceeding glad" he "greatly rejoicing" about his covering. Is that significant?
8) If the purpose of the prophet Dove's life is to provide a better understanding of the Holy Spirit, then is the role of "the gourd" a symbolic teaching of a covering or of atonement?
9) The Apostle Peter's father's name is Jonah. How does that fact play into this story? Surely it does, right?
10) Jonah's father's name is Amittai which means "My Truth". That "plays well" with the idea that "My Truth" would send Dove to teach us.
11) Is the Hebrew noun translated as "gourd" (קִיקָיוֹן) able to provide insight of Atonement? The fact that it covers Jonah's head and provides "a shadow" is a great start.
12) The "gourd" delivered Jonah from his grief! The word grief is in the KJV twenty-seven times, but this Hebrew word is only in the original Hebrew text three times. (Jeremiah 18:8, Jeremiah 23:14) Yes, another great sermon.

Summarizing, the best understanding of Atonement as a covering is provided in the Book of Dove (Holy Spirit). Our covering is Jesus, His Hebrew name is Yeshua which translated to English is Salvation. Salvation is our covering.

Glory to the King!

Chapter 9 Phr Phre (פר - פרה) – Bull Cow

Did you honestly have any idea that you would consider studying the Bible one Hebrew word at a time? It's dumbfounding to learn that by searching out the single spelling of a Hebrew word would eliminate a large portion of translated verses that you would have otherwise include. Did you have any idea that so many Hebrew words were translated as the same English word? That disqualifies the idea of a topic study using translations.

Are you beginning to see a pattern of the words we are searching out? We are searching out things you would have seen if you were in Jerusalem during the week of the triumphal entry. By now it should make sense that if all the letters are related to the Kingdom of God, then each word will have a Kingdom related understanding. It will become clear that the spelling of animals, trees, cities, plants, fragrances, spices, foods, nations, and people are all ordained. If every letter of the Hebrew alphabet has a Kingdom related meaning, then every word spelled by those letters has a Kingdom related definition. The more you study, the more clearly is His omniscience recognized. Let's continue by reviewing one of the most common stories of the cross, when they pierced His side.

John 19:37 KJV: But one of the soldiers with a spear pierced his side, and forthwith came there out blood and water

Let's search out this story and find clarity of God's plan for the water coming out of His side. But before we do, is it important to know about the water? The blood has been preached our entire life and the water is only mentioned while reading the verse. If the water came out with the blood, then surely it is equally as important, correct? That said, to prove this story will require searching out several words over the next five chapters. The first words we will search out are Calf, Bull, Bullock, or Heifer.

The word "Bull" or "Bullock" has been used in the KJV 148 times. *One* of the Hebrew words translated as Bullock is ephr הפר. The word (ephr הפר) is a young bull to be used as a sacrifice. This word has been used in Hebrew Old Testament (Tanakh) 39 times. The definition of the letters is that spell (ephr הפר) is, "Behold (ה) the Words (פ) of the Prince (ר)". What? Yes, the Hebrew word for a young bull to be sacrificed means "Behold the words of the prince!"

Wait a minute! So, there are 39 occurrences in the original Hebrew text where a "Sacrificed Bull" represents "Behold the Words of the Prince". The translations do not provide any distinction of these 39 occurrences from the other 109 occurrences of different Hebrew words also translated as Bull or Young Bull. Is it possible, or likely, that our Savior fulfilled the 40th occurrence of this word? If so, how? Coincidence?

To be clearer, understand that a Young Bull to be Sacrificed is the Hebrew word ephr (הפר) and a Bull is phr (פר).

The word Heifer occurs 19 times in the KJV nineteen times and is translated from several different Hebrew words. Once again, chapters of the tenacious efforts to reconcile the translation efforts have been removed from this book. Just know that the same Hebrew words translated as "Heifer" in the KJV are also translated as something other than "Heifer".

Sadly, translating a single word in the original text as different words in the KJV is a **VERY COMMON** occurrence! The Hebrew word (הדברים) translated as "Deuteronomy" as in the "Book of Deuteronomy" occurs 134 times in the original text and is never translated as "Deuteronomy". Only in the title of the Book is this word translated as "Deuteronomy". Sadly, often this word is translated as "things" or "matters".

After documenting and then removing pages of research, it was decided to summarize and reveal that the word (פרה) translated as "Heifer" is very similar to the word (הפר) also translated as "Young Bull" several times. The definition of the letters of this word (פרה) is "The Word (פ) of the Prince (ר) to be Revealed (ה)". Further research revealed the relationship between these two words and the water that poured from Jesus's pierced side.

Let's search out Numbers Chapter 19 and begin revealing why water poured out from Jesus's side when it was pierced. What is the significance of this water? Is it as significant as the blood?

Numbers Chapter 19 provides details of the Statute of the Red Heifer. Let's begin with Numbers 19:2.

Numbers 19:2 KJV: This is the *ordinance* (חקת) of *the law* (התורה) which the LORD hath commanded, saying, Speak unto the children of Israel, that they bring thee a *red* (אדמה)[18] *heifer* (פרה)[4] *without spot* (תמימה)[8], wherein is no blemish (aa), and upon which never came yoke:

This verse provides clear understanding that many of us are unaware of the significance of the water that poured from Jesus's side when it was pierced. Let's search out a few words from the original text of this verse that are not translated correctly and try to understand the impact if translated correctly.

<u>The Hebrew word Translated as "Spot" (תמימה)</u>

The word "spot" is in the KJV 24 times and the phrase "without spot" is in the KJV 11 times and this verse is the only time that the Hebrew word (תמימה) is translated as "without spot". To be clear, the other ten times the phrase "without spot" occurs in the KJV, it is not translated from this word (תמימה).

The Hebrew word (תמימה) translated as "without spot" in Numbers 19:2 is in the original text eight times, and this is the seventh occurrence, and the only it was translated as "without spot". The number seven in Hebrew means perfection and the number eight means protection and/or new beginnings. Has this verse been translated well enough for us to visualize the heifer as perfectly flawless?

What verse is the amazing eighth occurrence of this Hebrew word? Only by searching out this Hebrew word would we ever have an understanding that there is a difference between perfect, without spot, and flawless. Though the English definition of these three words is somewhat synonymous, the original Hebrew definition is very different.

The Hebrew word (תמימה) translated as "without spot" translates to "Flawless (תמים) to be revealed (ה)". The root Hebrew word flawless (תמים) is in the original Hebrew text an additional forty-nine times. Before the early 1970's the KJV was the only English translation of the "divine and inspired" word of God and *the word "flawless" is not in the KJV. It's also not in the NKJV* and it is only six times in the NIV. The number fifty in Hebrew represents "Jubilee", a time of rejoicing. Is it possible that our "flawless" Savior who fulfilled scripture is the 50th occurrence of this word that describes the red heifer?

How would "the church culture" be different if the word "flawless" were more common and able to be referenced correctly by scripture and verse? Would the eighth occurrence the word (תמימה) translated as "without spot" but means "flawless to be revealed" inspire additional understanding?

Psalm 19:7 KJV: The law of the Lord is perfect (תמימה), converting the soul: the testimony of the Lord is sure, making wise the simple.

Let's substitute "flawless to be revealed" into this verse and reveal the concealed prophecy.

Psalm 19:7 KJV: The law of the Lord is *flawless to be revealed* (תמימה), converting the soul: the testimony of the Lord is sure, making wise the simple.

Is this verse prophesying that our *flawless* Savior is the law? Let's continue searching out the water that poured from our Savior's side.

The Hebrew word Lawlessness (און)

The Hebrew word (און) meaning lawless, or lawlessness is in the original text 82 times. It is not in the Old Testament of the KJV or NKJV and is only once in the NIV. Again, how would our church culture be different if the words lawless or lawlessness were common and included in our Biblical vocabulary?

Many of us have parents that never went to church and out Bible vocabulary and culture came directly from the KJV. As we grew up, any church that did a better job of teaching directly from the KJV was perceived as increased Truth of Scripture. Few of us have experienced multiple near-death experiences and even fewer have ever visited a Christian Hebrew Bible Study group where they could hear how easy it is to learn Hebrew. There isn't a required path to hear "Learn Hebrew, it's easy!" Learn and validate everything you read in this book!

Researching the original Hebrew text will lead you to realize that your Biblical vocabulary and knowledge was founded and determined by the KJV translators. The removal and replacement of words like "flawless" and "lawlessness" and many more are proof that our Biblical vocabulary was not an accidental. Learn about the "Qere and Ketiv", an effort that began in the 10th and 11th century to eliminate words that are written from being spoken. The success of this process is why words were removed and there is natural discomfort hearing and speaking the words Torah, Yeshua, Elohim, and Yahweh in our church culture. Though nearly all the Hebrew nouns were not translated but rather transliterated into our English Bibles, the words flawless, lawless, Torah, Yeshua, Elohim, and Yahweh were totally removed from many of our

English translations. As we continue revealing the traditional lies from our birth, consider whether this effort was by design and why.

Many didn't learn how to read and study Hebrew words until late in life. Learn how to read and study the original Hebrew divine and inspired Word of God, everything else is a translation. That said, the original text will confirm that Jesus is our Salvation and will answer many questions left unanswered and not approachable topics. That said, we will search out Jesus, the name above all names, later in this book.

Our lack of knowledge about the water that poured from Jesus's side is not an accident. Let's continue this research by reviewing the Statue of Purification in Numbers 19:2-6.

Numbers 19:2-6 KJV: [2] This is the ordinance of the law which the LORD hath commanded, saying, Speak unto the children of Israel, that they bring thee a red heifer (פרה) without spot, wherein is no blemish, and upon which never came yoke:
[3] And ye shall give her unto Eleazar the priest, that he may bring her forth without the camp, and one shall slay her before his face:
[4] And Eleazar the priest shall take of her blood with his finger, and sprinkle of her blood directly before the tabernacle of the congregation seven times:
[5] And one shall burn the heifer (הפרה) in his sight; her skin, and her flesh, and her blood, with her dung, shall he burn:
[6] And the priest shall take **cedar wood**, and **hyssop**, and **scarlet**, and cast it into the midst of the burning of the **heifer**.

A common church slogan is "The Old Testament is the New Testament concealed and the New Testament is the Old Testament revealed". We will soon learn that all the items in verse six were at the cross. We will search out each of these words before revealing them in the Gospels. These four items were mixed in water that is referred to as "Water of Purification". Yes, Purification is another word that is not common in our church culture. We have already searched out cedar and wood. The Hebrew word translated as Wood in Numbers 19:6 is also the word translated as Tree.

Now let's continue searching out the word (פרה) translated as "Heifer". Earlier we revealed that the Hebrew spelling of the word (פרה) translated as Heifer in Numbers 19:2 is in the original Hebrew text four times. The first time this word was used is found in Genesis 35:11.

Genesis 35:11 KJV: And God said unto him, I am God Almighty: be fruitful (פרה) and multiply; a nation and a company of nations shall be of thee, and kings shall come out of thy loins;

The word is PROPERLY translated as fruitful. How is that possible? How can the word PROPERLY translated as Heifer and fruitful? Before revealing the understanding of how this is possible let's review and see that the word translated as Heifer in the remainder of Numbers Chapter 19 is spelled slightly differently. Let's look at Numbers 19:2,5.

Numbers 19:2,5 KJV: [2] This is the ordinance of the law which the LORD hath commanded, saying, Speak unto the children of Israel, that they bring thee a red heifer (פרה) without spot, wherein is no blemish, and upon which never came yoke:

[5] And one shall burn the heifer (הפרה) in his sight; her skin, and her flesh, and her blood, with her dung, shall he burn:

Notice that the Hebrew word (פרה) for a sacrificial Heifer before it is killed is spelled differently (הפרה) than after it is killed. The definition of the Hebrew letters of the word translated as Heifer before it is killed is, "The Words (פ) of the Prince (ר) to be Revealed (ה)". Think about what we learned in the Donkey Chapter. Jesus's words that He spoke on the cross were not understood while He was alive. Isn't this beautiful!

The definition of the letters of the Hebrew word translated as Heifer after it is sacrificed is, "Behold (ה) the Words (פ) of the Prince (ר) Revealed (ה)". Yes! The only difference is that after our Savior's death, His Words are understood, they are available to behold. The revelation of Words of the Prince is only available after He dies. You could even argue the revelation of His words weren't available until after His resurrection.

- Cedar - The Father (א) and His Son (ר) are Perfect (ז).
- Wood - See (ע) Righteousness (צ).
- Heifer (before death) - The Words (פ) of the Prince (ר) to be Revealed (ה).
- Heifer (after death) - Behold (ה) the Words (פ) of the Prince (ר) to be Revealed (ה).
- Hyssop – To be determined.

- Scarlet – To be determined.

Again, this is a list of what is added to the water for it to become purification water. Let's continue and search out Hyssop and Scarlet and then we will understand the purpose of the water that poured from His pierced side.

Chapter 10 Scarlet

We are searching out the ingredients that were added to the purification water listed in Numbers 19:6. Let's search out the word Scarlet.

Numbers 19:6 KJV: [6] And the priest shall take **cedar wood**, and **hyssop**, and **scarlet** (ושני תולעת), and cast it into the midst of the burning of the **heifer**.

There are two words (ושני תולעת) from the original text in Numbers 19:6 that combine and become translated as Scarlet in Number 19:6. The first Hebrew word is Vashni (ושני) which means "Two of" or "Double Dipped". The definition of the letters for this word is, "The Straight Up Man with the Nail (ו) was Destroyed (ש) and gave His Life (נ) by His Own Hand that does Mighty Deeds (י)".

The second word (תולעת) that combined with the first translates to Scarlet is Thuloth (תולעת) which means "Crimson" or "Worm". The definition of the letters that spell Crimson is, "The Covenant (ת) of the Straight Up Man with the Nail (ו) was Authorized (ל) for All to See (ע) on the Cross (ת)".

Pretty sure that double-dipped crimson is a new phrase for most of us. Let's look at Exodus 35:25 and Isaiah 1:18.

Exodus 35:25 KJV: And all the women that were wise hearted did spin with their hands, and brought that which they had spun, both of blue, and of purple, and of scarlet (ושני תולעת), and of fine linen.

Isaiah 1:18 KJV: Come now, and let us reason together, saith the LORD: though your sins be as scarlet, they shall be as white as snow; though they be red like crimson, they shall be as wool.

When reading and studying the use of crimson and scarlet, we are reminded of our Savior on the cross that surely had dried blood (crimson) as well as open wombs bleeding (scarlet) on His body and physically appeared to be "double dipped" while He declares, "Father, forgive them for they know not what they do.", Luke 23:34

Chapter 11 Azub (אזוב) – Hyssop

Earlier while studying the word Donkey, it was declared that we would search out the Hebrew Word translated as Hyssop used in John 19:29. Well, it's time.

Similar to the word "heifer", the Hebrew word for Hyssop has multiple spellings. The spelling of the word Hyssop used in the story of the Passover in Egypt is spelled slightly different that the Hebrew word Hyssop used in Numbers Chapter 19 in the description of the Statue of Purification. Let's compare the spelling of Hyssop in Exodus 12:22 with Numbers 19:6.

Exodus 12:22 KJV: And ye shall take a bunch of hyssop (אזוב), and dip it in the blood that is in the bason, and strike the lintel and the two side posts with the blood that is in the bason; and none of you shall go out at the door of his house until the morning.

Numbers 19:6 KJV: And the priest shall take **cedar wood**, and **hyssop** (ואזוב)[1], and **scarlet**, and cast it into the midst of the burning of the **heifer**.

The definition of Hyssop (אזוב) from the Hebrew letters is another of those that has a visual revelation. In the spelling of the Hebrew word (אזוב) translated as Hyssop in Exodus 12:22, the first (א) and last letters (ב) of the word spell father (abba אב) which is also God's (א) House (ב). The middle two letters are Zayin-Vav (זו) which means the Perfection (ז) of the Straight Up Man with the Nail (ו). So, the definition of Hyssop from the letters is, "The Perfect Straight Up Man with the Nail is inside the House of God, His Father." BEAUTIFUL, RIGHT!!!

Notice that the only difference in the spelling of Hyssop (ואזוב- אזוב) in these two verses is the first letter (ו) of the word (וַאזוב) in Numbers 19:6. That letter is the Hebrew letter Vav (וַאזוב). The Hebrew letter Vav (ו) means the Straight Up Man with the Nail. Since this Hebrew word has two Vavs (וַאזַוב) in its spelling, let's separate the definition of the letter. Let's consider the "Straight Up Man" is Jesus's sinless life and the "Nail" is His crucifixion. That said, definition of the letters in this word (ואזוב) is, "The sinless life of the Straight Up Man (ו) proved His Father (א) is Perfect (ז) and after the Nail (ו) returned to His Father's House (ב)". Glory to the King!

In the Book of Exodus's Passover story, the death angel saw the blood of the lamb sacrificed that was applied to the doorpost by dipping hyssop into the blood and striking the doorpost. God required the death angel to pass over these homes where the blood was applied with hyssop, "***The sinless life of the Straight Up Man*** (ו) ***proved His Father*** (א) ***is Perfect*** (ז) ***and after the Nail*** (ו) ***returned to His Father's House*** (ב)".

In Numbers 19:6 we see that hyssop is added to the sacrifice of the Heifer while it is burning. Now let's look at John 19:28-30.

John 19:28-30 KJV: [28] After this, Jesus knowing that all things were now accomplished, that the scripture might be fulfilled, saith, I thirst.
[29] Now there was set a vessel full of vinegar: and they filled a spunge with vinegar, and put it upon hyssop, and put it to his mouth.
[30] When Jesus therefore had received the vinegar, he said, It is finished: and he bowed his head, and gave up the ghost.

In verse 28 we see that only for the purpose of fulfilling scripture does Jesus declare that He is thirsty. What scripture did He fulfill? As we review these three verses, the translation has us focusing on the vinegar. Even in verse 30 it focuses Jesus's last words on Him receiving the vinegar.

Remember we discovered that the Heifer meant that we would not be able to understand the Words of the Prince until after the "Heifer" died? Well, would you be surprised to learn that the translators didn't understand His words? Do you see that it focuses on vinegar and not Hyssop? The Hyssop represents this is the last Mighty Deed of His Hand before He gives up the Ghost.

Numbers 19:6 says to cast the Cedar Wood, the Hyssop, and the Scarlet onto the burning Heifer. Do you see it?

Look at the "fires" of death upon our Savior's destroyed body. He is nailed to a tree (Wood) which means to ***See Righteousness***. The tree is made of Cedar which means the ***Father and the Son are Perfect***. His body is covered with dried Crimson and fresh Scarlet blood (double dipped) that tells us He was Destroyed and gave His Life by His Own Hand that does Mighty Deeds which means that He could have saved Himself if He wanted. The Hyssop that tells us that He is leaving to be with His Father. Now for us to understand His words, the Heifer must die.

There is one thing left that we haven't discussed. The Water. The Waters of Life (מים)! The definition of the letters that spell Waters is, "The Birth (מ) of The Hand That Does Mighty Deeds (י) from a Closed Womb (ם), a Virgin".

They pierced His side, and the Blood flowed for the remission of our Sins and the Water flowed to purify us from our Death.

The Water of Purification from our Death:

- Cedar - The Father (א) and His Son (ר) are Perfect (ז).
- Wood - See (ע) Righteousness (ץ).
- Heifer (before death) - The Words (פ) of the Prince (ר) to be Revealed (ה).
- Heifer (after death) - Behold (ה) the Words (פ) of the Prince (ר) to be Revealed (ה).
- Scarlet – He was destroyed by His own hands. He could have saved Himself.
- Hyssop – It is Finished, He is once again with His Father.

All of these were added to the Waters of Life, the Birth of the Hand that Does Mighty Deeds from a Virgin. The waters that flowed from His pierced side of His already dead body. The water that flowed from the Dead Heifer, which enables us to understand His words. He is our Lamb. He is our purification from death, the Water of Life!

Glory to the King!

Chapter 12 Oz (עז) – Goat or Strength

Let's continue searching out the translations of Hebrew nouns. The next word we will search out is the Hebrew root word for Goat or Strength which is Oz (עז). The definitions of the Hebrew letters that spell goat is Ayin (ע) which is the 13th letter of the alphabet and means eye and the last letter is Zayin (ז) the 7th letter of the alphabet and means Perfect and/or Sword. So, the definition of the word from the letters is "See Perfection" or "See a Sword".

The application of the definition of the letters for goat isn't as easy as what was clearly visible for the word (שה) lamb. Also, how can this one word represent both Goat and Strength? The Hebrew word Oz (עז) occurs in the original text fifty-three times and is translated many times as strength or goat. Similar to how we used the Hebrew name of *Moses* (משה) to reveal understanding about the *lamb* (שה), we will use the name *Boaz* (בעז) to reveal understanding about the *goat* (עז).

The story of *Boaz* (בעז), the kinsman redeemer, in the Book of Ruth is well known in most churches. His role as the kinsman redeemer of Ruth who is not an Israelite is a foreshadowing of how Christ redeemed all people and not just Israel. The name *Boaz* (בעז) translated to English is "In Him is Strength". As you can see the last two letters of Boaz's (בעז) name spell goat (עז). The first letter of Boaz's name is the Bet (ב) which is the 2nd letter of the Hebrew alphabet and means House. Another sign of strength is that Boaz is the name of one of the two posts in the vestibule of the temple which proves "In Him is Strength".

1 Kings 7:21 KJV: Then he set up the pillars by the vestibule of the temple; he set up the pillar on the right and called its name Jachin, and he set up the pillar on the left and called its name *Boaz* (בעז).

Let's reveal two goats that are used for a specific purpose which also have the root word of goat within their names. These two goats will reveal the strength of the goat and bring understanding to how Oz can represent a goat with great strength, the strongest spiritual animal in scripture. Let's review Leviticus 16:6-10.

Leviticus 16:6-10 KJV: [6] "Aaron shall offer the bull as a sin offering, which is for himself, and make atonement for himself and for his house.

⁷ He shall take the two goats and present them before the LORD at the door of the tabernacle of meeting.

⁸ Then Aaron shall cast lots for the two goats: one lot for the LORD and the other lot *for the scapegoat* (לעזאזל)⁴.

⁹ And Aaron shall bring the goat on which the LORD's lot fell, and offer it as a sin offering. ¹⁰ But the goat on which the lot fell *to be the scapegoat* (לעזאזל) shall be presented alive before the LORD, to make atonement upon it, and to let it *go as the scapegoat* (לעזאזל) into the wilderness.

These four verses have a lot to unpack, and it would be easy to drift into various topics by revealing more verses that of how Aaron made atonement UPON the goat. In summary, Aaron would lean (Hebrew word is Samech) on the goat. The goat is so strong that it would not fall. This act of leaning would then transfer all the sins of Israel to the scapegoat. The goat is strong enough to carry all those sins far from camp so they would never return. Now that is a strong goat!

Let's look deeper into the spelling of the scapegoat and see if it is even stronger. The Hebrew word translated as scapegoat is "For Azazel (לעזאזל)". Who is Azazel? Let's review several translations to see if we can determine what a scapegoat is and what "For Azazel" means.

- The NIV has a footnote that says, *"The meaning of the Hebrew for this word is uncertain;"*
- The LSB has a footnote that says, *"Lit goat of removal; or possibly a name: Azazel"*
- The NASB 1995 has a footnote that says, *"Lit goat of removal, or else a name: Azazel"*.

Ok, so we have a reference that the Hebrew word Azazel is acknowledged in some of the translations. Sadly verses 8, 10, and 12 of this chapter are the only places in the Bible that this word is used. Do we just give up? Never!

Later in the book we will provide more historical evidence of the evolution of the Books of the Canon. First, the word "Canon" is a Catholic term. In summary, ever since the formation of the Council of Nicaea the Roman Catholic Church has been the governing body of which books are in the Canon. Centuries later after the formation of the protestant churches, the decisions of the Roman Catholic Church to remove books from the "Canon" and deem them as no longer divine and inspired has been maintained without questioning from protestants. Well, Azazel is a well-known entity in the Book of Enoch, a book removed by the Catholic Church in 1684. That said, The Book of Enoch is still considered divine and inspired by the Ethiopian Bible and a few other cultures.

Without going into any further depth of research we will simply declare that Azazel is the Hebrew name of a fallen angel. You must do your own research to determine if you believe he is who he is implied to be.

Now, back to the scapegoat which in Hebrew means "For Azazel" goat. This goat takes all the sins of Israel and lays them on Azazel who will be held accountable for all sin on the day of judgment. This goat goes to the face of Azazel and forces him to take the blame for everything he is carrying. Wow, now that is a strong goat. You really need to confirm this. And don't believe it until you do. Of course, when you do prove it true you will have to ask yourself many more questions, right? Can you trust the compelling evidence about Azazel found in the Book of Enoch? If this evidence is true, then why was evidence that defines and condemns God's enemy removed from the Bible? Why hasn't the decisions of the Catholic Church in 1684 to remove Books from the Bible ever been revisited? Why now, how old were you when you learned about Azazel?

When you learn that the evidence exists, remember *"The Strength of a Goat"*.

Glory to the King!

Chapter 13 Et - The First and the Last

The *First letter and the Last* letter of the Hebrew alphabet spell the Hebrew word Et (את) also commonly referred to as "Alef-Tav". Nothing we will study from the original Hebrew text will impact the translations like learning about the word Et - Alef-Tav (את). This is the "Big One".

Revelation 22:13 KJV: I am Alpha and Omega, the beginning and the end, the first and the last.

In Revelation 22:13 Jesus, whose Hebrew name is Yeshua (ישוע), declares Himself to be Alpha and Omega, the *First and the Last*. Alpha and Omega are the first and last letters of the Greek alphabet. The Hebrew equivalent to Alpha and Omega is the Alef (א) and the Tav (ת) which is the word Et (את). The "Big Deal" about this word Et (את) is that it occurs 7,372 times in the Hebrew text, the Old Testament (Tanakh) *AND IS NOT TRANSLATED*. The Expanded Bible Translation (EXB) is the only English translation that acknowledges this word by displaying a very faint dot where it occurs.

How is this possible? The extent of the impact of this knowledge is related to the knowledge of the Hebrew alphabet. The more you know, the greater the impact of this issue. The Hebrew alphabet is debatably unlike any other alphabet. Those that know Greek would claim similarities.

Each letter of Hebrew has a numeric value, a definition, a paleo Hebrew pictograph symbol, a word that pronounces the letter and adds additional numerical and depth of definition, and a mystery of application within the scriptures. Each of the twenty-two letters is also associated with its adjacent letters. That said, the first letter Alef (א) is related to the second letter Bet (ב) and is also related to the last letter Tav (ת). This means that the Hebrew alphabet forms a circle and not a straight line.

The letter Alef (א) is "The God Letter" and has a value of one. The letter Tav (ת) means "Covenant" and its paleo Hebrew symbol is a "cross". The sentence formed from the definition of these two letters is, "God's (א) Covenant (ת) on the Cross (ת)".

Though there is much more to learn about the Hebrew alphabet, the question debated between the native Hebrew unbelievers of Yeshua and the Christians that learn how to read and research Hebrew is,

"Is our Savior declaring that He is the word Et (את)?
Was He literally referencing the "first and the last"
letters of His alphabet are His name?

Our Savior's transliterated name is Jesus, and His Hebrew name is Yeshua (ישוע) which translated means "Salvation". If Yeshua says that He is Et (את), then does that mean we can translate the word (את) as "Salvation"? If so, is it possible to exaggerate the impact of the translations if the word "salvation" is added to the Bible 7,372 times? Likewise, is it possible to exaggerate the impact of knowing and continuing to ignore this word in the Bible?

There is an alternative teaching that denies that the word Et (את) has a definition. They claim "God (א) Covenant (ת)" or "God (א) on the Cross (ת)" is a grammatical pointer that directs…etc. Is it possible that these are the same people that influenced the word את not to be revealed in the English translations? Could this issue have existed prior to the translation of the KJV? We know how the translators dealt with it, they simply ignored it and didn't even provide footnotes that it existed.

We won't mention names of people that provide Biblical research online, but we will confirm that there are people who have made courageous lifetime investments of Biblical research and documentation. Hopefully Traditions, Lies from Birth, becomes your personal documentation, something you can share with your children, all that you love, all that you have hurt, and all that has done harm to you. Choose to willfully and intentionally learn, document, and share what you have learned and how it differs from the lies that existed prior to our birth. Many of us have already experienced persecution from the courage to expose what we learn from the original Hebrew text. That said, as we get older, the persecution doesn't sting like it did when we were younger.

We love the Word of God. We learned to love when a new translation came out that added more insight to what the KJV provided. We never held the translators of various translations accountable to the original Hebrew text. We call every translation *"the divine and inspired"* word of God, even though the copyright is dated after we were born.

Many of us never considered calling our translations what they are. They are translations of the divine and inspired original Hebrew text. Yes, studying Alef-Tav - Et (את) brought many to this understanding.

Let's review how our Savior used the Alef-Tav - Et (את) to reveal His participation throughout His word by researching a few occurrences of Alef-Tav - Et (את) in the original Hebrew text of stories that many of us are familiar.

In the original Hebrew text, almost everyone mentioned in the genealogy of Abraham has Alef Tav (את) preceding their name the first time it is written. That said, in the Book of Ruth, Ruth's name does not. Ruth's name is simply "Ruth (רות)" until she is redeemed by Boaz. The next occurrence of her name she is Alef Tav-Ruth (את-רות), the Salvation (את) – Ruth (רות).

In the original Hebrew text Jonah's name does not have the Et (את) before his name until Jonah 1:15 where he is "lifted up" to be tossed into the sea. From the time Jonah is lifted-up to the time that the fish vomits him upon the shore, his name is Alef Tav Jonah (את-יונה), Salvation (את) – Jonah (יונה).

The stories of Alef-Tav (את) are endless. It is as though our Savior is placing a stamp from His signet ring on His Word throughout the scriptures. It's not surprising that the occurrence of Alef-Tav (את) begins in Genesis 1:1 where the word Et (את) stands alone twice in the verse but with a bit of uniqueness. Most that learn Hebrew spend weeks studying the original Hebrew text of Genesis 1:1. There is literally that much to unpack and all of it is beautiful.

בראשית ברא אלהים אֵת השמים ואֵת הארץ

HAARETZ V'ET HASHAMAYIM ET ELOHIM BARA BERESHET

Hebrew is read right to left so notice that Et (את) is in the verse twice. Notice also that the 2nd time it has the letter Vav (ו) in front. The Vav (ו) represents the Straight Up Man with the Nail. Would you find it interesting to learn that the word Et (את), the "First and the Last", precedes the word Hashamayim (השמים) which means "the heavens" and the word HaAretz (הארץ) means "earth"? Does that change your salvation? Well of course not! Does it make you adore the genius of your Creator's language? Yes! Does it bring adoration to the words of John, "In the beginning was the word…" Of course it does, our Savior is included in that verse! Increased revelation brings added adoration for *The Word* and brings new understanding to *The Word* becoming *Flesh*. The word Et (את) adds refreshing complexity and clarity to *The Word.*

ET – The First and the Last - את
The First(א) and the Last(ת), God's(א) Covenant(ת).

Chapter 14 The 5ᵗʰ Commandment

The 5ᵗʰ Commandment is in Exodus 20:12 and repeated in Deuteronomy 5:16.

Exodus 20:12 KJV: Honour thy father and thy mother: that thy days may be long upon the land which the Lord thy God giveth thee.

Deuteronomy 5:16 KJV: Honour thy father and thy mother, as the Lord thy God hath commanded thee; that thy days may be prolonged, and that it may go well with thee, in the land which the Lord thy God giveth thee.

Many are blessed and unaware of the point of contention with this commandment. The commandment doesn't say honor your mother and father *if they deserve it*. How are we to explain to a child of an abuser, an atheist, or a murderer that they must honor their mother and father just as a child of a Christian family honors their father? Yes, many of us have undertaken that effort and blessings to all of us that love children and do our best to serve our Savior in that effort.

If you're the child of an abusive home, please read this entire chapter! Read and learn about the ***SALVATION of our GOOD FATHER!***

Let's search out Exodus 20:12.

Exodus 20:12 KJV: *Honour* (כבד)[41] *thy father* (את-אביך) *and thy mother* (אביך-ואת): that thy days may be long upon the land which the Lord thy God giveth thee.

The word (כבד) translated as "Honour" occurs 41 times in the original text and the first occurrence is Genesis 12:10.

Genesis 12:10 KJV: And there was a famine in the land: and Abram went down into Egypt to sojourn there; for the famine *was grievous* (כבד-כי)[41] in the land.

No, wait a minute! Is the word (כבד) translated as "Honour" in the fifth commandment translated as *"grievous"*? We will search out the verse because there is much to tell but let's look at the second occurrence in Genesis 13:2 and see if we can get some clarity.

Genesis 13:2 KJV: And Abram *was* very *rich* (כִּי-כָבֵד)[41] in cattle, in silver, and in gold.

That didn't help! We will return to this verse but first let's continue doing what Jesus said to do in Matthew 4:4! The word (כִּי) translated as *"was"* occurs 4,377 times in the original text. The third occurrence is Genesis 41:31.

Genesis 41:31 KJV: And the plenty shall not be known in the land by reason of that famine following; for it *shall be* very *grievous* (כִּי-כָבֵד)[41].

The word (כבד) is translated as grievous again. Okay, this is the beginning of a stroll down *Confusion Street*. After walking a long way down this road, it will become very clear that this stroll is necessary! Let's continue our journey down *Confusion Street*.

Let's look at the tenth occurrence, the "It is finished" occurrence in Exodus 7:14.

Exodus 7:14 KJV: And the Lord said unto Moses, Pharaoh's heart is *hardened* (כבד), he refuseth to let the people go.

No, we can't stop! We must find commonality of how this word (כבד) *is translated.* The eleventh occurrence is the occurrence that represents a covering.

Exodus 8:24 KJV: And the Lord did so; and there came a *grievous* (כבד) swarm of flies into the house of Pharaoh, and into his servants' houses, and into all the land of Egypt: the land was corrupted by reason of the swarm of flies.

This doesn't make sense! How do we explain this? Let's look at the last occurrence, the 41st occurrence in the Book of Nahum. How old were you when you learned that the word (נחום) translated as "Nahum" means *"comforter"*? Let's look at the last occurrence, the 41st occurrence, the occurrence that follows the fortieth occurrence, of the word (כבד) found in The book of Comforter 2:9 (smile).

Comforter (Nahum) 2:9 KJV: Take ye the spoil of silver, take the spoil of gold: for there is none end of the store and *glory* (כבד) out of all the pleasant furniture.

Oh my, we have a mess to sort out! Note that it's only a mess because of the translation. Our Good Father didn't make this mess! Many of us use various concordances that repeatedly tell us that a particular word can have multiple meanings. Learn Hebrew and rid yourself of these concordances! Our Good Father made His language the easiest to learn! Join the millions of Christians that have learned to depend on our Father's words from His language.

To learn the truth about the original text requires an incomprehensible effort to clear out the knowledge that has been embedded into our minds from decades of church teaching that is debatably founded by Darby and Schofield. That said, the easiest way to sort out the beauty of the word (כבד) translated as "Honour" is to search out the words "Father" and "Mother". First let's look at this verse once again and recognize the words from the original text that were not translated into the KJV.

Exodus 20:12 KJV: ~~Honour~~ *Grieve* (כבד)[41] *thy father* (את-אביך) *and thy mother* (ואת-אביך): that thy days may be long upon the land which the Lord thy God giveth thee.

===================

Exodus 20:12 (Modified): ~~Honour~~ *Grieve* (כבד)[41] *thy Salvation father* (אֶת-אביך) *and thy Salvation mother* (וְאֶת-אמך): that thy days may be long upon the land which the Lord thy God giveth thee.

We just learned about the word Et (את), the *First and the Last*. The word Et (את) occurs nine times in the Ten Commandments and the word Vah-Et (ואת) occurs an additional three times. Our Savior, whose Hebrew name means Salvation, is included in this verse but 'who is our Salvation Father and our Salvation Mother? Is this referencing our DNA parents?

Yes, let's choose to search out "Salvation Father and Salvation Mother" to determine if it brings clarity to the 5th Commandment.

Oddly enough, the first mentioning of "Father and Mother" in the translations is also the first mentioning of "Salvation Father and Salvation Mother" in the original text. Let's look at Genesis 2:24.

Genesis 2:23-24 KJV: [23] And Adam said, *This* (זאת)[251] is now bone of my bones, and flesh of my flesh: *she* (לזאת)[5] shall be called Woman, because she was taken out of Man.

²⁴ Therefore shall a man leave *his father* (אֶת-אָבִיו) *and his mother* (וְאֶת-אִמּוֹ), and shall cleave unto his wife: and they shall be one flesh.

The Hebrew word (זאת) translated as *"This"* occurs 251 times in the original text. The definition of the letters that spell the word (זאת) is, "The Perfect Sword (ז) of Salvation (את)". "THIS" is far more than it seems.

The word (לזאת) translated as *"she"* occurs five times in the original text and the last occurrence is Jeremiah 5:7.

Jeremiah 5:7 KJV: ⁷ How shall I pardon thee *for this* (לזאת)[5]? thy children have forsaken me, and sworn by them that are no gods: when I had fed them to the full, they then committed adultery, and assembled themselves by troops in the harlots' houses.

Is Jeremiah 5:7 referring to the fall of man and woman in the garden? It continues to reveal that their children have forsaken Him. The definition of the letters that spell the word (לזאת) is, "The Authority (ל) of the Perfect Sword (ז) of Salvation (את)". Is God declaring that while in the garden, he gave the man and woman the authority and the sword of Salvation?

Is there a moment in Scripture where our Savior is not carrying a sword? Did our Savior carry a sword in the garden of paradise where there is no sin? Jesus came and gave us a sword. Is there any relationship between the word (לזאת) and our Savior providing us a sword just as it seems He provided man and woman in the garden?

Where there is no sin, there is no need for a sword. After the fall and expulsion from the garden, the woman is named Eve and Eve is never again referenced as (זאת) or (לזאת).

The first mentioning of the phrase "Salvation Father and Salvation Mother" is from a man that did not have a birth father nor a birth mother. He was created. The only way to explain Adam's declaration is to add your own personal conjecture. That said, let's provide additional truth that is seldom expressed or considered before we discuss this theological topic. Let's look at Genesis 1:27.

Genesis 1:27 KJV: ²⁷ So God created *man* (אֶת-הָאָדָם[140]) in his own image, in the image of God created he him; *male* (זכר)[106] *and female* (ונקבה)[8] created he them.

An awesome trick trivia question is to ask a Christian how many people God created. Most will quickly answer "one" and then realize that the woman (later named Eve, the mother of all living) was created also. What's interesting is that we have the declaration that woman was created in Genesis 1:27 and then we have the story of that moment in Genesis 2:21-25.

Let's continue our stroll down *Confusion Street* with the intent to add more beauty to the truth of Matthew 4:4.

The word (ונקבה) translated as *"and female"* occurs eight times in the original text and the last occurrence is Isaiah 36:6.

Isaiah 36:6 KJV: [6] Lo, thou trustest in the staff of this broken reed, on Egypt; whereon if a man lean (עליו)[404], it will go into his hand, *and pierce it* (ונקבה): so is Pharaoh king of Egypt to all that trust in him.

The word (ונקבה) translated as *"and female"* is translated as *"and pierce it"*. Yes, enjoy the stroll down *Confusion Street*. The stroll down *Confusion Street* is removing the barricades on the corner of *Tradition Avenue* and *Translation Circle* (smile). Oh, and the word (עליו) occurs 404 times and is not translated in this verse. In other occurrences it is translated as "on him". This verse is declaring that all who trust in Pharoah are leaning on Pharoah just as those who lean on the man whose palm was pierced. Those that know Hebrew, know that our Savior's Gospel is **LITTERED** throughout the original Hebrew text.

When our Savior's palms were pierced, He looked at the grief (honor) of His pierced mother, the female image that God created.

Are we capable of imagining Adam's and Eve's first days after being expelled from the garden? Can you imagine their exhaustive efforts to teach their children about a place so much better than the world that they were born in? Is it possible to exaggerate their grief? Is it possible that the 5th Commandment is teaching us that Adam and Eve are our examples of how to grieve for the Salvation of our children just as the "Father and Mother of all Living" grieved of the sin they brought upon all children to be born? Grieve as they grieved?

John 19:25-27 KJV: [25] Now there stood by the cross of Jesus his mother, and his mother's sister, Mary the wife of Cleophas, and Mary Magdalene.

[26] When Jesus therefore saw his mother, and the disciple standing by, whom he loved, he saith unto his mother, Woman, behold thy son!

[27] Then saith he to the disciple, Behold thy mother! And from that hour that disciple took her unto his own home.

Chapter 15 Seas and Days

There are few Hebrew words with as much depth of meaning as the word (ימים) translated as "the sea" which occurs 292 times in the original text. This word is so special! It has two Hebrew letter Yod (י י), and it has two Hebrew letter Mem (ם מ). The letter Yod (י) means "The Hand That Does Mighty Deeds" and the letter Mem (ם, מ) means a woman's womb. The letter Mem (ם, מ) is one of five Hebrew letters that has what is called a "Sofit" form which means it is spelled differently if it's the last letter of a word. If it's the last letter of the word, then it's a Closed or Virgin Womb (ם). Otherwise, it's an Open Womb (מ).

Let's look at the first occurrence of this word (ם, מ) in Genesis 1:10.

Genesis 1:10 KJV: [10] And God called the dry land Earth; *and the gathering together of* (ולמקוה)[1] *the waters* (המים)[96] *called he* (קרא)[88] *Seas* (ימים)[292]: and God saw that it was good.

Now, let's look at the third occurrence!

Genesis 8:10 KJV: [10] And he stayed yet other seven *days* (ימים)[292]; and again he sent forth the dove out of the ark;

WAIT! The word (ימים) translated as "Seas" in Genesis 1:10 is the same word (ימים) translated as "days" in Genesis 8:10? Yes, let's look at more occurrences.

- 4th Occurrence – Genesis 8:12 – translated as "**days**"
- 5th Occurrence – Genesis 17:12 – translated as "**days**"
- 6th Occurrence – Genesis 21:4 – translated as "**days**"
- 7th Occurrence – Genesis 21:34 – translated as "**days**"
- 10th Occurrence – Genesis 29:14 – translated as "**month**"
- 50th Occurrence – Leviticus 8:33 – translated as "**days**"
- 100th Occurrence – Numbers 28:24 – translated as "**days**"
- 150th Occurrence – 2 Samuel 14:2 – translated as "**long time**"
- 200th Occurrence – Job 2:13 – translated as "**days**"
- 290th Occurrence – Jonah 2:3 – translated as "**seas**"
- 291st Occurrence – Jonah 3:3 – translated as "**days**"
- 292nd Last Occurrence – Zechariah 8:4 – translated as "**age**"

Research revealed there are thirty occurrences of the word (ימים) translated as "Seas" and 262 occurrences of the same word (ימים) translated as something other than "Seas", most commonly "days" in the KJV. How is this possible?

There are 292 total occurrences, just eight shy of three hundred and the number three hundred represents "victory", and the number eight represents "New Beginnings", the great 8th Day, the beginning of eternity.

First, realize that this is only a problem for those that know Hebrew. The translations do not reveal any association between "seas" and "days".

Notice that both "seas" and "days" are plural. We have already shown that the plural form of a noun is attained by adding the two letters (ים) to the end of its spelling. That said, if we remove those two letters from the word (ימים) the remaining two letters is the word (ימ) but when the letter Mem (ימ) is the last letter it's spelled (ים) which occurs 91 times in the original text and is never translated as "day", it's always translated as "sea" with only a few exceptions.

- Joshua 18:14 and Ezekiel 47:20, the word (ים) is translated as "west".
- 2 Kings 25:13, 1 Chronicles 18:8, and Jeremiah 52:17 its translated as "sea" but it seems to be calling the Bronze Laver in the temple the Brazen "sea" and are also hyphenated with either "Et (את) Salvation" or "(דרך) The Way Of".

The purpose of dedicating an entire chapter to the word (ימים) is because it has additional depth of meaning. There are several Hebrew words that are spelled with a letter between two Yods (י י), the two hands that do mighty deeds and the greatest deed of all was our Savior keeping His hands on that cedar cross until his death.

The name Jesse, David's father, is spelled (ישי) and the letter Shin (ש) means "destruction". The spelling of the name Jesse reveals our Savior's destroyed body on the cross between those two hands that did a mighty deed. David's name "Beloved" and Jesse's name means "Gift".

The word (ימי) formed by the first three letters occurs 144 times in the original text and is translated as "days of". When the *days of* (ימי) our Savior were finished, He became a *gift* (ישי) on the cross.

Let's make a paragraph using the many revelations of the letters that spell "days" and "seas".

Over the years of *days* (ימים) since our Savior became a *gift* (ישי), the number who believe in the *days of* (ימי) our Savior who was born of a *virgin womb* (ב) is like the sand of the *seas* (ימים). That said, the **birth of many** (מים) **born** (מ) of the *water* (מים) are not believers that He was a *gift* (ישי) and believe the *days of* (ימי) his life ended because He was not the Son of God born of a *virgin womb* (ב).

Wait, we aren't done (smile)!

The Seas (ימים) and the Days (ימים) will both bring forth many that will be born again and believe in the virgin birth of our Savior. The sand of the seashore is where the seas meet every day (smile), and many will be born in every nation that will believe in the word (ימים), the one born of a virgin. Hence, the word (ימים) could also mean *"the believers of the nations"*, all nations including Israel.

Revelation 21:1 tells us that there will be no more sea. Does this mean that there will be no more water or no more nations? There is only one government in the millennium, His government that rest upon His shoulders.

Micah 7:19 KJV: [19] He will turn again, he will have compassion upon us; he will subdue our iniquities; and thou wilt cast all their sins into the depths of the sea.

Glory to the King!

Chapter 16   Fled

Congratulations! If you are still reading, then you have negotiated the conflict of the content of this book. Let's continue our efforts while honoring those persecuted for exposing the lies of passed down traditions.

After learning how to read and study Hebrew, a late life understanding of Matthew 4:4 would lead to searching the original Hebrew text one Hebrew word at a time. The results of that effort lead to believing this is exactly what our Savior was revealing from that verse. Our intent for the next five chapters is to take you on a journey of joyous understanding of Prophet Dove.

What a privilege it is to share the journey of researching each Hebrew word of the original text of the Book of Jonah. *Let's prove that this book is much easier to teach backwards.* Okay, we won't do it but when we are all done, you will agree!

There are few stories in scripture more impacted by the translation of one word than the story of Jonah is impacted by the *mistranslation* of the Hebrew word (לברח) translated as "flee" in Jonah 1:3. The truth of the story of Jonah can't be discovered until this is reconciled.

One of the passed down understandings before we were born is that the story of Jonah begins with Jonah rebelliously fleeing the presence of God. Jonah's name translated to English means "Dove". That passed down tradition burdens us with explaining how a rebellious prophet named Dove has any similarities with the heavens being opened and the Holy Spirit descending like a Dove after Jesus's baptism in Matthew 3:16.

Matthew 3:16 KJV: And Jesus, when he was baptized, went up straightway out of the water: and, lo, the heavens were opened unto him, and he saw the *Spirit of God descending like a dove*, and lighting upon him:

Jonah (יונה) means dove so Matthew 3:16 could have read "…he saw the *Spirit of God descending like a Jonah*, …".

There are many verses in this book that lead most churches to declare that Jonah was a rebellious prophet who after repenting of his sins returned to following God's will. Let's search out the first three verses of the Book of Jonah and determine if he is a rebellious prophet or an obedient prophet before searching out what is concealed in the entire Book of Dove.

Jonah 1:1-3 KJV: [1] Now the word of the Lord came unto Jonah the son of Amittai, saying,

[2] Arise, go to Nineveh (נינוה), that great city, and cry against it; for their wickedness is come up before me.

[3] But Jonah rose up to flee (לברח) unto Tarshish from the presence of the Lord, and went down to Joppa; and he found a ship going to Tarshish: so he paid the fare thereof, and went down into it, to go with them unto Tarshish from the presence of the Lord.

Spoiler Alert!

Let's begin this journey by sharing a maze of newfound understanding when we learn that the name Nineveh (נינוה) means "Fish Town". Yes! Fish Town! Jesus told the disciples that He would make them fishers of men. Then there are stories where He tells the disciples to cast their nets on the other side of the boat which results in them catching so many fish it almost tears the nets. If you know the story of Jonah, then you know that he gets swallowed and vomited by a fish. You also know that God has mercy on Fish Town. And what changes when we learn the prophet Nahum's (נחום) name translated to English is "Comforter" and become aware of the connection between Nahum and Jonah, or is it Dove and Comforter? Let's look at the first verse of the Book of Nahum.

Nahum 1:1 KJV: The burden of Nineveh. The book of the vision of Nahum the Elkoshite.

Hopefully this adds a level of desire to validate the Hebrew word that is **IMPROPERLY** translated as fled. The Hebrew word translated as "Elkoshite" is a unique word in the original text. The translation of that word is "Behold, God of the Stubborn (Obstinate)".

The contention is that there is an eternal message concealed in the truth of the story of Jonah that cannot be uncovered because of the claim that Jonah sinned when he fled from the presence of God rather than doing what he was told. Well, from the translation of the first three verses of Jonah, that is a difficult claim to argue. In fact, the only way to argue that point is to openly declare that the word "flee" in Jonah 1:3 is incorrectly translated.

Proving that the Hebrew word (לברח) translated as "flee" is a mistranslation is not difficult. What is difficult is proving it strongly enough to overrule the loyalty to this passed-down tradition that existed before we were born. That said, we will prove it is a gross mistranslation in several ways. When done, we will begin searching out the Book of Jonah in the next chapter without any contention that he is an obedient prophet that was not rebellious, and his works teach us about the Works of the Spirit of God.

Proof #1 of Mistranslation – The Definition of the Hebrew Letters

The definition of the Hebrew letters of the word (לברח) translated as "Flee" is, "The Authority (ל) of the House (ב) of the Prince (ר) Protects (ח)." That said, the two middle letters of this word (בר) spell the word Bar which means "Son", so the definition of the letters could also be, "The Authority of the Son Protects."

At first glance, there isn't a resemblance of fleeing nor rebellion. That said, if it isn't rebelliously fleeing then what is it? Well, if you don't know Hebrew then this doesn't change anything. Sadly, this isn't enough for many that know Hebrew to deny our loyalty to the passed down traditions. Let's move to our 2nd proof and return to the definition of the letters when the correct translation is more obvious.

Proof #2 of Mistranslation – Was verses 1-3 the entire conversation between Jonah and God?

What changes if we learn that the conversation in verses 1-3 was not the entire conversation or that there was another conversation prior to this? Yes, we will **_PROVE_** that verses 1-3 do not include the entire conversation that took place at that moment or that there was a prior conversation. This is why this story is easier to teach when we start from the end of the story.

Jonah 1:1-2 KJV: [1] Now the word of the Lord came unto Jonah the son of Amittai, saying,
[2] Arise, go to Nineveh, that great city, and cry against it; for their wickedness is come up before me.

Yes, there is proof within the Book of Jonah that there was more discussed before verse three. That proof is in Chapter 4.

Wait a minute! We must read the first three chapters and then in Chapter four we learn that the conversation in chapter one had more content than what was declared? So, we must go to the fourth chapter and then come back to the first chapter? Yes, or we will do what almost everyone before us has done; read the entire book of Jonah and totally miss what it says in the fourth chapter and then, decades later, only a few of us will finally see what we missed. ***Almost all of us miss Jonah 4:2 many times!***

Let's begin our journey of uncovering the "travels of the Dove". The dove was sent out three times in the story of Noah. Search and confirm that on the third occurrence, the dove never found rest. The second time it came back with a broken olive branch and the third time it didn't return. That said, there is no evidence that the dove ever found rest until it we read that it lighted upon Jesus in Matthew 3:16.

Okay, to prevent making multiple round trips, let's skip forward and peek to reveal what's concealed in Chapter 4. This is after Jonah has done what was requested in Jonah 1:2. This is after He went to Nineveh and ***preached one sentence***. Nineveh repented of their sins and God was merciful. After God extended mercy to Nineveh, Jonah ***prays*** in Jonah 4:2.

Jonah 4:2 KJV: And he prayed unto the LORD, and said, I pray thee, O LORD, *was not **this my saying*** (דברי)[300], when I was yet in my country? Therefore I *fled* (לברח) before unto Tarshish: for I knew that thou art a gracious God, and merciful, slow to anger, and of great kindness, and ***repentest thee of the evil***.

Again, this verse takes place after Ninevah repented and God spared Nineveh of his wrath. Jonah is praying and is telling God that this is what he told God would happen when he was yet in his country. The phrase "when I was yet in his country" would imply that this conversation took place before he "fled" the presence of God for Joppa. Review the verse and make sure you agree before continuing.

The revelation of the Book of Jonah is the case of
"Fled verses Jonah 4:2".
The revelation of the Prophet Dove will require
repeated round trips to Jonah 4:2.
It's crucial to consider the relationship between Dove
and John 14:26.

John 14:26 KJV: But the Comforter, which is the Holy Ghost, whom the Father will send in my name, *he shall teach you all things*, and bring all things to your remembrance, whatsoever I have said unto you.

In Jonah 4:2, it says, "when I was yet in my country (אדמתי)". If Jonah is a symbol of the Holy Spirit, then what country is he from?

2 Kings 14:25 KJV: He restored the coast of Israel from the entering of Hamath unto the sea of the plain, according to the word of the LORD God of Israel, which he spake by the hand of his servant *Jonah, the son of Amittai*, the prophet, which was of *Gathhepher*.

2 Kings 14:25 tells us that Jonah is from Gathhepher. Other Bible translations call it Gath-Hepher. This town is located about five miles south of Nazareth. Jonah is Galilean! The Book of Jonah doesn't declare that he is Galilean. Are we *"exceeding glad"* or do we *"greatly rejoicing"* that Jonah is Galilean just like Jesus. We will explain the difference later (smile).

THIS IS HUGE! There was a conversation between God and Jonah that took place in Galilee not mentioned in the beginning of the book. Of course, right?

How old were you when you learned that Jonah was from Galilee. How do you reconcile the addition of this information into the references of Jonah in the New Testament as well as the Book of Dove? Are the details of the conversation in Jonah 4:2 that take us back to the conversation of Jonah 1:1-3 similar to Noah sending out the dove and its return? Just like the dove in the story of Noah, the story of the prophet Dove requires re-traveling, re-reading, and re-interpreting the first three chapters after readying Jonah 4:2. The story of Dove requires multiple round-trip flights (smile).

The Hebrew word (אדמת) translated as "Country" is in the Tanakh (Old Testament) twenty-six times, but the Hebrew word (אדמתי) translated as "My Country" only occurs three times in the original text. Only three people in the Bible ever spoke the Hebrew word (אדמתי) translated as "My Country". They were Jonah, Job in Job 31:38, and God in 2 Chronicles 7:20.

Once again, this conversation either took place before the conversation in Jonah 1:1-3 or during that conversation. Nonetheless, Jonah 4:2 provides *new content* of a conversation between God and Jonah that took place prior or during the first conversation, correct?

In Jonah 4:2, Jonah says that this is why he fled to go to Tarshish. Stop, review, and agree that Jonah's *prayer* is making it clear that he knew Ninevah (Fish Town) would repent, and that God would be merciful. So, we know from this verse that Jonah and the LORD discussed Nineveh's repentance prior to him "fleeing" the presence of the Lord. That is not included in the beginning of the book. Does that change our loyalty to the passed down traditions?

Many of us have heard this story told over and over and it never included the fact that Jonah 4:2 occurred during or before the beginning of the book. Is it possible that Jonah's comment *"was not this my saying"* includes the entire story of the Book of Jonah up to this verse? Is it possible or is it absolutely true that everything in the Book of Jonah up to this verse is being referenced by Jonah in this prayer? Is it conceivable that everything, including what has not yet been shared, was included in that conversation?

Our research of Jonah 4:2 provides new understanding of the story, but it does not provide us with absolute clarity of whether the word "flee" is properly translated. That said, there is enough evidence that the jury is paying attention. The jury now has the *privilege* and *responsibility* to determine if Jonah is rebellious or obedient. We now have PROOF of new content of a conversation that makes it necessary to search out the translation of the Hebrew word (לברח) translated as "flee" with more openness. Was Jonah rebelliously fleeing the presence of God or was Jonah leaving for Joppa with the blessings, knowledge, and authority of God?

Proof #3 of Mistranslation – Where in the original Hebrew is this word used?

The word **flee** is in the KJV one-hundred-sixteen times. The word **fled** is in the KJV one-hundred-thirty-nine times. Yes, the two words flee and fled are in the KJV a combined total of two-hundred-fifty-five times. The Hebrew word (לברח) translated as flee in Jonah 1:3 is the same as the Hebrew word (לברח) translated as fled in Jonah 4:2. That word is in the original Hebrew text four times and the last two of those occurrences are in the Book of Jonah. That word is in the original text the same number of times as the dove was sent out by Noah. Coincidence? Are the passed down traditions crumbling? Let's review the other two occurrences as well as the root Hebrew word of this word.

In Genesis 31:27 we have the story of Laban finally catching up with Jacob and asking Jacob why he "fled".

Genesis 31:27 KJV: Wherefore didst thou flee (לברח) away secretly, and steal away from me; and didst not tell me, that I might have sent thee away with mirth, and with songs, with tabret, and with harp?

The *very condensed summarization* of the story of Laban and Jacob is that Laban, the father of Jacob's wives, abused Jacob's love for his daughter Rachel. Laban became aware of Jacob's God and the blessings of God upon Jacob and benefited from it. After twenty years of service, Jacob finally "fled" from Laban's house with his herds and family. There is more detail, but hopefully those that know this story would accept this quick summary that includes what appears to be Jacob "fleeing".

Two verses after Laban accuses Jacob of fleeing it tells us that God gave Laban a warning.

Genesis 31:29 KJV: It is in the power of my hand to do you hurt: but the God of your father spake unto me yesternight, saying, ***Take thou heed that thou speak not to Jacob either good or bad***.

Again, the Hebrew word translated as "fled" in the Jonah story is only in the Hebrew text four times and we are searching out the first occurrence. From this verse it seems clear that whatever this "fleeing" is, it is also protected by God. God is telling Laban that he cannot talk good or bad about the person that does this type of fleeing. Do you see that? That said, to be consistent, the definition of the word "fled" in the book of Jonah is not something that anyone can talk good or bad about. Do you see that? In fact, God told Laban, "Take heed". I view that as a warning to Laban and an endorsement to Jacob, do you agree? This does not appear to be viewed by God as a rebellious act. Agree? Not convinced?

Genesis 31:22-23 KJV: ²² And it was told Laban on the ***third day*** that Jacob was fled.
²³ And he took his *brethren* (את-אחיו) with him, and pursued after him seven days' journey; and they overtook him in the mount *Gilead* (הגלעד).

Laban was told "***on the third day***" that Jacob supposedly fled and pursued Jacob for "***seven days***". Craziness, right? This is the nineteenth occurrence of the Hebrew word translated as brother (אחיו) but only the second time in the original text that it is preceded by Alef-Tav (את) which means the

First and the Last. The first time was the birth of Abel in Genesis 4:2. Again, I view God's use of the word Et (את) as a stamp of something He approves.

Also, the letters that spell Gilead mean, "Behold (ה) Revelation (גל) of the Future (עד)". I have underlined the Hebrew root word "Reveal" that we searched out earlier. Gilead is on the east side of Jordan, and they are on a mountain. Surely, they can see the "future" promised land on the other side of the Jordan River.

The story of Laban pursuing Jacob is in Genesis Chapter 31. It's an awesome story but we are simply trying to validate how the word translated as "Fled" in Jonah 1:3 resembles the story of Laban pursuing Jacob. The conflict between Laban and Jacab reaches its conclusion in verse 42.

Genesis 31:42 KJV: Except the God of my father, *the God of Abraham*, and the fear of Isaac, had been with me, surely thou hadst sent me away now empty. *God hath seen mine affliction and the labour of my hands, and rebuked thee yesternight*.

We are seeing more and more clearly that the "fleeing" of Jacob was ordained by God. Let's continue researching what really happened and how this word "Fled" is used. First, we will look at Genesis 31:12.

Genesis 31:12 KJV: And he said, Lift up now thine eyes, and see, all the rams which leap upon the cattle are ringstraked, speckled, and grisled: *for I have seen all that Laban doeth unto thee.*

The story of Jacob and Laban is very interesting. Let's intentionally reduce it to researching out the use of the word **fled**. In Genesis 31:12 we see that *God is aware that Laban is abusing Jacob*. Does this apply to the Jonah story? Yes, it does. We will reveal who, why and how in Jonah Chapter 4.

Now let's look at Genesis 31:20, the verse where the translations claim that Jacob "fled" Laban to get an understanding of what Jacob really did. This verse uses the Hebrew root word of the word translated as **fled**.

Genesis 31:20 KJV: And Jacob *stole* (ויגנב) *away unawares* (את-לב) to Laban the Syrian, in that he told him not that he fled (ברח).

Yes, as you can see, the spelling of the Hebrew word translated as fled in this verse is **not** identical to the spelling in the book Jonah (לברח), rather it is the Hebrew root of that word. To better understand this verse, know that the Hebrew word translated as "stole" is only in the original Hebrew twice. Yes! What is awesome is that both times they are stealing the heart. The Hebrew word translated as "away unawares" is the word for Heart (לב). It is in the original Hebrew text two-hundred-two times. Can't explain why it is not translated as "stole Laban's heart". The word heart is also preceded with Et (את), the First and the Last, that we have discussed several times already. This is Jesus endorsing Jacob stealing Laban's heart by leaving. It appears Jacob's intent is not rebellious. So far, we don't have a hint of rebellion anywhere that this Hebrew word is translated as. WHAT IS CRAZY AMAZING is that the Hebrew word translated as **fled** in Genesis 31:20 is also used in Genesis 27:43 when Jacob's mother requested that he **flee** to Laban's house. Surely, we can agree that he left "with his mother's heart".

Genesis 27:43 KJV: Now therefore, my son, obey *my voice* (בקלי); *arise* (וקום), *flee* (ברח) thou to Laban my brother to Haran;

So, Jacob's mother tells him to "obey my voice; arise, flee", after they both participated in deceiving his father, Isaac, to giving him the blessings. Jacob is being told by his mother to flee from the wrath of his brother. Oh, how it would be awesome to divert and translate the love story in the two words (arise and flee) that Rebekah tells Jacob. Understand that there is no guarantee that she will ever see her son again and these are the two words she chose. I won't be diverted.

The **root Hebrew word** translated as "flee" in Genesis 27:43 and 31:20 is in the original Hebrew text eighteen times. Let's search out a "crowd favorite" that brings clarity to its meaning. Let's look at Exodus 14:5.

Exodus 14:5 KJV: And it was told the king of Egypt that the people fled (ברח): and the heart of Pharaoh and of his servants was turned against the people, and they said, Why have we done this, that we have let Israel go from serving us?

Surely you agree that we have an issue with the use of the word "fled" in this verse. God has just conquered Egypt with His might hand. He did it so well that the Egyptians willfully gave them all their wealth to take with them. Would you call that "fleeing"? Also, those that left weren't just from Israel.

Exodus 12:38-40 tells us that it was a mixed multitude of many nations. This isn't fleeing, it's a victory march!

Let's compare what Israel provided to Egypt with what Jacob provided to Laban. Israel brought the blessings of God to Egypt from the time of Jacob even until the time of Moses. Egypt was protected like no other country during the famine, and abused the blessings provided from Israel. Likewise, Laban abused the blessings provided by Jacob.

At the end of Exodus 14:5, it further supports our understanding when it says they let Israel go from serving them. Israel served Egypt; Jacob served Esau and got the blessing; and Jacob served Laban. In all three scenarios they left with the blessings they provide.

When Jacob obeyed his mother and "fled", he left with the blessings of God passed down from his father. When Jacob "fled" Laban, again he left and took the blessings of God with him. Laban knew this.

Now that we understand the root Hebrew word of "fled (ברח)" is leaving with blessings (the protection of the Son), we are finally ready to search out the fourth use of the Hebrew word translated as fled (לברח) twice in the story of Jonah. Let's look at Exodus 36:33.

Exodus 36:33 KJV: And he made the middle bar *to shoot through* (לברח) the boards from the one *end* (הקצה) to the other.

What is this verse? It occurs in one of the chapters that is revealing the construction of the tabernacle. The same Hebrew word (לברח) that is flee or fled in these other three instances is now being translated as "to shoot through". How do we make sense of this? Well, first it is quite clear that this is not a person so all the debates about obedience or rebellion don't apply in this verse.

We are trying to determine the character reference of this "middle bar" and how it could possibly relate to all the instances of the word translated as fled. Yes, we could have simply searched out this instance but instead we are doing exactly what Jonah did in Jonah 4:2 (smile). When we are done, we can only hope it makes an unforgettable impact on our understanding.

So, this middle bar plays a pivotal role in the tabernacle construction. Let's review Proof #1 where we defined the letters of this word.

The definition of the Hebrew letters of the word (לברח) translated as "Flee" is, "The Authority (ל) of the House (ב) of the Prince (ר) Protects (ח)." That said, the two middle letters of this word (בר) spell the word Bar which means "Son", so the definition of the letters could also be, "The Authority of the Son Protects."

That's it! The tabernacle is the House of the Son. This bar goes from ***END-TO-END***. Its purpose is to Protect the House of the Son. It alone has that authority.

Now that we know the Hebrew word can be defined by an object, we know that it is impossible for it to represent rebellion. This middle bar has the authority to protect the house of the Prince, the Son. Jonah left the presence of God with the authority to Protect the House of the Son. ***THERE WAS NO SIN OR REBELLION!*** The Prophet Dove is leaving the presence of God with His blessings!

This ends another traditional story that was passed down to before we were born. We will search out the Book of Jonah and reveal why this book is titled ***Traditions, Lies from Birth***. Let's search out and prove the righteousness of God's appointed prophets, especially Dove.

Several times the New Testament refers to "the law and the prophets", it never refers to "the law and the rebellious prophets". As we continue with the Traditions Series you will see a constant effort of God's enemy to reduce God, His name, His Son, His Son's name, and His prophets to nothing. At the time of our birth, the story of Prophet Dove is a story of a sinful man's salvation and returning to being the righteous prophet he was initially called to be. We will prove that the story of Dove, a symbol of the Holy Spirit, is a story of a righteous prophet worthy of being called the Book of Dove.

It will take time to process a new understanding of Jonah. That said, once the mistranslated sinful rebellion is no longer on his resume, we will see this story ***far*** differently.

Consider the impact of Jonah being righteous on Jesus's words in Matthew 12:42.

Matthew 12:42 KJV: For as Jonas was three days and three nights in the whale's belly; so shall the Son of man be three days and three nights in the heart of the earth.

Now we know that Jesus is referring to a righteous prophet named Dove rather than requiring us to negotiate the rhetoric of Jesus comparing himself to a sinful prophet. Yes, we will also prove the errors of passed down traditions about Jonah's prayer is Chapter 2.

Let's search out the Book of Dove without regard to passed down traditions from the poor translation of the word "Fled" that was the basis of the claim that he was a sinful, rebellious prophet. Let's search out how the Prophet Jonah, the Dove, provides additional understanding of the works of the Holy Spirit.

BONUS...

We didn't search out the Hebrew word for "middle bar". The original Hebrew says that the bar went from "End-to-End" and not "Side to Side". This bar Supported the House of the Son, the tent. This is the only bar that supports the structure from end to end. What geometric structure can be supported with one bar that reaches from end-to-end? Also, know that the phrase "end-to-end" is used many times in the construction of the tabernacle. Similarly, the eleven outer curtains of the tabernacle are connected end-to-end and not side-to-side. When connected, their width is 4 cubits and their length totals 314 cubits. The courtyard is 100 cubits by 50 cubits. Can you picture it? We will search out the tabernacle construction in a future book.

Glory to the King!

Chapter 17   Jonah "Dove" Chapter 1

In the previous chapter we searched out the Hebrew word translated as "fled" in Jonah 1:3. To accomplish that understanding required us to fast-forward to Chapter 4 and then return to Chapter 1 and apply what we learned. Prepare yourself, in the Book of Jonah you will constantly return to the previous chapters because of what you learn.

We have searched out words and now we are going to search out an entire book of the Bible, the Book of Jonah. To accomplish this requires that we introduce many interesting features of the original Hebrew text. Since the creation of the desktop computer, we can perform a word or phrase search of the KJV translation and now that feature also exist with the original Hebrew text. This capability provides the opportunity to reveal additional understanding about the original text that was never researched.

These features are constantly revealed in the Book of Jonah which has lots of unique Hebrew words that are literally only one time in the original text. It also has words that are only used within the Book of Jonah. We will also reveal the significance of the last occurrence of many Hebrew words. Knowing the features of Hebrew text does not make it a difficult language but rather makes it an interesting language. The opportunities for a lifetime of study and research are not a burden but rather a privilege. The many features of the Hebrew text will reveal the omniscience of our Creator like never witnessed before.

The Hebrew word (נינוה) translated as Nineveh is in the original text eleven times. In Hebrew, the number eleven means a covering and is considered "one short" of the number twelve which means a government. There are twelve apostles and twelve tribes of Israel, and their names are on the gates and walls of New Jerusalem. That said, there are many references of an 11th occurrence of a word in Jonah. Each of those occurrences is a testimony that the 12th occurrence is fulfilled by our Savior who established His government.

As mentioned earlier, Nineveh translated to English is "Fish Town" and occurs eleven times. The 9th and 10th occurrence of the word (נינוה) translated as Nineveh are in the book of Nahum. Nahum means Comforter. The 11th occurrence is in the book of Zephaniah which means "God has hidden". Is the 12th occurrence of "Fish Town" our Savior telling the disciples that He will make them fishers of men? Is it possible that Jonah is the concealed Old Testament shadow of that story?

Dove (Jonah) is going to Fish Town (Nineveh)
which is the burden of Comforter (Nahum 1:1)
and last mentioned by God Has Hidden (Zephaniah)
and our Savior (Salvation) is teaching the disciples
to become fishers of men.
**** Matthew 4:4 ****

The Book of Jonah is truly a journey of multiple round trips. Just as Noah sent out the Dove several times, Jonah has four chapters and researching the original text will have you constantly flipping pages. Noah's first dove left and returned with nothing. The second time the dove returned with a broken olive branch. Was Noah expecting a broken olive branch? Did Noah know what the broken olive branch represented? The dove made two "round trips" before that third flight and the next reference of a dove landing is mentioned at the baptism of our Savior. Again, reading and then returning to previous chapters is a recurring theme in the Book of Dove. Researching the original text of the Book of Jonah provides new revelations about scriptures we thought we understood. Let's enjoy going forwards and backwards, round trips, through the Book of Dove. Remember I warned you (smile)!

As mentioned earlier, the name Jonah translated to English is Dove. After learning Hebrew and the translation of several nouns, ask yourself why they weren't translated. Why aren't there footnotes in our Bible telling us the translation of these nouns. This book does not impose personal conjecture.

Learning how to read and research a Hebrew word is easy and you will spend the rest of your life searching out each of His Word(s). The good news is that you will never finish. An amazing example is the word (אשר) translated as "which". Did you know that one of Jacob's sons is named (אשר), "which"?

Because it is commonly known that the dove is a symbol of the Holy Spirit, is it possible that the story of Prophet Jonah is to teach us about the Works of the Holy Spirit? We are Christians, we know this story well, and we know the Holy Spirit. No way, right? Well, as mentioned in Psalm 25:2, let's do the ***Honor of Kings*** and ***search out*** the Book of Jonah and see what is concealed. Let's start with Jonah 1:1 or should that be Dove 1:1.

Jonah 1:1 KJV: Now the word of the LORD *came* (ויהי)[816] unto Jonah the son of *Amittai* (אמתי)[2], saying,

92

How old were you when you asked yourself "How the word of the Lord came to Jonah?" Yes, the Bible provides an answer. The word (ויהי) translated as "came" occurs 816 times in the original text and five times in the Book of Jonah. We will search out this word on its third occurrence in the Book of Jonah, Jonah 1:17.

As mentioned previously, Jonah's father's name Amittai translated to English means "My Truth". Ok, that's a good start! That's a great name for Dove's father (smile). Also, remember we learned earlier that the Apostle Peter's father is named Jonah.

Matthew 16:17 KJV: And Jesus answered and said unto him, Blessed art thou, Simon ***Barjona***: for flesh and blood hath not revealed it unto thee, but my Father which is in heaven.

Can you remember how old you were when you learned that "Barjona" in the KJV means "Son of Jonah"? This is not an endorsement of a translation, but the NKJV translates it as "Bar-Jonah" and the NIV translates it as "Son of Jonah".

None of us believe there is a minimum Final Test Score required for Salvation, but we do believe that without pursuing knowledge you are vulnerable to the passed down traditional lies that existed before we were born. Without the pursuit of knowledge, we would still believe the Father had forsaken His only begotten Son.

When are we old enough to respectfully question why men deemed worthy of translating the Bible wouldn't just say "Son of Jonah"? Did they have a separate translation for their kids? Surely, they wanted their children to know, right? Oh wait, did they have kids?

Jonah 1:2 KJV: Arise, go to *Nineveh* (נינוה)[11], *that great* (הגדולה)[31] city, *and cry* (וקרא)[13] *against it* (עליה)[174]; for *their wickedness* (רעתם)[15] *is come up* (עלתה)[14] before me.

The original text of Jonah has some very interesting features. The book has a lot of unique Hebrew words as well as the last occurrence of many Hebrew words. There are more unique features of the Hebrew text that will be explained as they occur. For example, the Hebrew word translated as Nineveh is in the original text eleven times. In Hebrew, the number eleven means a covering and is considered "one short" of the number twelve which references a government. There are twelve apostles and twelve tribes of Israel, and their names are on the gates and walls of New Jerusalem. That said, the Book of Jonah has the last occurrence of many words and several of those are the 11th occurrence which lends that our Savior fulfilled the 12th occurrence is in the Gospels.

The word (הגדולה) translated as "great" occurs 31 times in the original text and the last three occurrences (29th, 30th, and 31st) of this word are in the Book of Jonah. There are three different words from the original text translated as "great" in the Book of Jonah and they occur a combined eleven times (smile). Yes, there is additional understanding from searching out which word occurs in each verse. Note that this word (הגדולה) is spoken by God and He is telling Dove to go to the "great" city. Is the city "great" because God spoke of it or is it "great" because Dove is on his way with authority from God? This word occurs again in Jonah 3:2 and 4:11.

Jonah 1:3 KJV: But Jonah rose up to <u>**flee**</u> unto *Tarshish* (תרשיש) from the presence of the Lord, and went down to Joppa; and he found a ship going to Tarshish: so he paid the fare thereof, and went down into it, to go with them unto Tarshish from the presence of the Lord.

Wow, this puts a sudden stop to this theory, right? Not if you read the previous chapter! We proved that the original Hebrew word translated as flee was a mistranslation. We can now continue and know that Jonah left the presence of God with the authority to fulfill the work that God has set forth for him.

Again, the previous chapter also explained how Jonah 4:2 reveals that there was more content in the conversation between God and Jonah than was provided in the first verses of the book. It is conjecture to declare how much or how little of Jonah's ministry was planned before Jonah left God's presence with the authority to protect the House of the Son. Let's continue searching out the Book of Dove and validating the passed down traditional story.

Jonah 4:2 KJV: And he prayed unto the LORD, and said, I pray thee, O LORD, *was not this my saying*, when I was yet in *my country* (אדמתי)? Therefore I *fled* (לברח) before unto *Tarshish* (תרשיש): for I knew that *thou* (אתה) art a gracious God, and merciful, slow to anger, and of great kindness, and *repentest thee of the evil*.

Notice that it says, "***Therefore*** I fled". Jonah is now providing the reason that he fled. Again, is Jonah referring to everything that has happened in the book to this point and claiming that he fled because he **KNEW** that God was gracious, merciful, slow to anger, of great kindness, and would repent of His wrath on Nineveh? Jonah is claiming that he **KNEW** that Nineveh would repent, and he **KNEW** that God would spare them. And he **KNEW** all of this before he departed from the presence of God with God's blessings! The fact that Dove knew this should not surprise us. The fact he was informed by God should not surprise us. Let's look at John 14:26.

John 14:26 KJV: But the Comforter, which is the Holy Ghost, whom the Father will send in my name, ***he shall teach you all things***, and bring all things to your remembrance, whatsoever I have said unto you.

No, Jonah is not the Holy Ghost. Jonah is the Dove, a symbol of the Holy Ghost.

The story of Jonah is not one that you learn, it is one that you enjoy!

The journey of this story takes us through an amazing plot about the life of a faithful prophet referenced by our Savior as much or more than any other prophet. Don't memorize, enjoy! Don't be ***exceeding glad*** but rather ***Greatly Rejoice (to be explained later)!***

We have already discovered much about Jonah that many of us never knew, and we have only searched out verses 1:1, 1:2, part of 1:3 and part of 4:2. Let's finish searching out Jonah 1:3.

Jonah 1:3 KJV: [3] But Jonah rose up to **flee** unto Tarshish from the presence of the Lord, and went down to Joppa; and he found a *ship* (אניה)[2] going to Tarshish: so he paid the fare thereof, and went down into it, to go with them unto Tarshish from the presence of the Lord.

Let's search out the amazing word (אניה) translated as ship that only occurs twice in the original text. The other occurrence is Proverbs 30:18-19.

Proverbs 30:18-19 KJV: [18] There be three things *which are too wonderful* (נפלאו)[1] *for me* (ממני)[87], **yea,** *four* (וארבע)[39] *which I know* (ידעתים)[1] not: [19] The *way* (דרך)[201] *of an eagle in the air*; the *way* (דרך)[201] *of a serpent upon a* *rock*; the *way* (דרך)[201] *of a ship* (אניה)[2] *in the midst* (בלב)[27] *of the sea; and the way* (ודרך)[22] *of a man* (גבר)[51] *with a maid* (בעלמה)[1].

The original text of these two verses is the gift that keeps on giving! Let's start by searching out the word (דרך) translated as "way" which occurs 201 times in the original text. The first letter of this word (דרך) is the letter Dalet (ד) which means "door". The remaining two letters is the word (רך) which occurs a perfect seven times and means "tender". The way is a door of tenderness.

The word (אניה) translated as ship occurs twice in the original text and what's amazing is that if you remove the last letter, the letter Hey (ה) from the word (אניה), the remaining letters are the word (אני) pronounced "Ani" which occurs *698 times* in the original text. Let's look at Exodus 6:2.

Exodus 6:2 KJV And God spake unto Moses, and said unto him, *I am* (אני) the Lord:

** *The word* (אני) *means* <u>"I am"</u>. **

The phrase "I am" occurs 498 times in the KJV Old Testament and of course, the occurrences between the KJV and the original text do not reconcile but many times they do. Sure, some of us are aware that the words "I am" occur many times in the Bible but did we have any idea that it occurred 698 times in the original text?

The definition of the letters of the word (אניה) translated as "ship" is, "*I am* (אני) *to be Revealed* (ה)". Jonah went to Joppa and found *I am to be revealed (ship)* headed to Tarshish. This is one of only two times this word is used in the original text! Coincidence? How does this impact on our views and understanding to the boat ride?

Proverbs 30:19 says that one of the four wonderful things that the *"way of"* cannot be explained is the way of a ship in the midst of the sea. The word (בלב) translated as "in the midst" occurs 27 times in the original text and means "in the heart". One of the four wonderful "ways of" is the way of "I am to be revealed" in the heart of the sea. Is Proverbs 30:19, where we find the only other occurrence of the word (אניה) translated as "ship", revealing that Jonah's story on the ship will reveal *the wonderful way of I am in the heart of the sea*?

Isn't Proverbs 30:18-19 beautiful? Learn Hebrew! Don't trust anyone's translation of interpretation of the words spoken by our God in His language. Hebrew is incredibly easy to learn. It has been witnessed that some have learned how to read and research Hebrew in as little as seventeen days. Don't trust this book, validate it!

Notice that the word (נפלאו) translated as *"which are too wonderful"* is unique. This description of wonderful is a unique expression of wonderful unlike anything we consider to be wonderful (smile).

The letter Mem (מ) is the first letter of the word (ממני) in Proverbs 30:18 translated as *"for me"* which means this word should be translated as *"from me"*. The word (ממני) occurs 87 times in the original text and the first occurrence is Genesis 22:12 when God tells Abraham, "*...seeing thou hast not withheld thy son, thine only son from me* (ממני)." When the letter Mem (מ) is the first letter of a word it is translated as "from" and not "for".

Notice that Proverbs 30:18 seems to single out the fourth uniquely wonderful thing from God. Is it possible that the understanding of *"the wonderfulness"* of the four examples of *"the way"* is revealed in the *fourth "way of"*?

Proverbs 30:19, provides the four *"ways of"* from God that are too wonderful to explain. The fourth *"way of"* in Proverbs 30:19 is "and the way of a *man* (גבר) *with a maid* (בעלמה)". The word (גבר) translated as "man" occurs 51 times in the original text and is most often translated as "master". The word (בעלמה) translated as "with a maid" is unique, only spoken by God one time. The first letter of this word is the letter Bet (ב) which when it is the first letter of a word, it is translated as "in". The last letter of this word is the letter Hey (ה) and when it is the last letter it means "to be revealed". The word (עלמ) from the remaining three letters occurs 6 times in the original text and five of those occurrences are in the Book of Daniel (4:3. 4:34, 7:14, 7:18, and 7:27) where it is translated as "everlasting" or "for ever and ever". The fourth "way of" is *the way of a Master in the everlasting to be revealed"*. Invest in the 45-day effort to learn Hebrew and prove this to yourself and your family!

At the end of Jonah 1:3, Jonah is on a boat headed to Tarshish. Recall that there is also a boat story in the New Testament where Jesus boarded a boat with his disciples to go to the other side, Luke 8:22-25. If our newly found understanding that Dove is aboard a ship that will reveal the wonderful way of "I am" in the heart of the sea, then the *plot should thicken* by comparing these two stories. Let's search out and compare the boat stories from the Book of Jonah and the Gospel of Jesus.

Let's give the boat story in the Book of Jonah the name "Jonah's boat" and likewise we will call the story in the Gospels "Jesus's boat".

First, we know that Jesus is a Galilean from Nazareth and earlier we learned from 2 Kings 14:25 that Jonah, son of Amittai, is from Gath-Hepher which is a small town about five miles south of Nazareth. Jonah is Galilean as well. Both boats have a Galilean on board.

- Jonah is Galilean.
    o   Jesus is Galilean.

Jonah 1:1 and 2 Kings 14:25 also tells us that Jonah's father's name is Amittai which translates to English as My Truth.

- Jonah is Galilean.
    o   Jesus is Galilean.
- Jonah's father is My Truth
    o   Jesus's Father is Yahweh. It's okay to call him My Truth in this story. Agree?

Let's review John 7:52.

John 7:52 KJV: They answered and said unto him, Art thou also of Galilee? Search, and look: for out of Galilee ariseth no prophet.

In John 7:52 a Pharisee tells Nicodemus to search the scriptures and see that no prophet ever came out of Galilee. This verse claims that Jesus is not a prophet because he is unaware of Jonah or unaware that he came from Galilee or both. Both Jesus and Jonah are declared not to be prophets within the same verse.

How is it possible? How can this Pharisee that supposedly studies the scriptures be unaware of Jonah? Is there a chance that when Jonah departed that he did it without anyone noticing him? That's a little humorous, right? Well, let's watch this story play out and see if it becomes clear why this Pharisee is not aware of Jonah.

- Jonah is Galilean.
    o   Jesus is Galilean.
- Jonah's father is My Truth

- o Jesus's father is Yahweh. I'm okay with calling him My Truth in this story. Agree?
- Didn't believe Jonah was a prophet (John 7:52).
  - o Didn't believe in Jesus was a prophet (John 7:52).

Jonah gets on his boat in Joppa and is headed to Tarshish. Joppa in Hebrew means "Beautiful". An internet search, which is subject to change from day-to-day, reveals that the Hebrew translation of Tarshish is "Yellow Jasper". Let's look at the translation of the word (תרשיש) in Ezekiel 1:16.

Ezekiel 1:16 KJV: The appearance of the wheels and their work was like unto the colour of a *beryl* (תרשיש): and they four had one likeness: and their appearance and their work was as it were a wheel in the middle of a wheel.

Most Christians are aware that each stone on the breastplate of the High Priest represents one of the sons of Jacob, but they are unaware that many times God conceals a message by revealing a stone. Now we know that the name Tarshish is a transliteration and not a translation and we also know that it represents a precious stone. Ezekiel 1:16 tells us that it's beryl. The beryl stone represents Jacob's son Naphtali on the breastplate. Likewise, the jasper stone represents Jacob's son Benjamin. Let's look at the NIV translation of Ezekiel 1:16 and see if we can get a majority vote of translation of Tarshish.

Ezekiel 1:16 <u>NIV</u>: This was the appearance and structure of the wheels: They sparkled like *topaz* (תרשיש), and all four looked alike. Each appeared to be made like a wheel intersecting a wheel.

The NIV translation of Tarshish isn't beryl or jasper, it's topaz. Topaz is the stone that represents Jacob's son Simeon. Other English translations translate Tarshish as Chrysolite or Olivine.

The BIG question now is, "Does this really matter?" Most Christians will agree that when we arrive in a scenario where we have a Hebrew word translated several different ways by various English translations, that we just say. "Oh well" and continue without resolution. Most Christians don't recognize nor get upset that they have just validated their "divine and inspired" translations to be flawed. But there are a few Christians that get "spitting" mad about it. Some get so mad that they learn Hebrew. When they return and report their findings of what Tarshish means, they are persecuted with words we won't repeat.

The Hebrew word (תרשיש) translated as Tarshish occurs 25 times in the original text and is always transliterated as Tarshish or one of five different stones. Knowing the correct stone is *VITAL* to our research because each stone represents one of the sons of Jacob on the High Priest breastplate. If we know the stone, then we know which son. If we know which son, then we can search out that the meaning of that son's name which will reveal the correct translation of Tarshish and the destination of Jonah's boat. Our creator conceals beautiful truths using stones. Always consider this exercise when you encounter a stone in your research.

If you don't know Hebrew, the research effort to determine the correct stone is both frustrating and inconclusive.

What happens if your research concludes it's the jasper stone, the last stone on the 4th row of the High Priest Breastplate and represents the tribe of Benjamin whose name means "Son of My Right Hand". If that was the right stone, it would make this story far easier to search out, right? Dove, who represents the Holy Spirit, gets on a boat headed from "Beautiful" (Joppa) to "The Son of My Right Hand" (Tarshish – yellow Jasper). That would be an awesome story to tell! Well, until we try to explain why Jonah was hurled into the sea and never reached Tarshish, The Son of My Right Hand.

Even knowing Hebrew will require tenacity to conclude that Tarshish is the topaz stone and represents the tribe of Simeon whose name means "Hearing". Later we will contend with why something as simple as translating a stone correctly is mistranslated. For now, we will simply reveal the beauty of knowing it's the Topaz. This is PERFECT! Let's search out why.

The significance of *hearing* is a character trait described consistently throughout the Bible and is almost always concealed. It's most often concealed through the stories of people in the Bible named Simeon. The Bible is littered with concealed references of the ability to hear or not hear.

- Joseph kept Simeon (hearing) in prison until the brothers returned with Benjamin (the son of my right hand). Wow, that adds to our story!
- Moses blessed the tribes of Israel, but he did not bless Simeon (hearing). A sign that Moses knew that Israel would not hear, and the gentiles would.
- Jesus said, "those who have ears, let them hear."

- The Holy Spirit gets on a boat and is headed to Hearing.
- Jesus is brought to the temple on the 8th day and is circumcised by a "just and devout" man named Simeon. Coincidence? (Luke 2:25-26)

Luke 2:25-26 KJV: [25] And, behold, there was a man in Jerusalem, whose name was *Simeon*; and the same man was just and devout, waiting for the consolation of Israel: and the Holy Ghost was upon him.
[26] And it was revealed unto him by the Holy Ghost, that he should not see death, before he had seen the Lord's Christ.

Jesus departed Capernaum and in Matthew 8:18 it tells us He simply headed to the other side. Capernaum means Village of Nahum. Village in Hebrew means to **cover** or **protect**, and Nahum in Hebrew means **Comforter**. Let's add that to our list of Books of the Bible with their translated names.

- Book of Friend (Ruth)
- Book of Dove (Jonah)
- Book of the Comforter (Nahum)

Yes, the book of Nahum translated to English is the Book of the Comforter. Oh my, this is crazy amazing, right? So, Jesus is departing the Covering of the Comforter to go to the other side.

Jonah is departing Beautiful to go to Hearing and Jesus is departing the Covering of the Comforter to go to the other side. Oh Lord, please provide us an English translation that includes the correct translation of these nouns!

- Jonah is Galilean.
  - Jesus is Galilean.
- Jonah's father is My Truth
  - Jesus's father is Yahweh. (a.k.a. My Truth?)
- Didn't believe Jonah was a prophet (John 7:52)
  - Didn't believe in Jesus was a prophet.
- Jonah's boat is departing Beautiful and headed to Hearing.
  - Jesus's boat is departing the Covering of the Comforter to go to the other side.

In Jonah 1:3 it tells us that Jonah paid a fare before getting on the boat, but we know that Jesus did not. We will document and search this out while continuing the story.

- Jonah is Galilean.
  - Jesus is Galilean.
- Jonah's father is My Truth
  - Jesus's father is Yahweh. (a.k.a. My Truth?)
- Didn't believe Jonah was a prophet (John 7:52)
  - Didn't believe in Jesus was a prophet.
- Jonah's boat is departing Beautiful and headed to Hearing.
  - Jesus's boat is departing the Covering of the Comforter to go to the other side.
- Jonah pays a fare.
  - Jesus does not pay a fare.

In both stories they go to the bottom of the boat and sleep.

- Jonah is Galilean.
  - Jesus is Galilean.
- Jonah's father is My Truth
  - Jesus's father is Yahweh. (a.k.a. My Truth?)
- Didn't believe Jonah was a prophet (John 7:52)
  - Didn't believe in Jesus was a prophet.
- Jonah's boat is departing Beautiful and headed to Hearing.
  - Jesus's boat is departing the Covering of the Comforter to go to the other side.
- Jonah pays a fare.
  - Jesus does not pay a fare.
- Jonah goes to sleep at the bottom of the boat.
  - Jesus goes to sleep at the bottom of the boat.

Let's review the passengers on the boats. Jonah's boat has gentile unbelievers. Jesus's boat has His Disciples, Jewish believers.

WAIT! Do we agree that Jonah's boat has gentile unbelievers? We have gentile unbelievers headed to Tarshish which means Hearing, **CORRECT** (screaming with a smile)? But the Book of Jonah never tells us whether they arrived. Coincidence? ***NO WAY!*** When do the gentile unbelievers finally hear? In the Book of Acts after the resurrection, right?

- Jonah is Galilean.
  - Jesus is Galilean.
- Jonah's father is My Truth
  - Jesus's father is Yahweh. (a.k.a. My Truth?)

- Didn't believe Jonah was a prophet (John 7:52)
  - Didn't believe in Jesus was a prophet.
- Jonah's boat is departing Beautiful and headed to Hearing.
  - Jesus's boat is departing the Covering of the Comforter to go to the other side.
- Jonah pays a fare.
  - Jesus does not pay a fare.
- Jonah goes to sleep at the bottom of the boat.
  - Jesus goes to sleep at the bottom of the boat.
- Jonah's boat has gentile unbelievers.
  - Jesus's boat has disciples, Jewish believers.

This is where it gets interesting. It would seem as though the two stories take different paths. In Jonah 1:4 God sends a "great wind" into the sea and the ship was "like to be broken", but not "filled with water". Note that it doesn't say there was a storm, it's a wind, a great wind sent by God. Consider that on the Day of Pentecost there was a sound like a rushing mighty wind. Just saying! Coincidence? Let's see what happens next on Jesus's boat.

In Luke 8:23 we learn that there came down a storm of wind. Hmm, is "came down a storm of wind" the same as "a great wind sent by God"? In Acts 2:2 it tells us that on the Day of Pentecost that "suddenly there came a *sound* from heaven as of a rushing mighty wind".

Is there any chance that the wind came from the same place for these two boats? Jonah's boat with gentiles is experiencing wind from God and their boat is breaking, while Jesus's boat is experiencing wind and taking on water (apparently from waves) and it is sinking. The unbeliever's boat is breaking while the believer's boat is taking on water.

Sometimes a boat will break if there are too many fish, other times it will take on water. Just saying! Coincidence?

- Jonah is Galilean.
  - Jesus is Galilean.
- Jonah's father is My Truth
  - Jesus's father is Yahweh. (a.k.a. My Truth?)
- Didn't believe Jonah was a prophet (John 7:52)
  - Didn't believe in Jesus was a prophet.
- Jonah's boat is departing Beautiful and headed to Hearing.

- o Jesus's boat is departing the Covering of the Comforter to go to the other side.
- Jonah pays a fare.
    - o Jesus does not pay a fare.
- Jonah goes to sleep at the bottom of the boat.
    - o Jesus goes to sleep at the bottom of the boat.
- Jonah's boat has gentile unbelievers.
    - o Jesus's boat has disciples, Jewish believers.
- Jonah's boat experiencing wind from God and about to break.
    - o Jesus's boat experiences wind (from God?) and is about to sink.

Now we have an amazing profound divergence between these two stories. At this moment the men on both boats are fearing their lives and each is going to approach Jonah or Jesus to save them. Let's see the divergence of how the unbeliever and the believer are saved.

On Jonah's boat they are doing everything possible to save themselves. They throw everything overboard to lighten the load. Is it fair to say that the fare Jonah paid was thrown overboard? Hmm, how do we apply that? The Hebrew word for Fare (שכרה) in Jonah 1:3 is only used one time in scripture. Upon research you will also find this to be the only time in the translations that "a fare" is paid. Note that an offering or a tithe are not the same as paying a fare. Don't you love it when Hebrew and the English translation agree?

The definition of the Hebrew letters for this word (שכרה) translated as *fare* is, "The destruction (ש) of the hand that covers (כ) the prince (ר) will be revealed (ה)". Furthermore, the root noun (שכר) of this word is in the Hebrew text 29 times and means "being irritated". Coincidence? Thirty is the number that represents betrayal. Is it possible that the unique occurrence of Jonah paying a fare (שכרה) is a shadow of the 30th occurrence of our Savior being betrayed and paying a ransom? Dove is the only person in scripture to pay a fare and our Savior is the only one willing to pay the ransom. Coincidence?

The gentile passengers on Jonah's boat are praying to their gods. Notice that they are not bailing water. Their boat isn't sinking, it's breaking. Finally, they awaken Jonah and ask him how he can sleep at such a time, and they request that Jonah pray to his God as they have been praying to theirs.

On Jesus's boat, there isn't any hint in the story that the men did anything, not even prayer. Likewise, they awaken Jesus and asks Him to save them.

Believers know where to find salvation, unbelievers need help to learn where to find salvation.

- Jonah's boat - the unbelievers do everything they can before awakening Jonah and asking him to join them in the effort to save them. They don't ask Jonah to save them, they simply ask for his help.
    o Jesus's boat - the believers awaken Jesus and ask for Him to save them.

We know that the last bullet point of these two stories is that the men on both boats will be saved but now we get to search out the beautiful understanding of salvation for unbelievers (gentiles) and believers (Jews).

On Jonah's boat the unbelievers had no idea that Jonah would awaken from sleep and tell them what they must do to be saved. The first thing they did was cast lots to see which of them was the cause of this windstorm. These men are aware that this is an act of God, but they are pagans and don't know which god. It seems clear that Jonah is participating in this effort of casting lots. Wait, these are gentiles, and they are casting lots. They are using a custom taught in the Law's of God? Where did they learn to do that?

After casting lots they learn that this is Jonah's "fault" and they ask him four questions 1) his occupation, 2) where he was from, 3) what country he was from, 4) what people he is.

Now let's review what happens next on Jesus's boat. Remember, this is a boat of believers. Luke Chapter 8 makes it clear that all twelve disciples are with him.

Several of these men are accustomed to the weather changes on the Sea of Galilee but like Jonah's boat this wind is like none before. These men know the sea, they're fishermen. Surely, they did what they knew to do while the boat was taking on water. Surely, their experience of what to do led them to believe it was a lost cause, so they awakened Jesus. Scripture describes their amazement when they witness the miracle, proof they didn't wake him up to knowingly perform this miracle.

How about some conjecture... The disciples had no idea that Jesus possessed authority over the wind. Is it possible that when they awakened him, they were holding a bucket to help bale water (smile)? Play it out the way you like, but from the time the wind started to the moment they feared death, do we think they just sat there? It also seems apparent that they didn't pray. They woke up the Son of God to ask him to bail water (smile). Yes, that is a conjecture, fun conjecture.

They awaken Jesus and He rebuked the wind and the raging water. Then in Luke 8:25 Jesus asks them, "Where is your faith?" Understand that prior to getting on the boat, Jesus shared the parable of the Sower and the seed. They are with Jesus, and they are "hearing". Oh wait, after the unbelievers hurled Jonah off the boat, they continued their journey to Tarshish which means "hearing". The passengers on both boats have ears to hear (smile)!

Let's search out the Book of Jonah and reveal the story never told.

Jonah 1:4 KJV: [4] But the Lord *sent out* (הטיל)[1] *a great* (גדולה)[72] *wind* (רוח)[214] into the sea, and there was a *mighty* (גדול)[179] *tempest* (סער)[2] in the sea, *so that the ship* (והאניה)[1] *was like* (חשבה)[2] *to be broken* (להשבר)[1].

The superscript number of the words from the original text reveals how many times the word occurs in the original text (the Tenakh, Hebrew Old Testament). There are three unique words in this verse and two other words that only occur twice in the original text. Prepare to be "like a dove" and make multiple round-trip flights throughout the Book of Jonah back to Jonah 1:1-4.

Let's search out these words that come from the mouth of God and reveal more of the story not told.

The word (הטיל)[1] translated as "sent out" is unique. Whatever your view of God "making or sending" a "great wind" in the sea, add to that understanding that this is something God only did one time in the entire Old Testament. However, the word "sent" occurs 678 times in the KJV. Though the word "sent" is very common in our vocabulary and the KJV, this ***HEBREW WORD*** (הטיל) ***IS UNIQUE*** in the original text.

The word (חשבה) translated as "was like" occurs twice in the original text and the other occurrence is Genesis 50:20.

Genesis 50:20 KJV: [20] But as for you, ye thought evil against me; but God *meant it* (חשבה)[2] unto good, to bring to pass, as it is this day, to save much people alive.

In Genesis 50:20, Joseph is explaining to his brothers that God devised a way to make something good from his brother's evil against him. God only did this twice and the other occurrence is the events of Jonah's boat ride to Tarshish. Now we know that God's intent to "sent out" a great wind is meant for good. The unbelieving gentile passengers are unaware that everything they are about to encounter is from God and meant for good. ***Again, only two times in the Old Testament does God use something that seems bad and devises it for good.***

Note that the first time God did this, all nations, including Israel, benefited from Joseph's preparations of the world-wide famine. Is our Savior's death and burial something that was meant for bad, but our Good Father devised it good for all nations by the resurrection of His Son? Is the resurrection the third occurrence that fulfills these two Old Testament occurrences?

Jonah 1:5 KJV: [5] Then *the mariners* (המלחים)[1] were afraid, and cried every man unto his god, *and cast forth* (ויטלו)[1] *the wares* (את-הכלים)[34] that were *in the ship* (באניה)[1] into the sea, *to lighten* (להקל)[2] *it of them* (מעליהם)[13]. But Jonah *was gone down* (ירד)[51] into *the sides of the ship* (הספינה)[1]; *and he lay* (וישכב)[54], *and was fast asleep* (וירדם)[1].

This verse contains the translation of five unique words from the original text.

Let's search out the unique word (המלחים) from the original text translated as "the mariners". Why would the prophet Jonah get on a ship with mariners? The word "mariners" occurs five times in the KJV, all in the Old Testament, but this word (המלחים) translated as "mariners" only occurs one time in the original text.

The Hebrew word Canaan means merchant. Mariners are merchants on ships. These merchant **"mariners** (a unique word)" **"cast forth** (a unique word)" their "wares" that were **"in their ship** (a unique word)" into the sea **"to lighten** (twice in the original text)" the load. While all of this is taking place, Jonah is laying **"fast asleep** (a unique word)".

Does revealing that most of this verse is translated from words spoken by God one time arouse a desire for more understanding of what is taking place? While consider the impact of this uniqueness, consider that this is the last occurrence of the word (את-הכלים) translated as "the wares" and it's the last occurrence of the word (וישכב) translated as "and he lay". You don't have to be Hollywood's best private detective to know this verse has depth *far* beyond the sum of the translated English. And we will ignore the word (אֶת) this time, just like the translators did 7,372 times in the translation of the KJV.

This would be an excellent time to reconsider the beauty of knowing that Jonah is not a rebellious prophet that sinfully fled from the presence of God. Rather, his presence on the ship is a gift to the "*sappy ones* (לחים)", the grapes ripe for the harvest. Mariners (הַמַּלָּחִים), behold (ה) from (מ) the grapes (לַחִים).

Searching out the words of Jonah 1:5 is a **wonderful exercise** but documenting that effort would take an estimated fifty pages. The most difficult part of that effort is explaining and documenting the variance between the meaning of these words and how they are translated.

Jonah 1:6 KJV: [6] So *the shipmaster* (רַב הַחֹבֵל[2] [186]) came to him (וַיִּקְרַב)[24], and said unto him, What (מַה)*30* meanest thou (לְךָ)[965], O sleeper (נִרְדָּם)[5]? arise, call upon thy God, if so be that God *will think upon us* (יִתְעַשֵּׁת)[1], *that we perish* (נֹאבֵד)[2] not.

The word (נֹאבֵד) translated as "that we perish" occurs twice in the original text. We will search out this word on its last occurrence in Jonah 3:9.

The underlined words from the original text are the last occurrence of the word. That said, there are thirty more occurrences of the word (מה) translated as "What". Does this imply that the last occurrence of this word, found in Malachi 3:13, will reveal betrayal?

The word "shipmaster" occurs in the KJV two times, the other occurrence is Revelation 18:17. This word is translated by combining two words (רב החבל) from the original text. The first word (רב) occurs 186 times in the original text and is most often translated as "many". The second word (החבל) occurs twice in the original text and the other occurrence is 2 Samuel 8:2.

2 Samuel 8:2 KJV: [2] And he smote Moab, and measured them with a line, casting them down to the ground; even with two lines measured he to put to death, and *with one full line* (הַחֶבֶל) to keep alive. And so the Moabites became David's servants, and brought gifts.

So, the two words (רב החבל) from the original text that are translated as "shipmaster" means "many in a full line". The beginning of Jonah 1:6 is, "*Many in a full line* came to him (וַיִּקְרַב)…"

The word (ויקרב) translated as "came to him" occurs 24 times in the original text and in all occurrences, it is the verb "brought". The many in full line didn't come to Jonah, but rather, Jonah is bringing them near to him. Does that sound familiar?

Let's continue and search out Jonah 1:7.

Jonah 1:7 KJV: [7] And they said every one to his fellow, Come, *and let us cast* (ונפילה)[1] *lots* (גורלות)[8], that we may know (ונדעה)[8] *for whose cause* (בשלמי)[1] this evil is upon us. *So they cast* (ויפלו)[29] *lots* (גורלות)[8], *and the lot* (הגורל)[24] *fell* (ויפל)[50] upon Jonah.

There are two unique words from the original text translated in this verse. Again, the other words from the original text are the last occurrence of those words in the Hebrew Old Testament.

We have revealed several words that occur twenty-nine times in the original text and pointed out the potential that the thirtieth occurrence, which represents betrayal, could be our Savior's fulfillment of the word. Could the 30th occurrence of the word (ויפלו) translated as "So they cast" be another one of those scenarios? That said, since the number eight represents "New Beginnings" and the number nine represents "Truth", is it also possible that the next occurrence of the word (גורלות) translated as "lots" which occurs eight times is when they cast lots for our Savior's garments? If so, that would be the ninth occurrence and reveal that our Savior is fulfilling "truth".

The revelation of the occurrences of His Words brings additional revelation of the beauty and omniscience of the Divine and Inspired Word of God from His Holy Language.

Jonah 1:8 KJV: [8] Then said they unto him, *Tell us* (הגידה)[18], we pray thee, for whose cause this evil is upon us; What is thine *occupation* (מלאכתך)[4]? *and whence* (ומאין)[8] comest thou? what is thy country? and of what people art thou?

This verse is the beginning of collaboration between Jonah and the mariners that influences the traditional passed down idea that the storm is a curse of evil and that it's Jonah's fault because he sinfully fled from the presence of God. But we have already revealed that Jonah didn't flee sinfully, rather he fled with the authority to do God's will. Let's continue and prove this storm will wonderfully reveal "I am" and that *Jonah is a faithful prophet.* Is it becoming more clear that Dove, son of My Truth (Amittai), is doing the will of the Father and teaching men what they must do to be saved?

Consider that the mariner's experience is how the spirit works. He brings turbulence into our lives to persuade us to seek and find the right path.

Yes, again, the three words revealed in Jonah 1:8 from the original text are the last occurrence of those words.

The last occurrence of the word (ומאין) translated as "and whence" is a role reversal of the first occurrence. The first occurrence is in Joshua 9:8 and that chapter tells the story of how the Hivites tricked Joshua and the elders of Israel. They claimed to be ambassadors of Yahwey to get Israel to make a vow with them. They successfully acted out the lie of their fake identity with props of worn clothes and old wine skins (smile, sound familiar) and received a vow from Israel that saved their towns from the destruction of Israel as it claimed the promised land.

The Hivites came as imposters of good, and now the prophet Dove seems to be disguising himself as something bad. He even paid a fare to be on the boat. While on the boat with pagans, he is awaiting the opportunity to teach them something good, how to be saved.

Jonah 1:9-10 KJV: [9] And he said unto them, I am an Hebrew; and I *fear* (ירא)[49] *the Lord* (ואת-יהוה), *the* God (אלהי)[502] of *heaven* (השמים[236]), which hath made *the sea* (את-הים) *and the dry land* (ואת-[5]היבשה).
[10] Then were the men exceedingly afraid, and said unto him. Why hast thou done this? For the men knew that he *fled* (ברח)[18] *from the presence of* (מלפני)[50] the Lord, because he had told them.

Jonah 1:9 is unexplainable until we have abandoned the passed down traditional story. That said, the word Et (את) appears 12 times in the Book of Jonah. The only two occurrences of the word Vah-Et (ואת) in the Book of Jonah are also in this verse. Recall that (את) is the First and the Last letters of Hebrew and our Savior said that He is the First and the Last. It is impossible to exaggerate the significance of these words in Jonah 1:9.

Jonah 1:9 is also the fifteenth occurrence of the word (עברי) translated as Hebrew. The number fifteen means redemption.

Jonah 1:10 reveals that the mariners were "exceedingly afraid". Very likely, anyone who hears what Jonah told these men in the previous verse would be "afraid"?

The number fifty in Hebrew represents "Jubilee". Every seven years is a jubilee year, a year of rest. The year following every seventh jubilee, the 50th year, is a Jubilee of Jubilees. The 50th year is another year of rest; no crops are to be planted, even the land gets rest. That said, the word (ירא) translated as "fear" occurs 49 times in the original text. Could Philippians 2:12-13 where we are to seek our own salvation with fear and trembling be an example of the 50th occurrence that fulfills these forty-nine Old Testament occurrences?

The number eighteen in Hebrew represents bondage or freedom from bondage. Isn't it interesting the word (ברח) translated as "fled" occurs on its last occurrence, the 18th occurrence, in Jonah 1:10 where pagan mariners are visited by the prophet Dove and are told how to be saved, freed from bondage?

Jonah 1:11 KJV: [11] Then said they (ויאמרו)[5] unto him, What *shall we do* (נעשה)[53] unto thee, that the sea *may be calm* (וישתק)[2] *unto us* (מעלינו)[7]? for the sea wrought, and was tempestuous.

The word (נעשה) translated as "shall we do" occurs 53 times in the original text and the first occurrence is Genesis 1:26, *"And God said, **Let us make** (נעשה) man in our image, after our likeness: and let them have dominion..."* Wow, right? The mariners are declaring to Jonah that whatever he tells them to do, they will do.

The second occurrence of the word (נעשה) translated as "shall we do" is found in Exodus 19:8, *"And all the people answered together, and said, All that the Lord hath spoken **we will do** (נעשה). And..."*

The third occurrence is found in Exodus 24:3, *"And he took the book of the covenant, and read in the audience of the people: and they said, All that the Lord hath said **will we do** (נעשה), and be obedient.*

Though it can't be proven, could the 54th occurrence of the word (נעשה) translated as "shall we do" be found in Acts 2:37?

Acts 2:37 KJV: [37] Now when they heard this, they were pricked in their heart, and said unto Peter and to the rest of the apostles, Men and brethren, ***what shall we do?***

No surprise to learn that the word (ויאמרו) translated as "Then said they" occurs five times in the original text, and this is the fourth occurrence. The number four reveals a door.

No, this book doesn't preach (smile). Each of us must rightly divide the Word of Truth. Glory to the King.

Jonah 1:12 KJV: [12] And he said unto them, *Take me up* (שאוני)[2], *and cast me forth* (והטילני)[1] *into the sea; so* shall *the sea* be calm (וישתק)[2] *unto you* (מעליכם)[7]: *for* (כי)[4,231] I *know* (יודע)[40] *that* (כי)[4,231] *for my sake* (בשלי)[2] *this* (הזה)[704] *great* (הגדול)[89] *tempest* (הסער)[1] *is upon you* (עליכם)[101].

The word (שאוני) translated as "Take me up" occurs twice in the original text. The phrase "take me up" is translated as "lift me up" by two English translations (LSB and YLT).

The word (והטילני) translated as "and cast me forth" has a footnote in the NKJV that declares this literally means "hurl me into the sea".

This verse has several slightly misworded translations that when combined lead us back to the traditional passed down idea that this storm is Jonah's fault because of his sin. The traditional story does not reveal what's taking place with "the mariners", it portrays them as victims of Jonah's sin.

This verse and the following verses will reveal the truth that Jonah's participation on this boat is an act of intercession for the salvation of these men. Dove is revealing **"...*the way of a ship* (אניה)[2] *in the midst of the sea; and...*"** from Proverbs 30:19. Recall that the word (אניה) translated as "ship" only occurs in this story of Jonah and Proverbs 30:19. Coincidence?

The word (הדברים) **means** "These are the words" and occurs in the original text 134 times, but Christians are most familiar with the only time it was translated into Greek by the KJV translators. Yes, the KJV translators provided the Greek translation of this word as the title of the Book of Deuteronomy. The English name of the Book of Deuteronomy is "These are the words". The root noun (דבר) of the word (הדברים) occurs in the original text nearly 1,200 times and is most often translated as "a thing" or "these things".

Let's look at Proverbs 25:2 one more time!

Proverbs 25:2 KJV: It is the glory of God to conceal *a thing* (דבר)[798]: but the *honour of kings* is to <u>search out</u> *a matter* (דבר)[798].

The definition of the letters of the word (דבר) translated as "a thing" is, "The (ד) to the Son (בר)".

Let's return to searching out Jonah 1:12.

Look at the words from the original text of Jonah 1:12 and consider that two are unique and three only occur twice. This is the only time in the original text of the Old Testament where ***"these words from the original text"*** tell the story of a prophet openly declaring ***"a way for a ship in the midst of the sea"***. Dove tells the mariners that he is why this unique tempest (rushing mighty wind) is upon them and they must cast him into the sea for the waters to be calmed and they be saved.

Christians that know how to read and research Hebrew are aware that this book is as guilty of intentionally not providing the complete story, there is so much more to share. Hence, this is Volume #1. This print, the 2nd Edition of Volume #1, was published after Traditions, Lies from Birth Volume #2 on October 5, 2024. Again, apologies to anyone who endured reading the 1st Edition of this book!

The omniscience of the Word of God concealed in the order of occurrences of words in the original text provides unprecedented added revelation. That said, because this is Volume #1, it was decided to disprove the traditional lies without leaning on the revelations provided by the order of occurrences. Yes, the 53rd, 32nd, and 41st occurrences of a word do reveal incredible revelation, and those revelations reconfirm the truth of the original text and further expose the lies of the passed down traditions. Volume #2 of this series will be forthcoming to reveal the omniscience of our Father's order of occurrences of "Deuteronomy - these words" to confirm truth and reveal the traditional lies from before we were born.

By now, hopefully we are beginning to believe the truth about righteous prophet Dove who was sent to teach us about the works of the spirit.

Let's continue searching out Jonah's

Jonah 1:13 KJV: [13] Nevertheless *the men rowed hard* (ויחתרו)[1] *to bring* (להשיב)[32] it to *the land* (היבשה)[5]; but they could not: for the sea *wrought* (הולך)[41], *and was tempestuous* (וסער)[4] *against them* (עליהם)[222].

The word "Nevertheless" is implied by the translators and not in the original text.

The word (ויחתרו) translated as "the men rowed hard" is unique. Consider the idea that the men departed from Israel, then had an encounter with Dove, and now they are trying to return to "the dry land", to unbelieving Israel. Dove is still on the boat and the "rushing mighty wind" is still blowing. Dove has already told them how to be saved. They must lift him up and hurl him to his death.

Jonah 1:14 KJV: [14] Wherefore they cried (ויקראו)[32] unto the Lord, and said, We beseech thee, O Lord, we beseech thee, let *us not perish* (נאבדה)[1] for this man's *life* (בנפש)[17], and lay not upon us ***innocent*** (נקיא)[2] blood: for thou, O Lord, hast done as it *pleased* (חפצת)[5] thee.

The word (ויקראו) translated as "Wherefore they cried" occurs 32 times in the original text and this is the 30th occurrence. The number thirty represents betrayal. Coincidence?

The word (נאבדה) translated as "us not perish" is unique. The last letter of the word is the letter Hey (ה) which means "to be revealed". The remaining letters (נאבד) occurs twice in the original text. The first occurrence of this word was Jonah 1:6 where it is translated as "we shall perish" and in this verse it is translated as "we are perishing". We will continue to search out this word (נאבד) when we get to the last occurrence in Jonah 3:9.

The word (בנפש) translated as "life" is most often translated as "soul of".

The word (נקיא) translated as "innocent" only occurs twice in the original text. The mariners are praying that they are not judged for the "soul of" Jonah's *innocent* blood.

Wait! Both the traditional passed down story and the translation of these verses hint that Jonah is NOT innocent blood! Yet, this verse reveals that after hearing Jonah's words, these men believe him to be innocent. ***It's as though "they find no fault in him"*** (smile). Coincidence?

That's correct! Read this verse again and decide for yourself if the words of these men "at sea" resemble the words of Pilate when our Savior was judged on "dry land". In verse nine, Jonah declared that he fears His God that created "the sea" and the "dry land". Coincidence?

Jonah 1:15 KJV: [15] *So they took up* (וישאו)[43] Jonah (את-יונה), *and cast him forth* (ויטלהו)[1] into the sea: and the sea *ceased* (ויעמד)[73] *from her raging* (מזעפו)[1].

We have all heard much teaching about the Holy Ghost or Holy Spirit depending on your denomination. Thankfully all denominations teach of the meekness and beauty of the Spirit. The Book of Dove is not about Dove, it's about the lives that Dove impacts, the lives that Dove loves, the lives that Dove willfully gives his life to save, the lives that lifted him up, the lives that Dove "fled" from God knowing he would impact. Yes, there are many more.

Our Savior (innocent blood) was buried on "dry land" and Jonah (innocent blood) was being buried "at sea", correct? This verse has two unique words from the original text and the two other words revealed from the original text are the last occurrence of these two words.

It is **CRUCIAL** that we recognize that Jonah's name is preceded by Et (את) for the first time. More on that later, ***but don't' forget*** that the moment they lifted up Jonah, his name is preceded by Et (את)!

We haven't searched out the revelation and omniscience of the last occurrence of each word our Father speaks, especially when the word occurs many times like 43 or 73 times like the two words in this verse. Let's search out the translation of these two words, then we will search out the omniscience of "the last occurrence" of each word that our Father speaks.

The word (וישאו) translated as "So they took up" occurs 43 times in the original text and the first occurrence is Genesis 7:17.

Genesis 7:17 KJV: [17] And the flood was forty days upon the earth; and the waters increased, and bare up the ark, *and it was lift up* (וישאו)[43] above the earth.

The same word (וישאו) translated as "So they took up" is translated as "and it was lifted up". Hmm... Recall that the tenth occurrence of a word will reveal "it is finished". The 10th occurrence of the word (וישאו) is Judges 2:4.

Judges 2:4 KJV: [4] And it came to pass, when the angel of the Lord spake these words unto all the children of Israel, that the people *lifted up* (וישאו)[43] their voice, and wept.

After our Savior said, "It is finished", the people at the cross lifted up their voice and wept. Again, this word (וישאו) means "lifted up".

Now, let's search out the omniscience of the last occurrence of the word (וישאו) that is repeatedly translated as "lifted up". Most Christians are aware of the many occurrences of the number forty in scripture, and most are also aware that that any time you see this number, it will reveal "a test".

After our Savior fasted for forty days and forty nights, He was tempted (tested). The 40th occurrence of the word (וישאו) is Ezekiel 32:24.

Ezekiel 32:24 KJV: [24] There is Elam and all her multitude *round about her grave, all of them slain, fallen by the sword, which are gone down uncircumcised into the nether parts of the earth*, which caused their terror in the land of the living; yet have they *borne* (וישאו)[43] their shame with them that go down to the pit.

We won't be diverted and search out this verse, but the word translated as "lifted up" is translated as "borne". This verse reveals the *results* of a test. It reveals that they are *"lifting up"* their shame (sin) from the pit. It reveals the "death and burial of sin slain by the sword".

Our Savior's temptation, proved to be "the death of sin" who was tempting Him and the beginning of His ministry. Is it possible that the Words of God in the original text provides us revelation of the Gospel on the 40th, 41st, 42nd, and 43rd occurrence of each word from His original language? No way, right? What changes if this is found to be true? Nothing? No, this book doesn't preach, it joyously reveals the beauty of our Father's word. The 41st occurrence of this word (וישאו) is Ezekiel 32:25 (yes, the next verse).

Ezekiel 32:25 KJV: [25] *They have set her a bed in the midst of the slain with all her multitude: her graves are round about him*: all of them uncircumcised, slain by the sword: though their terror was caused in the land of the living, yet have they *borne* (וישאו)[43] their shame with them that go down to the pit: he is put in the midst of them that be slain.

Is it blatantly clear that the 41st occurrence of this word (וישאו) reveals the second occurrence of sins death by the sword and the burial of sin? Notice that *"all of them uncircumcised, slain by the sword"*. They are "lifting up" their sin from the pit.

The phrase "son of man" occurs 192 times in the KJV. It occurs more times in the Book of Ezekiel (92) than it does in the New Testament (84). What does that mean? Lord willing, it will be revealed in Traditions, Lies from Birth Volume 5. Yes, research has been compiled and we have already planned several upcoming volumes to this series. The "omniscience" of the order of these volumes will be revealed in Traditions, Lies from Birth Volume 3, "The Birth of the Light of the World".

The 42nd occurrence of the word (וישאו) translated as "lifted up" occurs in Ezekiel 32:30. No surprise that it occurs in Ezekiel, the "son of man" book, right?

Ezekiel 32:30 KJV: [30] There be the princes of the north, all of them, and all the Zidonians, which are gone down with the slain; with their terror they are ashamed of their might; and they lie uncircumcised with them that be slain by the sword, *and bear* (וישאו)[43] their shame with them that go down to the pit.

The 42nd occurrence of this word reveals the third consecutive occurrence of the uncircumcised ones who died from the sword are "lifting up" their sin from the pit. For the third time they are "bearing" their own sin, they are "lifting up" their sin.

Let's look at the 43rd and last occurrence of this word (וישאו) translated as "lifted up".

Jonah 1:15 KJV: [15] *So they took up* (וישאו)[43] Jonah (את-יונה), *and cast him forth* (ויטלהו)[1] into the sea: and the sea *ceased* (ויעמד)[73] *from her raging* (מזעפו)[1].

The mariners, who have not been slain by the sword. and are not in the pit and are "lifting up" the innocent blood of Dove and they are going to cast him into the sea. Let's look at John 12:31-33.

John 12:31-33 KJV: [31] Now is the judgment of this world: now shall the prince of this world be cast out.

³² And I, if I be lifted up from the earth, will draw all men unto me.
³³ This he said, signifying what death he should die.

In Jonah 1:15, it's not surprising to learn that the word (ויטלהו) translated as "and cast him forth" is unique. Is it coincidence that this only happened once in the Old Testament and once in the New Testament?

We will not search out the word (ויעמד) translated as "ceased" and references "the sea". Neither will we search out the unique word (מזעפו) translated as "from her raging". That said, is the phrase "and the sea ceased from her raging" related to Revelation 21:1 where it says, "…and there was no more sea."? A hint? The number seventy in Hebrew represents "The Nations".

This book is written by and likely read by a Christian. Christian's love exalting our Savior. Learning Hebrew doesn't make you deny Christ, rather it provides countless opportunities to "lift up" our Savior from His original Hebrew text. His name is not translated into any English translation, it's transliterated.

In the previous chapter we learned about the word Et (את). The word Et (את) occurs twelve times in the Book of Jonah. The number twelve represents authority of government. Jonah 1:15 is the third occurrence of the word Et (את) in the Book of Jonah and ***the first time Et (את) precedes Jonah's name.*** Our Savior proclaimed that He is Et (את), the First (א) and the Last (ת). Well, if He is Et (את) then Et (את) is Him. His name is Yeshua which means Salvation. ***The mariners "lifted up Salvation – Jonah" and cast him into the sea.*** At the worst moment of his life, Salvation (Yeshua) is with Jonah.

Salvation, the First and the Last,
is with Jonah throughout his journey in the fish.

Let's continue searching out the Book of Jonah and be aware of the word Et (את), ***the First and the Last***, in the Book of Dove.

Jonah 1:16 KJV: ¹⁶ Then the men feared the Lord (את-יהוה) exceedingly, *and offered* (ויזבחו)¹⁵ a sacrifice unto the Lord, *and made* (וידרו)¹ vows.

The men didn't fear the Lord, Yahweh (יהוה), they feared the Lord, Yahweh (את-יהוה). What's the difference? How do we translate (את-יהוה)? Our Savior's Hebrew name is Yeshua which means Salvation. He said that He is the First and the Last. If Salvation is the First and the Last, then the First and the

118

Last is Salvation. This isn't difficult! The men feared the Salvation of the Lord.
Glory to the King!

The word (ויזבחו) translated as "and offered" occurs fifteen times in the
original text and this is the last occurrence. The number fifteen represents
redemption. Just another coincidence?

The word (וידרו) translated as "and made" is unique. The first and last
letters of this word is the Vav (וַיִּדְרוּ). The word (ידר) from the remaining three
letters (ידר) occurs three times. The first and second occurrences are found in
Numbers 6:21.

Numbers 6:21 KJV: [21] This is the law of the Nazarite *who hath vowed* (ידר)[3],
and of his offering unto the Lord for his separation, beside that that his hand
shall get: according to the vow *which he vowed* (ידר)[3], so he must do after the
law of his separation.

The letter Vav (ו) is the sixth letter of the Hebrew alphabet and means
"the straight up man with a nail". Not surprising that this word (וידרו) is unique.
Dove taught these men to make unique vows (וַיִּדְרוּ) with the First (וַ) and the
Last (וּ) who is yet to come, the straight up man with a nail, the Vav (ו).

Jonah 1:17 KJV: [17] Now the *Lord* (יהוה)[6,007] *had prepared* (וימן)[5] a *great*
(גדול)[179] *fish* (דג)[1] *to swallow up* (לבלע)[3] ___Jonah___ (את[7,372]-יונה[27]). *And* (ויהי)[816]
Jonah (יונה)[27] *was in the belly of* (במעי)[2] *the fish* (הדג)[1] three days and three
nights.

The Bible is littered with once in the history of man events. Let's
search out the original text of one of the most amazing events of the Bible.

The word (וימן) translated as "prepared" occurs five times in the
original text and the first occurrence is Nebuchadnezzar preparing food for
Daniel and his three friends Hananiah, Mishael, and Azariah whom are more
commonly known to by their Babylonian names Shadrach, Meshach, and
Abednego. The remaining four occurrences are in the Book of Jonah, and this
verse is the first of those four occurrences. All four occurrence of the word
(וימן) are quite remarkable because they are being performed by God.

The first thing God "prepared" in the Book of Jonah was a great fish
(דג). The word (דג) translated as "fish" is unique and the definition of the letters

is, "The Door (ד) of Wealth (ג)". The Hebrew pronunciation of the word (דג) fish is "Dog" (smile). It isn't likely that the humor or a dog swallowing a dove exist in any other language.

This fish (דג) was a "*great* (גדול) *fish* (דג)". There are three words translated as "great" in the Jonah story.

- (גדול) – 2 times in Jonah – verses 1:4, 1:17
- (גדולה) – 6 times in Jonah – verses 1:4, 1:10, 1:16, 3:3, 4:1, 4:6
- (הגדולה) – 3 times in Jonah – verses 1:2, 3:2, and 4:11

These three words all contain the root noun (גדול) and occur a total of eleven times. The number eleven represents a covering. The root noun word (גדול) is translated as "mighty" in Jonah 1:4 and Jonah 1:17 is its last occurrence in the Book of Jonah.

The word (גדול) translated as "great" occurs twice in the Jonah story and this is the last occurrence. Now, we get to consider why God used this word. Is the fish great because of its size or is it great because it was "prepared" by God or is it great because it has the privilege to swallow up Jonah or is it a combination of these three?

What's the difference between these three words translated as great? Well, not knowing Hebrew makes this question seem daunting but the difference isn't something that requires years of Biblical Hebrew research. The difference of these words is something that is recognizable almost immediately after learning the Hebrew alphabet. The root noun (גדול) means that God has declared something to be great, in this case a fish, and we must determine why. The second spelling of the word (גדולה) translated as great adds the letter Hey (ה) as a suffix so the word (גדולה) means "Great to be Revealed". The third spelling of the word (הגדולה) translated as great has the letter Hey (ה) as a prefix and a suffix which means "Behold Great Revealed".

Let's make a *return flight* and apply this understanding to Jonah 1:4.

Jonah 1:4 (Modified): But the Lord **_sent out_** (הטיל)[1] a ~~great~~ **_great to be revealed_** (גדולה)[72] *wind* (רוח)[214] into *the sea* (הים), and *there was a* (ויהי)[816] ~~mighty~~ **_great_** (גדול)[179] *tempest* (סער)[2] in the sea, *so that the ship* (והאניה)[1] ~~was like~~ **_meant it_** (חשבה)[2] *to be broken* (להשבר)[1].

We have searched out the words that are italic, bold, and underlined.

Church has correctly taught us to realize when Jesus repeats Himself. We pay close attention when He says, "Verily, verily…" That said, there are many times when scripture repeats itself "in the spirit" of the words rather than the "context" of the word. Noticing when this happens adds new revelations or knowledge to the verse.

In Jonah 1:4, consider whether the "**_great_** (גדול) *tempest* (סער)", is a result "**_greatness to be revealed_** (גדולה) *wind* (רוח)" that was sent by the Lord. Let's search out the word (רוח) translated as "wind".

The word (רוח) translated as "wind" occurs 214 times in the Tanakh but only twice if the Book of Dove and the number two represents a witness. The church has correctly taught us that "the wind" often references "the spirit". That said, the word "wind" occurs 140 times in the KJV Old Testament, and the word "spirit" occurs an additional 236 times in the KJV Old Testament. That said, to audit the translation of this word (רוח) translated as "wind" would require hundreds of pages. Let's search out the first seven occurrences.

- **1ˢᵗ Occurrence Genesis 6:17** KJV And, behold, I, even I, do bring a flood of waters upon the earth, to destroy all flesh, wherein is the **_breath_** (רוח) of life, from under heaven; and every thing that is in the earth shall die.
- **2ⁿᵈ Occurrence Genesis 7:15** KJV And they went in unto Noah into the ark, two and two of all flesh, wherein is the **_breath_** (רוח) of life.
- **3ʳᵈ Occurrence Genesis 7:22** KJV All in whose nostrils was the **_breath_** (רוח) of life, of all that was in the dry land, died.
- **4ᵗʰ Occurrence Genesis 8:1** KJV And God remembered Noah, and every living thing, and all the cattle that was with him in the ark: and God made **_a wind_** (רוח) to pass over the earth, and the waters assuaged.
- **5ᵗʰ Occurrence Genesis 26:35** KJV Which were a grief of **_mind_** (רוח) unto Isaac and to Rebekah.
- **6ᵗʰ Occurrence Genesis 41:38** KJV And Pharaoh said unto his servants, Can we find such a one as this is, a man in whom the **_Spirit_** (רוח) of God is?
- **7ᵗʰ Occurrence Genesis 45:27** KJV And they told him all the words of Joseph, which he had said unto them: and when he saw the wagons which Joseph had sent to carry him, the **_spirit_** (רוח) of Jacob their father revived:

Within the first seven occurrences this word (רוח) is translated as breath, wind, mind, and spirit. Which one is it? Could it possibly be all four along with the many other ways it's translated in the remaining 207 occurrences? Many Christians recognize this word (רוח) is pronounced "Ruach" and represents "Spirit". Substitute the word "spirit" in the first seven occurrences and see that it's applicable.

Now we can apply this understanding to Jonah 1:4.

Jonah 1:4 (Modified): But the Lord ***sent out*** (הטיל)[1] ~~great~~ ***greatness to be reveal the*** (גדולה)[72] ~~wind~~ ***spirit of Him*** (רוח)[214] into *the sea* (הים), and *there was a* (ויהי)[816] ~~mighty~~ ***great*** (גדול)[179] *tempest* (סער)[2] in the sea, *so that the ship* (והאניה)[1] ~~was like~~ ***meant it*** (חשבה)[2] *to be broken* (להשבר)[1].

As mentioned earlier, Jonah 1:4 is a pivotal verse to continue disproving the passed down traditional story of Dove. Let's search out the unique word (והאניה) translated as *"so that the ship"*.

** The amazing word (והאניה) translated as "so that the ship". **

Two of the last three words from the original text of Jonah 1:4 is unique and the other only occurs twice. Searching out these three words will raise questions about the translation efforts of the KJV. Know that these unspoken questions will be addressed in Traditions, Lies from Birth Volume 2. Yes, prepare yourself for an amazing revelation of the original text.

The left four letters (אניה) of the unique word (והאניה) translated as *"so that the ship"* occurs twice in the original text and is translated as "ship". Recall that we searched out the occurrence of this word (אניה) in Jonah 1:3. Recall that the only other occurrence of the word (אניה) translated as "ship" occurred in Proverbs 30:18-19 "… the wonderful … way of a ship…" We also learned that the word means "I AM to be revealed". That said, the definition of the letters of the word (והאניה) translated as *"so that the ship"* is, "The Straight Up Man with the Nail (ו) Reveals (ה) I AM (the Father אני) to be Revealed (ה)". Does this resemble John 14:6 …no man cometh unto the Father, but by me."?

Let's search out the unique word (להשבר) translated as "to be broken". Once again, we face the daunting task of validating a unique Hebrew word from the original text. And once again, by removing the ***First and the Last*** letters, the word (השב) from the remaining three letters occurs seventeen times in the original text and the first occurrence is Genesis 20:7.

Genesis 20:7 KJV Now therefore *restore* (השב)[17] the man his wife; for he is a prophet, and he shall pray for thee, and thou shalt live: and if thou restore her not, know thou that thou shalt surely die, thou, and all that are thine.

The occurrences of the word (השב) validate that this word means "restore". Now that we know the root noun (השב) of the word (להשבר) translated as "to be broken" means "restore", we can add the definition of the First and Last letters that were removed. The definition of the letters of this unique word means, "The Authority (ל) to Restore (השב) is the Prince (ר)".

Watch and become aware that Jonah was not sent to the House of Israel, his own country. Every work that God requests of Jonah is done with gentiles. Jonah is Galilean, watch and see that and all his work reveals he was sent to the gentiles.

To further support that the gentiles on Jonah's boat did not repent is the unique Hebrew word translated as "making vows" used in this verse. Again, we know that the "time of the gentiles" begins in the New Testament Book of Acts, after the resurrection. Jonah, the Old Testament Prophet, was sent to the gentiles.

Jonah's boat story is contained in the first chapter of Jonah. Yes, there is crazy more that we will share about the Book of Dove as we continue but here is a bonus. The Hebrew root word for fish in Jonah 1:17 is spelled (דג). This is the only time that this root word for fish is used in the Hebrew text. The definition of the Hebrew letters of this word is, "The door of wealth" or "The door of the spirit". Glory to the King!

Glory to the King!

Chapter 18 – Jonah Chapter 2

Learning and researching the original Hebrew text is a gift that just keeps on giving, *nevertheless* (smile) the passed down traditions of "the church" has a loud subliminal message for Christians that the original text is only for the Jews. There are very few Christian churches that endorse and teach from the original text. Most churches either openly teach or subliminally warn that their members, Christians, from engaging in any effort to validate the English translations.

Oh my. How do we explain Jonah Chapter 2? I was in my mid-40's when an amazing friend introduced me to the phrase, "It's time to spend some of my collateral". He was referring to the need to reference his good deeds of the past with our boss to attain a favor. Yes, at our jobs this usually isn't a good day.

If I have mustered any favor, then I am requesting that you grant me a couple of pages of explanations while we overrule several HUGE traditions that were passed down before I was born. Jonah Chapter 2 is a very simple chapter to understand but because the passed down traditions believed that Jonah was a rebellious prophet that sinfully fled from the presence of God, this chapter is misunderstood as well. I promise that this chapter will be 100% understood but it will require that you unlearn everything ever taught about Jonah repenting. Jesus never repented because he never sinned. If the Dove is representing the Holy Spirit, then this chapter cannot be related to repentance. Be patient and enjoy as we search out Jonah Chapter 2. After finishing this chapter, I want all my collateral returned. I will need it repeatedly! (smile)

Let's begin our study of Chapter 2.

Jonah 2:1 KJV: Then Jonah *prayed* (ויתפלל) unto the Lord his God out of the *fish's* (הדגה)[3] *belly* (ממעי)[4],

The words pray, prayed, and prayer are a total of 343 times in the Old Testament. That said, there are many Hebrew words translated as prayed. The Hebrew word translated as "prayed" in Jonah 2:1 is only in the original Hebrew text nineteen times.

WAIT! Here I go screaming again. (smile) Mark, are you telling me that different types of prayer in scripture are spelled differently in Hebrew? Yes, let's look at a few. Let's do a mini searching out of the Hebrew words translated as pray, prayed, or prayer.

The first time "pray" was used in the KJV was Genesis 12:13.

Genesis 12:13 KJV: Say, *I pray thee* (נא), thou art my sister: that it may be well with me for thy sake; and my soul shall live because of thee.

The Hebrew word translated as prayer in Genesis 12:13 is Na (נא) and is in the Hebrew Old Testament 407 times. Obviously, this Hebrew word is translated as something other than prayer many times. The phrase "I pray thee" is in the KJV 158 times and is always the Hebrew word Na (נא). This word is synonymous with "Please" in our culture.

The Hebrew word translated as prayer in Genesis 23:13 (שמעני) is only three times in the original Hebrew text. It is translated as "hear me" in verse eleven and it is translated as "hearken unto me" in verse fifteen. These verses are within the discussion of Abraham negotiating for the burial place for his wife, Sarah. This is not an instance of actual prayer.

I know, if you are like me, you likely never considered what type of prayer Jonah was praying. He is just praying, right? The first time that the Hebrew word translated as prayed in Jonah 2:1 is used is found in Genesis 20:7.

Genesis 20:7 KJV: Now therefore restore the man his wife; for he is a prophet, and he shall pray (ויתפלל) for thee, and thou shalt live: and if thou restore her not, know thou that thou shalt surely die, thou, and all that are thine.

This is the story of Abimelech and Abraham. What's important here is that Abimelech must get Abraham to pray for him or he will die. Likewise, Jonah is praying for somebody so that they can live. Jonah is not praying for himself. Again, this is not a prayer of repentance. Let's now look at Abraham's prayer.

Genesis 20:17 KJV: So Abraham prayed (ויתפלל) unto God: and God **healed** Abimelech, and his wife, and his maidservants; and they bare children.

This is Abraham's prayer for Abimelech, his wife, and his maidservants. It seems that they were already sick prior to Abraham praying. Now we know that Jonah is praying for somebody, now we must figure out who.

Let's search out the word (מֵעֵי) translated as "belly".

Jonah 2:1 KJV: Then Jonah *prayed* (וַיִּתְפַּלֵּל) unto the Lord his God out of the *fish's* (<u>הַדָּגָה</u>)[3] *belly* (<u>מְּעֵי</u>)[4],

The word (מֵעֵי) translated as "belly" occurs four times in the original text and this is the last occurrence (denoted by underline). The first occurrence of the word (מֵעֵי) occurs in 2 Samuel 16:11.

2 Samuel 16:11 KJV: And David said to Abishai, and to all his servants, Behold, my son, which came forth *of my bowels* (מֵעֵי)[4], seeketh my life: how much more now may this Benjamite do it? let him alone, and let him curse; for the Lord hath bidden him.

Is it clear that Jonah is not in the digestive system of this fish? It will become clearer that Jonah is not in the digestive stomach in a few more verses. That said, the first two letters that spell this word (מֵעֵי) are the letter Mem (מ) which means a woman's womb. Coincidence? There is two Mems (מִמ)! Is this suggesting "born again"? Let's enjoy the journey through Jonah Chapter Two!

Let's review Jonah 1:17. Note that the number of times each Hebrew word is found within the original text as a superscript at the end of the word.

Jonah 1:17 KJV: Now the LORD had *prepared* (וַיְמַן)[5] a great *fish* (דָּג)[1] to *swallow up* (לִבְלֹעַ)[1] *__Jonah__* (אֶת-יוֹנָה). And Jonah was *in the belly of* (בִּמְעֵי)[2] *the fish* (הַדָּג)[1] three days and three *nights* (לֵילוֹת)[4].

This is the second time Jonah's name is preceded by Et (אֵת). The fish swallowed **אֵת-Jonah**. Our Savior, the *first* (א) *and the last* (ת), was with Jonah! This is a *SMALL* detail that is not provided in any English translation!

The Hebrew word translated as "prepared" is used in the original Hebrew text five times and four of those are in the Book of Jonah. The first instance is in Daniel 1:5, and it is translated as appointed. King Nebuchadnezzar appointed menus for the three men he would later sentence to the furnace. Other translations translate all five occurrences of this word as appointed. God _appointed_ a "great fish" to swallow Jonah.

So, Jonah is praying from the <u>belly</u> of the great fish. The Hebrew word translated as "belly" in this verse is not referring to the "stomach". This Hebrew word is only twice in the original text and the other occurrence is Ruth 1:11 where Naomi tells her daughter-in-law's that she is unable to conceive sons for them to marry.

Ruth 1:11 KJV: And Naomi said, Turn again, my daughters: why will ye go with me? are there yet any more sons in _my womb_ (במעי), that they may be your husbands?

Yes, the same Hebrew word (במעי) that is translated as "belly" in Jonah 1:17 is also translated as "womb" in Ruth 1:11. Wow! Where do we go with this! Is it obvious that the "great fish" that was "appointed" by God did not swallow Jonah for nourishment? Is it possible that wherever Jonah is located within the "belly" of this fish, that God is trying to symbolize that Jonah is becoming an example of being born again?

The Hebrew word (דג) translated as fish is pronounced "Dog". Yes, the dove was swallowed by a dog which is really a fish (smile). Though the play on words likely only exists with the English translation, you can't make this up! The definition of the letters of Dog is, "The door (ד) of wealth (ג)" or "The door of the spirit". The Dove was swallowed by the Door of the Spirit.

The Dove is interceding from the womb (belly) of the Dog. Is it a coincidence that the word for fish transliterates into English as dog? There are many stories in scripture relating to something being "swallowed up". Few of those stories include vomiting and even fewer include vomiting from the womb.

Now is a good time to recall that this entire story was planned before Jonah ever left Galilee. Remember Jonah 4:2? Jonah is a prophet so cannot be considered omniscient therefore Jonah 4:2 provides insight that God and Jonah visited during or before the beginning of the book and planned everything that Jonah was going to do. This prayer is more proof that Jonah is not surprised about his plight. He is interceding while inside the womb (belly) of a fish. Who could do that other than Dove?

Dove and Dog are only the beginning of a maze of understanding of the English translation of Hebrew words. A *great* maze. Let's travel through the maze of names and their translated meanings and see if it will help us understand Jonah and his prayer.

We have already discussed how Peter's father's name is Jonah. We know that Peter's name was Simon until Jesus changed it. We know that Peter means Rock. We know that Rock represents Christ. We know that Jesus's Hebrew name translates to Salvation, and we also know that Joshua's name translated to English is, "God is Salvation". Wait! Did we search out that Joshua's name is also spelled identical to Yeshua's in Nehemiah 8:17? Yes, Joshua's name is spelled identical to our Savior's Hebrew name. Wow, right? Peter, the son of Jonah, is Peter, the Rock that Jesus will build His Church. Peter, the Rock, walked with Salvation (Jesus). Jonah, the Dove, was swallowed by a Fish and the Hebrew word for Fish is pronounced Dog. Wait, are we missing something? Joshua! Yes, I forgot to mention Jesus's and Joshua's "dog".

Most of us are unaware that Joshua whose name means God is Salvation, had a dog. Well, he "kind of" had a dog. Yes, knowing about Joshua and his loyal dog plays a huge role in understanding Dove. Understanding Joshua's Dog will help to understand Dove on the ship (*I AM to be revealed*) in the ~~midst~~ heart of the sea.

Can we recall the story where Jesus, whose Hebrew name means Salvation, had an encounter with someone that He rightfully called a "Dog". Remember? Matthew 15:21-28 tells the story of the woman that *came from the coast* that had a daughter vexed with a devil. The disciples asked Jesus to send her away, but He stayed quiet. After the woman, who wasn't from Israel, pleaded her case, Jesus asked her if He should take the children's bread and cast it to the dogs. She wasn't offended, she knew she was a foreigner and replied that even the dogs get the crumbs that fall from the Master's table. Jesus's reply is Matthew 15:25.

Matthew 15:25 KJV: Then Jesus answered and said unto her, O woman, great is thy faith: be it unto thee even as thou wilt. And her daughter was made whole from that very hour.

Even while "The Prince" walked among us He did not withhold ministering to all nations. There are many stories in the Gospels where our Savior blessed, loved, and shared with people from nations other than Israel. If the Gospel of Jesus, our Salvation, is for all, then would we not expect that the same be true when Joshua took Israel into the promised land? Does the Bible consistently reveal that our Creator loves all nations, and Israel is his first love that began with His Covenant with Abraham? Let's review Joshua's dog and then we will be ready to search out Dove's prayer.

Joshua's Dog…

It is impossible to talk about Joshua without talking about Caleb just like it is impossible to talk about Jesus without talking about Peter.

Most Christians are unaware that Caleb was not born a son of the tribes of Israel. Sure, he is from the tribe of Judah, but he wasn't born of the sons of Judah. Caleb's father's name is Jephunneh. Caleb's brother is Kenaz and Kenaz had a son named Othniel, the first Judge in the Book of Judges. All of these men are descendants of Edom, the name given to Jacob's brother Esau.

Joshua 14:6 is one of a few places that tells us "Jephunneh the Kenezite". Though it isn't documented in scripture, Jephunneh proselytized into the tribe of Judah. The Hebrew word Jephunneh is in the original Hebrew text twenty-four times and means to "Turn around" or "Change direction".

1 Samuel 14:47 KJV: So Saul took the kingdom over Israel, and fought against all his enemies on every side, against Moab, and against the children of Ammon, and against Edom, and against the kings of Zobah, and against the Philistines: and whithersoever he *turned himself* (יפנה - Jephunneh), he vexed them.

Yes, the definition of Jephunneh, Caleb's father's name, is the "Change Direction", the same definition as Repentance! Kenaz, Jephunneh's son, name means "Bright". The name Caleb, Jephunneh's other son, means "All Heart". Caleb had a daughter named Achsah which means "Beauty Beyond the Vail". Kenaz's son Othniel's name means "Lion of God". Othniel, Lion of God, married his cousin Achsah, Beauty Beyond the Vail. Othniel was the first Judge of Israel in the Book of Judges. *Just like a Christian, everyone mentioned in this paragraph was not born into Israel.*

Oh wait, Caleb whose name means "All Heart" is the Hebrew word for Dog. Joshua and his loyal dog led the people to the promised land (smile).

What does Joshua's dog story, Jesus's dog story, Othniel, Jephunneh, and Kenaz have to do with Jonah's prayer? It proves "God So Loves the World" didn't start after Jesus went to the cross. God's love for the world started the moment he breathed into the nostrils of Adam. Jesus the same yesterday, today, and forever.

Abraham's prayer, Jonah's prayer, and Jesus's prayer in John 17 are for the lives of others. Jonah is praying for the nations just like Jesus prayed for all. Jonah is Dove! Surely you can see it now. Jonah IS NOT REPENTING! Jonah is interceding.

After three days in the belly of the fish, Jonah returns to being Dove. And now we will see that it openly declares that people repent! It's just like the Gospel story. It's just like Jesus said! After Jesus was resurrected, people repented!

There is a prayer that we have titled *"The Lord's Prayer"*. Let's search out the prayer of Dove and determine if the *TRUTH FROM THE ORIGINAL TEXT* proves this prayer worthy to be called *"The Holy Spirit's Prayer"*. Is that possible? Let's set the standard required to be called *"The Holy Spirit's Prayer"* so high that we consider this an impossibility! Set the requirements so high that the mere thought of this existing borderlines blasphemy. Now we are ready to search out Jonah's prayer.

Let's search out Dove's nine verse prayer (Jonah 2:2-10) and reveal the Hebrew words that are *only found in this Chapter* of Jonah and other words from the original text that will bring shame to the passed down traditional story portraying this as Jonah's prayer of repentance. There are several unique words from the original text that provide glorious uniqueness of this prayer.

Jonah 2:2 KJV: [2] *And said* (ויאמר)[2,084], *I cried* (קראתי)[26] *by reason of mine affliction* (מצרה)[7] *unto the Lord* (לי אל-יהוה), *and he heard me* (ויענני); *out of the belly* (<u>מבטן</u>)[16] *of hell* (<u>שאול</u>)[394] *cried I* (שועתי)[5], *and thou heardest* (<u>שמעת</u>)[45] *my voice* (<u>קולי</u>)[23].

All the underlined words revealed from the original are the last occurrence of those words. That said, this book has repeatedly required us to entertain a new Biblical Study exercise that we have called "the rule of occurrences". The rule of occurrences is merely what the modern-day church would call "A Biblical Word Study". Howbeit, attempting this effort using the English translations would not reveal the omniscience of the order of occurrence of each word that *"proceedeth out of the mouth"* of our Father's original text, Matthew 4:4. *LEARN THE HEBREW ALPHABET! IT'S EASY!*

Hopefully, by now the rule of a words occurrences has made an impression. The first word that we will search out from Dove's prayer will have an impact on our depth of understanding of how our Creator ordered His Words. Let's search out the word (שמעת) translated as "thou heardest".

The word (שמעת) translated as "thou heardest" occurs 45 times in the original text and this is the 45th occurrence, the last occurrence. After researching all the occurrences of this word, there are few occurrences where God spoke, and somebody listened. On the third occurrence Abraham listened, and it would be a conjecture to find another occurrence where God spoke, and man listened. That said, on the 30th occurrence, man spoke, and God listened. On the 45th occurrence, Dove spoke, and God listened.

Consider the difficulty of an interpreter explaining the interpretation of words interpreted to each participant of a conversation. Now consider the magnitude of importance to translate the words spoken by Dove during his prayer of intercession (*not repentance*). All Christians that know how to read and research Hebrew will concur that trying to explain the depth of Dove's prayer to someone that doesn't know Hebrew is an effort of futility. Basically, if you did it wonderfully, because the reader doesn't know Hebrew, they would quit reading and likely discard the book. The proof that this is true is found by reading the KJV translation of Jonah Chapter two. After reading, you will agree that most of the verses require excessive amounts of conjecture to provide an explanation and the 45th occurrence of the word (שמעת) translated as "thou heardest" is another blatant example.

We have searched out many words and associated the rules of occurrences to these words. What's so special about the 45th occurrence that makes this effort of sharing its meaning so difficult? Well, there are two issues with the 45th occurrence that make this effort nearly impossible. The first issue is that it is also the last occurrence of this word. The other reason is that these occurrences reveal that man loses and regains his ability to hear. What's even more amazing is that man's ability or willingness to hear is mostly revealed by him hearing or not hearing other people but the last occurrence is God listening to Dove.

The first example of this word (שמעת) is Genesis 3:17 where God is telling Adam that because he listened to his wife's voice and did not do as God instructed. Though it was an act of disobedience, man could hear and listened. The 44th occurrence is Nebuchadnezzar hearing of Daniel. Again, it's not our "man of choice" but nonetheless, after many occurrences revealing not being heard, *MAN HEARS!*

The result of man hearing is unfathomable. After man can hear, the 45th occurrence is God waiting to hear from man what He has been waiting to hear, hence, it is spoken by Dove. "Dove" knows all things, right? He knows what the Father wants to hear. Sadly, for those that don't read or research Hebrew, Dove speaks it in Hebrew.

We will refrain from commenting on the context of the translation and declare that "The Dove's Prayer" is so beautiful that it's near impossible to search it out without feeling as though you are participating in a monumental hack.

Imagine taking a road trip and sitting in the back seat and sleeping the entire eight hours while someone else drove. You both got to the destination, but the driver took a journey while you took a nap. That said, some take the journey to learn Hebrew so that they can search out the original text, while other depend on a book author.

One of the hundreds of sight-seeing beauty during this journey is the word (שמעת) translated as "thou heardest" and you are witnessing the difficulty to explain the degradation and recovery of mans ability to hear. This book and the translators are incapable of sharing the story of the history of this word. To thoroughly understand this word requires the driver or passenger to know Hebrew and to stay awake. Any attempt to translate the story of this word into another language would require the translator to write pages of talk for an hour. A one-word English translation doesn't do it justice! This is true for many Hebrew words.

Learn Hebrew and take that journey! Don't depend on anyone's efforts to reveal the truth of God's original text, especially not English translators! Especially not "The Dove's Prayer".

Jonah 2:2 KJV: [2] *And said* (ויאמר)[2,084], *I cried* (קראתי)[26] *by reason of mine affliction* (מצרה)[7] *unto the Lord* (לי אל-יהוה), *and he heard me* (ויענני)[6]; *out of the belly* (מבטן)[16] *of hell* (שאול)[394] *cried I* (שועתי)[5], *and thou heardest* (שמעת)[45] *my voice* (קולי)[23].

The word (שאול) translated as "hell" is also the name of Israel first king, King Saul. This word (שאול) is also translated as "unseen" and "sheol". So, Saul's name is the transliteration of the word (שאול) that is also translated as "unseen", "sheol", and in this verse "hell".

Recall the story of the appointment of King Saul found in 1 Samuel 8. Samuel, the first prophet, warned the people not to do this, but they wouldn't listen. Let's search out *1 Samuel 8:10-18*, and consider whether the prophet provides clarity that the king will lead them to the unseen, to sheol.

1 Samuel 8:10-18 KJV: [10] And Samuel told all the words of the Lord unto the people that asked of him a king.
[11] And he said, This will be the manner of the king that shall reign over you: He will take your sons, and appoint them for himself, for his chariots, and to be his horsemen; and some shall run before his chariots.
[12] And he will appoint him captains over thousands, and captains over fifties; and will set them to ear his ground, and to reap his harvest, and to make his instruments of war, and instruments of his chariots.
[13] And he will take your daughters to be confectionaries, and to be cooks, and to be bakers.
[14] And he will take your fields, and your vineyards, and your oliveyards, even the best of them, and give them to his servants.
[15] And he will take the tenth of your seed, and of your vineyards, and give to his officers, and to his servants.
[16] And he will take your menservants, and your maidservants, and your goodliest young men, and your asses, and put them to his work.
[17] He will take the tenth of your sheep: and ye shall be his servants.
[18] And ye shall cry out in that day because of your king which ye shall have chosen you; and the Lord will not hear you in that day.

Does that provide a fair description of Saul, or hell?

Is anyone allowed to question these multiple methods that the Bible provides an English version of the same word from the original text? How are we to know when an English word is transliterated or translated? Do we have the authority to express concern? Do we have the right to be mad? Does it really matter?

We are searching out the prayer of the prophet Dove and we have questions. Have we abandoned the traditional story that teaches this is a prayer of repentance? Do we simply continue searching out words from the original text with no regard we are finding errors of translation? Dare we speak aloud the question that are not approachable?

The third letter of the Hebrew alphabet it the letter Gimel (ג). The paleo Hebrew pictograph for this letter is a camel. If you look at this letter, it somewhat resembles a camel. The camel is a symbol of wealth. In fact, Abraham's unnamed servant took ten camels of great wealth in his quest to retrieve a bride for Isaac, Abraham's son. The Holy Spirit is also a symbol of great wealth, and the Dove is a symbol of the Holy Spirit. The remainder of Dove's prayer contains untranslatable wealth.

Below is the remainder of "The Dove's Prayer". Note that all the words revealed from the original text are either only found in the Book of Jonah, or they are the last occurrence of the word. Correct, the number of words in each verse that are either the last occurrence of that word or only found in the Book of Dove is unfathomable. These words are the fulfillment of "The Dove's Prayer". ***LEARN THE HEBREW ALPHABET! IT'S EASY!***

Jonah 2:3 KJV:[3] *For thou hadst cast me* (ותשליכני)[2] *into the deep* (מצולה)[4], *in the midst of* (בלבב)[3] *the seas* (ימים)[292]; *and the floods* (ונהר)[5] *compassed me about* (יסבבני)[2]: *all thy billows* (וגליך)[2] *and thy waves* (משבריך)[3] *passed* (עברו)[44] *over me.*

[4] *Then I* (ואני)[179] *said* (אמרתי)[82], *I am cast out* (נגרשתי)[1] *of thy* (מנגד)[24] *sight* (עיניך)[62]; *yet* (אך)[158] *I will look* (להביט)[1] *again* (אוסיף)[11] *toward thy holy* (קדשך)[20] *temple* (אל-היכל)[26].

[5] *The waters* (מים) *compassed me about* (אפפוני)[3], *even to the soul* (נפש)[140]-(עד)[1,095]): *the depth* (תהום)[21] *closed me round about* (יסבבני)[2], *the weeds* (סוף)[29] *were wrapped* (חבוש)[2] *about my head* (לראשי)[7].

[6] *I went down* (ירדתי)[2] *to the bottoms* (לקצבי)[1] *of the mountains* (הרים)[62]; *the earth* (הארץ)[935] *with her bars* (ברחיה)[1] *was about me* (בעדי)[10] *for ever* (לעולם)[157]: *yet hast thou brought up* (ותעל)[14] *my life* (חיי)[36] *from corruption* (משחת)[14], *O Lord my God.*

[7] *When my soul* (נפשי)[173] *fainted* (בהתעטף)[2] *within me* (עלי)[246] *I remembered* (זכרתי)[9] *the **Lord*** (את-יהוה): *and my prayer* (תפלתי)[20] *came in* (ותבוא)[21] *unto thee* (אליך)[248], *into thine holy* (קדשך)[20] *temple* (אל-היכל)[26].

[8] *They that observe* (משמרים)[2] *lying vanities* (הבלי-שוא)[38]-[3]) *forsake* (יעזבו)[3] *their own mercy* (חסדם)[1].

[9] *But I* (ואני)[179] *will sacrifice* (אזבחה)[2] *unto thee* (לך)[965] *with the voice of* (בקול)[76] *thanksgiving* (תודה)[15]; *I will pay that* (אשלמה)[2] *that* (אשר)[4,838] *I have vowed* (נדרתי)[2]. *Salvation* (ישועתה)[2] *is of the Lord* (ליהוה)[577].

[10] *And the Lord spake unto the fish* (לדג)[1], *and it vomited* (ויקא)[1] *out **Jonah*** (יונה-את) *upon the dry land* (היבשה)[5].

REMEMBER!
Salvation, the First and the Last,
is with Jonah throughout his journey in the fish.

The (ה) Searching out of Verse Three…

The words from the original text of this verse are some of the most challenging to explain and reveal the depth of understanding not provided in the translations. That said, though there will be far more depth of understanding provided, it will still be incomplete. The eleven words of this verse are more complex than any verse we have searched out. For example, this verse contains the second occurrence of the word (ימים) translated as "seas". An entire chapter was devoted to this word so that its complexity could be explained without interrupting the efforts to search out this verse.

Again, we are searching out one verse at a time so that no memorization is required, simply enjoy the effort for each verse Yes, there are days of prayer and discussion with others to provide the best understanding of each word, Matthew 4:4.

Jonah 2:3 KJV:[3] *For thou hadst cast me* (ותשליכני)[2] *into the deep* (מצולה)[4], *in the midst of* (בלבב)[3] *the seas* (ימים)[292]; *and the floods* (ונהר)[5] *compassed me about* (יסבבני)[2]: *all thy billows* (וגליך)[2] *and thy waves* (משבריך)[3] *passed* (עברו)[44] *over* me.

The underlined words from the original text are either the last occurrence of the word or the word only occurs in the Book of Jonah. Also, learn that there is almost no punctuation in the Hebrew text and that punctuations are also from translation. Below is the original text of Jonah 2:3 and notice that it does not have any punctuation. That said, the commas of translation are merely grammar, but the semi-colons and colons need to be searched out to verify they aren't impacting the context. Recall that Hebrew is read from right to left.

ותשליכני מצולה בלבב ימים ונהר יסבבני כל-משבריך וגליך עלי עברו

Let's search out the words of Jonah 2:3!

The word (ימים) is translated as "the seas"! Remember this from the previous chapter? Dove is not whining about being in sea water, he's declaring

135

that he was cast amongst the nations to bring forth (ימים) *"the believers of the nations"*.

The word (ותשליכני) translated as "For thou hadst case me" is close to the literal definition but it lacks depth of meaning and purpose of this word. Recall that Moses "flung" a tree into the waters of Marah (Exodus 15:23-26) and the bitter waters became sweet. Oddly, the word (ותשליכני) is using the same verb used by Moses. ***How is Jonah being "cast" into "the sea" related to Moses's tree that was "flung" into the waters of Marah?***

The word (מצולה) is translated as "into the deep" but the first letter of this word is the letter Mem (מ) which is translated as "from". The word (צל) occurs six times in the original text and is translated as "shadow". The last letter of this word is the letter Hey (ה) which means revelation and/or grace. The middle letter is the letter Vav (ו) which means the "Straight Up Man with the Nail". The Vav (ו) letter is our Savior's letter and is used as a connector, hence the nails in His hands connect. Notice that the Vav (ו) is between the two letters that spell the word (צל) translated as "shadow" and the last occurrence is later in this prayer. Coincidence? If you are in a shadow, then something is covering you and providing shade from the sun. The word (מצולה) truly means "from the covering that provides me shade and grace".

The word (בלבב) translated as "in the midst of" occurs three times in the original text and this is the last occurrence. The word (לב) means "heart". The name Caleb (כלב), Joshua's loyal companion, means "all heart" and is also the word for "dog". The ***first and the last*** letter of this word (בלבב) is the Bet (ב) which means "house" but when it's the first letter of a word it is translated as "in" when it's the last letter it is commonly translated as "of". Though the literal translation of this word (בלבב) is likely "in the heart of" it seems clear that the heart (לב) is being taken from inside the house (ב ב). The word (בב) does not exist in the original text.

Notice that Dove is speaking of borders and how the nations at his borders are leaning or pressing against him. The word (ונהר) is singular and translated as "and the streams" occurs 5 times and this is the last occurrence, the fifth occurrence. The first occurrence is Genesis 2:10.

Genesis 2:10 KJV:[10] And a river (ונהר)[5] went out of Eden to water the garden; and from thence it was parted, and became into four heads.
[11] The name of the first is Pison: that is it which *compasseth* (הסבב)[1] the whole land of Havilah, where there is ***gold***;

The fifth occurrence of a word means revelation and/or grace. The omniscience of our Good Father placed the fifth occurrence in the words spoken by Dove from the fish, the Door of Wealth. At the end of the fish journey, Jonah miraculously finds himself on the sands of the seashore.

In Genesis 2:11, the word Havilah means "a stretch of sand". God told Abraham that his seed would be as the sand of the sea and now Dove has a miraculous arrival on the sand of the seashore. Is Dove's arrival and journey across *a stretch of sand* (Havilah) to *Fish Town* (Nineveh) an act of God fulfilling His promise to bless the seed of Abraham, the nations?

Jonah 2:3 KJV:[3] *For thou hadst cast me (וַתַּשְׁלִיכֵנִי)[2] into the deep (מְצוּלָה)[4], in the midst of (בִּלְבַב)[3] the seas (יַמִּים)[292]; and the floods (וְנָהָר)[5] compassed me about (יְסֹבְבֵנִי)[2]: all thy billows (וְגַלֶּיךָ)[2] and thy waves (מִשְׁבָּרֶיךָ)[3] passed (עָבְרוּ)[44] over me (עָלָי)[246].*

================

Jonah 2:3 (Modified): [3] ***For thou hadst cast me (וַתַּשְׁלִיכֵנִי)[2] from the covering that provides me shade and grace (מְצוּלָה)[4], into the heart of (בִּלְבַב)[3] nations (יַמִּים)[292]; and the streams (וְנָהָר)[5] surround and lean upon me (יְסֹבְבֵנִי)[2]: your clouds (וְגַלֶּיךָ)[2] and your waves (מִשְׁבָּרֶיךָ)[3] you pass (עָבְרוּ)[44] over me (עָלָי)[246].***

The word (וְנָהָר) translated as "and the streams" occurs five times in the original text and the word is not plural. The first occurrence, Genesis 2:10, is translated as "river". The problem is that the words "river" and "stream" occur in the KJV 241 times, but this word only occurs five times and this is the last occurrence. Even more troubling is that if we remove the letter Hey (ה), then the remaining word (וְנֵר) occurs six times and it means "lamp of". Yet another issue is that the last two letters of this word (וְנָהָר) spells mountain. The definition of the letters is, "Yeshua (ו) is a Lamp (נֵר)" or "Yeshua's (ו) Life (נ) on the Mountain (הר)". Let's continue our research and determine if this word means "lamp".

The word (יְסֹבְבֵנִי) only occurs twice in the original text and both occurrences are in the Book of Dove. The middle letters spell the word (סבב) which occurs three times in the original text and means to surround something. The remaining letters of this word (יני) is a unique word from Psalm 141:5 and translated as "break" in the phrase "shall not break the head of me". The word (יני) means "repudiate" or "reject something as though it has no authority". The word (יְסֹבְבֵנִי) means "surrounded by those who reject me".

Let's apply these two words and continue…

Jonah 2:3 KJV:[3] *For thou hadst cast me (וַתַּשְׁלִיכֵנִי)[2] into the deep (מְצוּלָה)[4], in the midst of (בִּלְבַב)[3] the seas (יַמִּים)[292]; and the floods (וְנָהָר)[5] compassed me about (יְסֹבְבֵנִי)[2]: all thy billows (וְגַלֶּיךָ)[2] and thy waves (מִשְׁבָּרֶיךָ)[3] passed (עָבָרוּ)[44] over me (עָלַי)[246].*

================

Jonah 2:3 (Modified): [3] ***For thou hadst cast me (וַתַּשְׁלִיכֵנִי)[2] from the covering that provides me shade and grace (מְצוּלָה)[4], into the heart of (בִּלְבַב)[3] nations (יַמִּים)[292]; and your lamp (וְנָהָר)[5] is surrounded by those who reject you (יְסֹבְבֵנִי)[2]: your clouds (וְגַלֶּיךָ)[2] and (כֹּל)[3,143] your waves (מִשְׁבָּרֶיךָ)[3] you pass (עָבָרוּ)[44] over me (עָלַי)[246].***

The two words (וְגַלֶּיךָ) and (מִשְׁבָּרֶיךָ) are translated in reverse order. The proof is that the word (וְגַלֶּיךָ) translated as "your clouds" begins with the letter Vav (ו) which is translated as "and" when it's the first letter of a word. The verse should say, "… your waves and your clouds …"

The word (מִשְׁבָּרֶיךָ) translated as "your waves" occurs three times in the original text and this is the last occurrence. The third occurrence of a word is supposed to reveal wealth or the spirit. That said, it's difficult to declare either wealth or spirit in the KJV translation but our **Modified** version has the words ***covering, grace, heart, and lamp*** which validates our research.

The two words (וְגַלֶּיךָ) and (מִשְׁבָּרֶיךָ) both end with the letters (יךָ) which mean "of you". The definition of the letters of the word (וְגַלֶּיךָ) is, "And (ו) the Revelation (גל) of You (יך)".

If we remove (יך) from the word (מִשְׁבָּרֶיךָ), the remaining word (מִשְׁבָּר) occurs twice in the original text and both occurrences (2 Kings 19:3 and Isaiah 37:3) translate this as "ready to give birth". The word (מִשְׁבָּרֶיךָ) means "ready to give birth of you".

Let's apply this understanding and review our final modified version.

Jonah 2:3 KJV:[3] *For thou hadst cast me (וַתַּשְׁלִיכֵנִי)[2] into the deep (מְצוּלָה)[4], in the midst of (בִּלְבַב)[3] the seas (יַמִּים)[292]; and the floods (וְנָהָר)[5] compassed me about (יְסֹבְבֵנִי)[2]: all thy billows (וְגַלֶּיךָ)[2] and thy waves (מִשְׁבָּרֶיךָ)[3] passed (עָבָרוּ)[44] over me (עָלַי)[246].*

================

Jonah 2:3 (Modified): [3] *For thou hadst cast me (וַתַּשְׁלִיכֵנִי)[2] from the covering that provides me shade and grace (מְצוּלָה)[4], into the heart of (בִּלְבַב)[3] nations (יַמִּים)[292]; and your lamp (וְנָהָר)[5] is surrounded by those who reject you (יְסֹבְבֵנִי)[2]: all (כֹּל)[3,143] ready to give birth of you (מִשְׁבָּרֶיךָ)[3] and the revelation of you (וְגַלֶּיךָ)[2] you pass (עָבָרוּ)[44] on me (עָלַי)[246].*

The (ה) Searching out of Verse Four...

Jonah 2:4 KJV: [4] *Then I (וַאֲנִי)[179] said (אָמַרְתִּי)[82], I am cast out (נִגְרַשְׁתִּי)[1] of thy (מִנֶּגֶד)[24] sight (עֵינֶיךָ)[62]; yet (אַךְ)[158] I will look (לְהַבִּיט)[1] again (אוֹסִיף)[11] toward thy holy (קָדְשֶׁךָ)[20] temple (אֶל-הֵיכַל)[26].*

The word (וַאֲנִי) translated as "Then I" is one of those words that reveals the chasm between translation and the original text. The word (וַאֲנִי) occurs 179 times and this is the first of three times it occurs in the Book of Dove. This word (וַאֲנִי) means *"And I AM"*. Yes, the word (אֲנִי) occurs an additional 698 times and means *"I AM"*.

There are words in scripture that we are very familiar with, such as Judah (יְהוּדָה) which occurs 684 times and Israel (יִשְׂרָאֵל) which occurs 2,267 times but the words (וַאֲנִי) and (אֲנִי) occur a total of 877 times and most Christians can only quote the words "I AM" when He spoke to Moses on Mt. Sinai.

The word (יְהוּדָה) translated as "Judah" is a transliteration of his name which means "Praise", yet the word "Judah" is quite common in our church vocabulary. That said, so is the name "Israel". The word (יִשְׂרָאֵל) transliterated as "Israel" means "One who struggles with God". Recall that Jacob was given this name after wrestling with an angel (Genesis 32:24-32). The transliteration of the words (וַאֲנִי) and (אֲנִי) are supposed to be as common to the church vocabulary as Judah and Israel. That said, the transliteration of the words Et (אֵת) and Vah-Et (אֵת) which occur a total of 9,623 times should also be far more common to the church than Judah or Israel. Yet, the words Et (אֵת) and Vah-Et (אֵת) are rarely translated and NEVER translated correctly. The words (וַאֲנִי) and (אֲנִי) are also rarely translated or transliterated correctly.

With great pleasure, behold the truth about the translation of the first two words from the original text of Jonah 2:4, *"And I AM (וַאֲנִי) spoke of me (אָמַרְתִּי)"*.

After Jonah 2:3, "I AM" is about to speak, NOT Jonah. The word "Then" is added by the translators and is not part of the original text.

Take thirty days and learn the Hebrew letters. Don't trust this book, check it and prove it, just as you should check and prove the translation of the KJV done by men for the sake of King James I, and just as you should check anyone you are trusting to assist you and/or your family's efforts to seek and find.

The word (נגרשתי) translated as *"I am cast out"* is unique. Again, if we remove **the first and the last** letters the remaining letters are the word (גרשת) which is another unique word that describes the unique event where Cain declares that God has "driven me out". So, "Cast Out" and "Driven Me Out" are very similar. Now, let's add the definition of the two letters that were removed. When the letter Yod (י) is at the end of a word, it adds the word "My" to the word. The letter Nun (נ) means life. So, the definition of the letters of the unique word (נגרשתי) is "I cast out the life of Me".

The word (אמרתי) translated as "said" occurs 82 times and this is 80th occurrence and it is better translated as "spoke of me". Below is the modified version of Jonah 2:4 with more documentation to follow.

Jonah 2:4 KJV: [4] *Then I* (ואני)[179] *said* (אמרתי)[82], *I am cast out* (נגרשתי)[1] *of thy* (מנגד)[24] *sight* (עיניך)[62]; *yet* (אך)[158] *I will look* (להביט)[1] *again* (אוסיף)[11] *toward thy holy* (קדשך)[20] *temple* (אל-היכל)[26].

===============

Jonah 2:4 (Modified): [4] ***And I AM*** (ואני)[179] ***spoke of me*** (אמרתי)[82], ***I cast out the life of Me*** (נגרשתי)[1] *from in front of* (מנגד)[24] *your eyes* (עיניך)[62]; *yet* (אך)[158] *I will look* (להביט)[1] *again* (אוסיף)[11] *toward thy holy* (קדשך)[20] *temple* (אל-היכל)[26].

The ***Bold-Italics*** is what we have already searched out.

The word (מנגד) as "of thy" occurs 24 times in the original text and this is the last occurrence. Again, we see that the first letter is the letter Mem (מ) which means "from". The remaining three letters is the word (נגד) which occurs 55 times in the original text and means "in front of".

The word (עיניך) translated as "sight" occurs 62 times in the original text and means "your eyes" or "the eyes of you". It doesn't mean "sight", it means putting something before "your eyes" so you will see it. If something is removed from in front of "your eyes" then you can't see it any longer.

The word (אך) translated as "yet" occurs 158 times in the original text and the is the 155th occurrence and the only occurrence in the Book of Dove.

This word (אך) means "Yea" but is translated as "surely", "yet", "for", etc. The word "Yea" occurs 965 times in the KJV Old Testament.

The next issue is that the next two words of this verse "...*I will look* (להביט)[1] *again* (אוסיף)[11] ... " are translated in reverse order. Below is a screenshot of this verse in Hebrew showing that the word (אוסיף) comes before the word (להביט). Hebrew is read from right to left.

ואני אמרתי נגרשתי מנגד עיניך אך אוסיף להביט אל ־ היכל קדשך

qdsh·k   eikl - al   l·ebit   ausiph   ak   oini·k   m·ngd   ngrshthi   amrthi   u·ani

Before we search out these two words "(להביט) *and* (אוסיף)", let's apply what we have searched out and put them in proper order in our modified verse.

Jonah 2:4 (Modified): [4] *And I AM* (ואני)[179] *spoke of me* (אמרתי)[82], *I cast out the life of Me* (נגרשתי)[1] *from in front of* (מנגד)[24] *your eyes* (עיניך)[62]; *yea* (אך)[158] *again* (אוסיף)[11] *I will look* (להביט)[1] *toward thy holy* (קדשך)[20] *temple* (אל-היכל)[26].

The word (אוסיף) translated as "again" occurs eleven times in the original text which implies that our Savior is the fulfillment and 12th occurrence of this word. The 12th occurrence means authority or government. Let's look at 1 Kings 12:11.

1 Kings 12:11 KJV: [11] And now whereas my father did lade you with a heavy yoke, *I will add* (אוסיף) to your yoke: my father hath chastised you with whips, but I will chastise you with scorpions.

The word (אוסיף) means "I will add".

The word (להביט) translated as "I will look" is unique. Let's not lose sight that the words in Jonah 2:4 are *I AM* speaking *OF* Jonah. If we remove the first letter, the word (הביט) from the remaining letters occurs six times in the original text. Let's look at Psalm 33:13.

Psalm 33:13 KJV: [13] The Lord *looketh* (הביט) from heaven; he beholdeth all the sons of men.

The word (הביט) is translated as "looketh". Notice that the first letter of this word is the letter Hey (ה) which means revelation and/or grace. If this letter is the first letter of a word and is intended to represent revelation, then we can remove it to see what we are supposed to behold. That said, if we remove this letter then the word from remaining letters does not exist in the original text. The letter Hey (ה) in this verse represents grace! We must continue seeking to determine the root noun of this verse.

To search out the root noun of this word, let's once again remove *the first and the last* letter of this word (להביט). The word (הבי) from the remaining letters is another unique word found in Ruth 3:15.

Ruth 3:15 KJV: [15] Also he said, *Bring the vail* (הבי) that thou hast upon thee, and hold it. And when she held it, he measured six measures of barley, and laid it on her: and she went into the city.

The name Ruth (רות) means friend. The unique word (הבי) is translated as "Bring the vail". Now if we remove the letter Hey (ה) which means grace, the remaining word (בי) occurs 159 times in the original text and is translated as "in me". Boaz told Ruth to "Bring the vail" because he had *grace* (ה) *in him* (בי) for her.

The unique word (להביט) translated as "I will look" has amazing depth of meaning! Before we apply our efforts to the definition of this word, let's recall that Jonah's father's name is Amittai which means "My Truth". Now, let's combine what we have searched out and add the definition of the two letters removed. The letter Lamed (ל) that was removed means authority and the letter Tet (ט) that was removed means *Truth*. The definition of this word is, "The authority (ל) of Grace In Me (הבי), My Truth (ט)".

Before we apply the efforts of what was searched out about these two words "(להביט) *and* (אוסיף)", let's consider how much liberty we will give to our efforts. Let's minimize our efforts to seek and find by declaring that a dove is just a bird. Surely our Creator isn't putting this much investment into the many dove stories throughout scripture. We won't seek and find the sacrificial purposes of the dove. Surely, God's purpose of a prophet named Dove couldn't possibly conceal play the significant role of grace that we are finding in Jonah 2:4. Let's look at the first occurrence of Jonah's name.

2 Kings 14:24-26 KJV: [24] And he did that which was evil in the sight of the Lord: he departed not from all the sins of Jeroboam the son of Nebat, who made Israel to sin."
[25] He restored the coast of Israel from the entering of Hamath unto the sea of the plain, according to the word of the Lord God of Israel, which he spake by the

hand of his servant Jonah, the son of Amittai, the prophet, which was of Gathhepher.
[26] For the Lord saw the affliction of Israel, that it was very bitter: for there was not any shut up, nor any left, nor any helper for Israel.

This is where we learned that Jonah's father is name Amittai which means "My Truth". It's also where we learned that Jonah is from Gathhepher which revealed that he is Galilean. Now we can see that Jonah was a servant of God, the prophet. Because King Jeroboam didn't to Jonah, there isn't a helper for Israel. This is the only visit from Dove in Israel. Coincidence? Consider that so far, everyone that meets Dove, is saved by obvious miraculous events.

We are almost done, but let's apply what we have searched out (seek and find) into our modified version and compare it to the KJV translation.

Jonah 2:4 KJV: [4] *Then I* (ואני)[179] *said* (אמרתי)[82], *I am cast out* (נגרשתי)[1] *of thy* (מנגד)[24] *sight* (עיניך)[62]; *yet* (אך)[158] *I will look* (להביט)[1] *again* (אוסיף)[11] *toward thy holy* (קדשך)[20] *temple* (אל-היכל)[26].

=================

Jonah 2:4 (Modified): [4] *And I AM* (ואני)[179] *spoke of me* (אמרתי)[82], *I cast out the life of Me* (נגרשתי)[1] *from in front of* (מנגד)[24] *your eyes* (עיניך)[62]; *yea* (אך)[158] *I will add* (אוסיף)[11] *the authority of My grace, My Truth* (להביט)[1] *toward thy holy* (קדשך)[20] *temple* (אל-היכל)[26].

The final two words of "toward *thy holy* (קדשך) *temple* (אל-היכל)" are also translated in reverse order. Again, view the screenshot of this verse from the original text. Yes, this is a common occurrence in translations.

ואני אמרתי נגרשתי מנגד עיניך אך אוסיף להביט אל ־ היכל קדשך

qdsh·k   eikl - al   l·ebit   ausiph   ak   oini·k   m·ngd   ngrshthi   amrthi   u·ani

Notice that there are two words (אל-היכל) from the original text that are combined and translated as "temple". The first word (אל) occurs 4,374 times and is translated as *"to"*.

The second word (היכל) occurs 26 times and this is the 22nd occurrence. The word (היכל) means *"the (ה) temple (יכל)"*. So, the two words (אל-היכל) translated as *"temple"* mean *"to (אל) the (ה) temple (יכל)"*.

The word (קדשך) occurs 20 times in the original text, and this is the 19th occurrence. The last occurrence is also in this chapter. The translation of this verse would lead us to understand that the temple is holy. By translating these two words in the correct order we will see that *the holiness of God is in the temple*. We have witnessed countless times that the temple and tabernacle are able to be desecrated. Jesus witnessed the temple being defiled by the tables of the money changers. The tabernacle and temple are not always holy, but our God is always holy.

Let's apply what we have searched out to our final modified version.

Jonah 2:4 KJV: [4] *Then I* (ואני)[179] *said* (אמרתי)[82], *I am cast out* (נגרשתי)[1] *of thy* (מנגד)[24] *sight* (עיניך)[62]; *yet* (אך)[158] *I will look* (להביט)[1] *again* (אוסיף)[11] *toward thy holy* (קדשך)[20] *temple* (אל-היכל)[26].

===============

Jonah 2:4 (Modified): [4] *And I AM* (ואני)[179] *spoke of me* (אמרתי)[82], *I cast out the life of Me* (נגרשתי)[1] *from in front of* (מנגד)[24] *your eyes* (עיניך)[62]; *yea* (אך)[158] *I will add* (אוסיף)[11] *the authority of My grace, My Truth* (להביט)[1] *to the temple* (אל-היכל)[26] *of thy holiness* (קדשך)[20].

Let's remove the original text and view Jonah 2:1-4 (Modified).

Jonah 2:1-4 (Modified): Then Jonah interceded unto the Lord his God out of the fish's womb,

[2] And said, I cried by reason of mine affliction unto the Lord, and he heard me; out of the womb of hell cried I, and thou heardest my voice.

[3] For thou hadst cast me from the covering that provides me shade and grace, into the heart of nations; and your lamp is surrounded by those who reject you: all ready to give birth of you, and the revelation of you, you pass on me.

[4] And I AM spoke of me, I cast out the life of Me from in front of your eyes; yea I will add the authority of My grace, My Truth to the temple of thy holiness.

The (ה) Searching out of Verse Five...

Jonah 2:5 KJV: [5] *The waters* (מים)[265] *compassed me about* (אפפוני)[3], *even to the soul* (נפש)[140]-(עד)[1,095]: *the depth* (תהום)[21] *closed me round about* (יסבבני)[2], *the weeds* (סוף)[29] *were wrapped* (חבוש)[2] *about my head* (לראשי)[7].

The word (מים) translated as *"The waters"* occurs 265 times in the original text and this is the only occurrence in the Book of Dove. This word is spelled like the word (ימים) translated as "seas" but does not include the first letter. Since there aren't two Yods (מָיִם) as there are in the word (יָמִים). The word (מִים) means, "The birth (מ) of many (ים)". This implies that there will be many born that will not believe. Jonah is surrounded by unbelievers.

The word (אֲפָפוּנִי) translated as *"compassed me about"* occurs three times in the original text and this is the last occurrence. Recall that the word (יְסֹבְבֵנִי) in Jonah 2:3 was also translated as *"compassed me about"* in the KJV. Notice that the word (אֲפָפוּנִי) has the letter Vav (ו) in the middle. The letter Vav (ו) is "The Straight Up Man with the Nail", it's a connector. Our Savior was nailed and lifted up on a cross. It's as though He was connecting heaven and earth.

Because the letter Vav (ו) is a connector, it is often translated as the word "and". If we remove this letter, then the remaining word (אֲפָפֻנִי) is unique and found in 2 Samuel 22:5.

2 Samuel 22:5 KJV: [5] When the waves of death *compassed me* (אֲפָפֻנִי), the floods of ungodly men made me afraid;

Wow, the words of this verse belong in the book of Jonah (smile). The word (אֲפָפֻנִי) is translated as "compassed me". And after adding the letter Vav (ו), ***The Straight Up Man with the Nail***, the word is translated as "compassed me about". That's a correct translation except it leaves out why. They compassed Jonah to ask about the Vav (ו), right?

The other two occurrences of the word (אֲפָפוּנִי) translated as *"compassed me about"* occur in the Book of Psalm.

1st Occurrence - Psalm 18:4 KJV: [4] *The sorrows of death **compassed me*** (אֲפָפוּנִי), *and the floods of ungodly men made me afraid.*

2nd Occurrence - Psalm 116:3 KJV: [3] *The sorrows of death **compassed me*** (אֲפָפוּנִי), *and the pains of hell gat hold upon me: I found trouble and sorrow.*

What's the difference? In Jonah 2:5, the third and last occurrence of this word, Dove is not encompassed by "the sorrows of death", he is encompassed by (מִים) "The waters", the birth (מ) of many (ים). The Dove is compassed by those born of the water! *Many of the living, born of the water,* (מִים) *compassed Dove about* (אֲפָפוּנִי) the Vav (ו).

There are two words (עד-נפש) translated as *"even to the soul"*. The word (עד) translated as "even" occurs 1,095 times in the original text and is almost always translated as "unto" or "until", but there is something special about many of the Hebrew words that only have two letters. Many of the words spelled with two letters often reveal a deeper understanding if you research the spelling backwards.

The backward spelling of the word (עד) is the word (דע) which occurs eight times in the original text and means "Know you". Again, the number eight means New Beginnings! So, the definition of the two words (עד, דע) should provide incredible understanding. The definitions are, "know you (דע)" and "unto (עד)". Well, that was a big flop (smile)!

Let's look at the definition of the letters. The definition of the letters of the word (עד) translated as "unto" is, "See (ע) the Door (ד)". Now the two definitions are "Know you" and "see the door" (smile).

The word (נפש) translated as "to the soul" occurs 140 times and is correctly translated.

The word (תהום) translated as *"the depth"* occurs 21 times in the original text and the first occurrence is Genesis 1:2.

Genesis 1:2 KJV: ² And the earth was *without form* (תהו)[10], and void; and darkness was upon the face of *the deep* (תהום)[21]. And the Spirit of God moved upon the face of the waters.

The word (תהום) translated as "the depth" is translated as "the deep" ***but notice that the spelling of the word*** (תהו) ***translated as "without form" is very similar.*** The only difference in the spelling is that the word (תהום) translated as "the depth" has the letter Mem (מ) at the end. And, because it's the last letter of the word, it's the Sofit Mem (ם). We know that the Sofit Mem (ם) represents a woman's virgin womb so the translation of these two words does not reconcile. That said, the word (תהו) translated as "without form" is also translated as "confusion" in Isaiah 34:11 and several translations translate this word as "chaos".

The word "chaos" is not in the KJV or NKJV but is found in almost all other translations. The CLV translation translates all ten occurrences of the word (תהו) as "chaos". Now, if we add the Sofit Mem (ם) to the end of the word (תהו) then the definition of the word (תהום) translated as "the depth" in Jonah 2:5 is, "The Chaos of the Closed Worm" or "The Chaos of the Virgin". ***THAT***

MAKES SENSE! Surely, everyone struggled believing that Joseph's and Mary's first born was conceived by the Holy Ghost. We have clear evidence in the scripture that it caused *CHAOS*.

The word (תהו) translated as "without form" occurs 10 times in the original text. It would require a few pages to search out Isaiah 45:19 and reveal that it blatantly confirms the word (תהו) means "chaos" or "confusion", so the word (תהום) means "Chaos (תהו) of the Virgin Birth (ם)". Some translations translate the word (תהום) as "abyss" which stirs up more chaos (smile). Learn Hebrew and confirm for yourself that Jonah is praying from the womb of the fish and referencing the chaos of our Savior's virgin birth.

Let's apply our efforts…

Jonah 2:5 KJV: [5] *The waters (מים)[265] compassed me about (אפפוני)[3], even to the soul (נפש[140]-עד[1,095]): the depth (תהום)[21] closed me round about (יסבבני)[2], the weeds (סוף)[29] were wrapped (חבוש)[2] about my head (לראשי)[7].*

====================

Jonah 2:5 (Modified): [5] ***Many born of the water (מים)[265] compassed me about the Straight Up Man with the Nail (אפפוני)[3] who sees the door of the soul (נפש[140]-עד[1,095]): chaos of your virgin birth (תהום)[21] closed me round about (יסבבני)[2], the weeds (סוף)[29] were wrapped (חבוש)[2] about my head (לראשי)[7].***

We have already searched out the word (יסבבני) from its first occurrence in Jonah 2:3. The word (יסבבני) means *"is surrounded by those who reject you"*.

The word (סוף) translated as "the weeds" occurs 29 times in the original text and this is the only occurrence in the Book of Dove. The number 30 means betrayal, so the next occurrence of this word would reveal betrayal. Almost every occurrence of this word (סוף) refers to the Sea of Weed which is what we know to be the Red Sea. This word (סוף) is singular and three times it is translated as "end" in the book of Ecclesiastes.

The word (חבוש) translated as "were wrapped" occurs twice in the original text and is translated as "bind" in Ezekiel 24:17.

Let's view our final modified version…

Jonah 2:5 KJV: [5] *The waters (מים)[265] compassed me about (אפפוני)[3], even to the soul (נפש[140]-עד[1,095]): the depth (תהום)[21] closed me round about (יסבבני)[2], the weeds (סוף)[29] were wrapped (חבוש)[2] about my head (לראשי)[7].*

===============

Jonah 2:5 (Modified): [5] *Many born of the water (מים)[265] compassed me about the Straight Up Man with the Nail (אפפוני)[3] who sees the door of the soul (נפש[140]-עד[1,095]): chaos of your virgin birth (תהום)[21] is surrounded by those who reject you (יסבבני)[2], the end (סוף)[29] they are bound (חבוש)[2] to the authority of my head (לראשי)[7].*

The (ה) Searching out of Verse Six…

Jonah 2:6 KJV: [6] *I went down (ירדתי)[2] to the bottoms (לקצבי)[1] of the mountains (הרים)[62]; the earth (הארץ)[935] with her bars (ברחיה)[1] was about me (בעדי)[10] for ever (לעולם)[157]: yet hast thou brought up (ותעל)[14] my life (חיי)[36] from corruption (משחת)[14]*, O Lord my God.

Remember, all of the words underlined are either the last occurrence of the word in the original text or only found in the Book of Dove.

The word (ירדתי) translated as "I went down" occurs twice in the original text and is translated the same in both occurrences. That said, the word has two Yods (י י) which represents the two hands that did mighty deeds on the cross. The word (ירדתי) is implying that Jonah's action is a might act just like our Savior. Several translations translate this word (ירדתי) as *"I descended"*.

The word (לקצבי) translated as "to the bottoms" is unique and its translation is priceless. So, the last occurrence of the word (ירדתי) translated as "I went down" takes us to a unique place translated as "to the bottoms". Yahweh was rejected by the sons of the earth when He visited them at the bottom of Mount Sinai. Both the Father and the Son were rejected by the sons of the earth when they visited them at the *"bottoms of the mountains"*.

Again, this prayer is the second occurrence, the second and last time "descending" is mentioned in the original text. There is increased understanding to reveal the first occurrence of the word (ירדתי) translated as "I went down" without revealing where it's located. You can find it but enjoy reading the first ~~coming~~ occurrence of this word.

> *I went down into the garden of nuts to see*
> *the fruits of the valley,*
> *and to see whether the vine flourished*
> *and the pomegranates budded.*

Let's continue searching out verse six with the mindset to recognize the chasm between the description of the two occurrences of the word (ירדתי) translated as "I went down".

The word (ברחיה) translated as "with her bars" is unique. The verse says, "the earth *with her bars* (ברחיה)".

Once again, we have a unique word (ברחיה) that is partially transliterated as well as partially not translated. The first two letters (בר) of this word spells "Bar" as in the common phrase "Simon **Bar**jona" in Matthew 16:17. "Bar" means "son", and some would say this is Aramaic.

The word from the remaining three letters (חיה) of the word (ברחיה) occurs 32 times in the original text and the first occurrence is Genesis 1:20.

Genesis 1:20 KJV: [20] And God created great whales, and *every living* (חיה) creature that moveth, which the waters brought forth abundantly, after their kind, and every winged fowl after his kind: and God saw that it was good.

Let's apply what we have searched out.

Jonah 2:6 KJV: [6] *I went down* (ירדתי)[2] *to the bottoms* (לקצבי)[1] *of the mountains* (הרים)[62]; *the earth* (הארץ)[935] *with her bars* (ברחיה)[1] *was about me* (בעדי)[10] *for ever* (לעולם)[157]: *yet hast thou brought up* (ותעל)[14] *my life* (חיי)[36] *from corruption* (משחת)[14], O Lord my God.

================

Jonah 2:6 (Modified): [6] *I went down* (ירדתי)[2] *to the bottoms* (לקצבי)[1] *of the mountains* (הרים)[62]; *the earth* (הארץ)[935] *with her sons and every living thing* (ברחיה)[1] *was about me* (בעדי)[10] *for ever* (לעולם)[157]: *yet hast thou brought up* (ותעל)[14] *my life* (חיי)[36] *from corruption* (משחת)[14], O Lord my God.

The word (בעדי) translated as *"was about me"* occurs ten times in the original text and this is the tenth occurrence. The tenth occurrence of a word will reveal the crucifixion story. Note that the first letter of this word (בעדי) is the letter Bet (ב), and when it's the first letter it means "in". Also, the last letter of this word is the letter Yod (י), and when it's the last letter it will often means "my". The remaining two letters are the word (עד) we searched out in the previous verse and means *"see the door"*. Jonah is saying that "In (ב) Me (י) See (ע) the Door (ד)".

Our Savior was betrayed and sent to His death on dry land and the prophet Dove is betrayed and sent to his death in the sea. Coincidence? Reconsider Jonah 1:9 where Dove told "the shipmaster", *"...I am an Hebrew; and I fear the Lord, the God of heaven, which hath **made the sea and the dry land**."*

The words (חיי) and (משחת) are translated in reverse order. The word (משחת) comes before the word (חיי).

The word (משחת) translated as "from corruption" occurs 14 times in the original text and this is the last occurrence. The number fourteen reveals life. The first occurrence of this word is Genesis 31:13.

Genesis 31:13 KJV: [31] I am the God of Bethel, where thou *anointedst* (משחת) the pillar, and where thou vowedst a vow unto me: now arise, get thee out from this land, and return unto the land of thy kindred.

When something is anointed, it has arisen from corruption. The translation of the word (משחת) as "from corruption" and "anointed" are synonymous but we aren't taught that, and we don't recognize it when we see it.

The word (ותעל) translated as *"yet hast thou brought up"* occurs 14 times in the original text and this is the last occurrence. The number fourteen in Hebrew represents *"LIFE"*. The tenth occurrence of a Hebrew word will reveal the crucifixion. The tenth occurrence of the word (ותעל) is 2 Chronicles 18:34.

2 Chronicles 18:34 KJV: [34] And the battle *increased* (ותעל) that day: howbeit the king of Israel *stayed himself up* (מעמיד)[1] in his chariot against the Syrians until the even: and about the time of the sun going down he died.

The tenth occurrence of a word will reveal the crucifixion. Is it coincidence that in the same verse where the tenth occurrence of the word (ותעל) occurs we also have the unique word (מעמיד) translated as "stayed himself up"? A King (Ahab) *"stayed himself up"* on the tenth occurrence of the word *"increased"*. This is more proof that the 14th occurrence of the word (ותעל) translated as *"yet hast thou brought up"* in Jonah 2:6 represents *God has brought up **LIFE**.*

Let's search out the amazing word (חיי).

**** *The amazing word* (חיי) ****

The word (חיי) translated as *"my life"* occurs 36 times in the original text and Jonah 2:6 is the last occurrence. The translated text leads us to view this as Jonah referencing his life. Let's search out the first occurrence.

Genesis 23:1 KJV: [1] And Sarah was an hundred and seven and twenty years *old* (חיי): these were the years *of the life* (חיי) of Sarah.

Hmm… It seems simple enough, right? Sarah lived 127 years. What's strange is that the first and second occurrences of this word (חיי) are in this verse, and both reference the years of Sarah's life. Why wouldn't it be Adam or Noah? What's even more odd is that the third occurrence is Abraham. Yes, this is ***VERY SIGNIFICANT!*** And why or how does this word (חיי) translate to "old" and "of the life"?

Let's look at Genesis 5:5.

Genesis 5:5 KJV: [5] And all the days that Adam lived (חי) were nine hundred and thirty years: and he died.

So, what's the difference between "the years *of the life* (חיי) of Sarah" and "Adam *lived* (חי)"? Why is this so important? Is it coincidence that the Lord made a covenant with Abraham and the first occurrence of the word (חיי) is Sarah (smile)?

First, we will search out Genesis 16:16 to determine whether the word (חיי) means "old".

Genesis 16:16 KJV: [16] And Abram was fourscore and six years old, when Hagar bare Ishmael to Abram.

Neither the word (חיי) or the word (חי) occurs in Genesis 16:16. And no, the word "fourscore" is not Hebrew, it's British influence into the scriptures.

There are 117 occurrences of the phrase "years old" in the KJV Old Testament. The researchers of this book did not search out each occurrence but after searching out several, neither the word (חיי) or the word (חי) was found in those verses. Hence, the word (חיי) does not mean "old". Let's look at the direct translation of Genesis 16:16 without correcting it to readable English grammar *to get an example of the liberties taken* by the translators as well as the modern-day new translations and their explanations.

Genesis 16:16 (Original Text): [16] *And Abram* (ואברם) *son of eighty* (בן - שמנים) *year* (שנה) *and six* (ושש) *years* (שנים) *in to birth Hagar* (בלדת-הגר) *Salvation-Ishmael* (את-ישמעאל) *to Abram* (לאברם).

We can agree that the direct English would require some work for it to be readable but nonetheless, each of us would have taken our own liberties as did the Brits with their "fourscore" influence. They also added the "years old" phrase of how we denote someone's age. Then in Genesis 23:1 many of the other translations declared that the word "old" was translated from the word (חיי). And the spinning wheel of incompetence is passed on from generation to generation until it meets the age of the computer where the liberties of translation, otherwise known as errors, can be searched out and documented. Of course, exposing those errors comes at a great price.

Let's look at Genesis 23:1 once again and this time we will include the words from the original text that were not translated.

Genesis 23:1 KJV: [1] And (ויהיו) (חיי) Sarah was an hundred and seven and twenty years old: these were the years *of the life* (חיי) of Sarah.

Let's look at John 17:6-7 to introduce a potential New Testament understanding of the word (חיי).

John 17:6-7 KJV: [6] I have manifested thy name unto ***the men which thou gavest me out of the world***: thine they were, and thou gavest them me; and they have kept thy word.
[7] Now they have known that all ***things*** whatsoever thou hast given me are of thee.

John 17:7 was included to further influence nausea every time we see the words "thing" or "things" in the translations (smile).

Jesus is referencing the disciples as *"the men which thou gavest me out of the world"*.

The word (חיי) occurs twice in Genesis 23:1. It's so interesting to witness how the translations try to fit the other occurrence of this word into their documentation. The Blue Letter Bible edition at the time this book was published declares that the first occurrence is translated as *"old"* in Genesis 23:1. That said, the word (חיי) is the second word of the verse just before Sarah's name and it's not translated. The first two words of Genesis 23:1 from the original text were not translated.

Again, ***it is crucial to be confident of the meaning*** of this word. Let's look at the third occurrence.

Genesis 25:7 KJV: [7] And these are the days of the years of Abraham's life (חיי) which he lived (חי), an hundred threescore and fifteen years.

The problem is that the word (חיי) translated as *"life"* occurs before Abraham's name in the original text. Most if not all churches teach the truth that Christians are grafted into the seed of Abraham. There are multiple verses in the New Testament where people declare Abraham to be their father. The word (חיי) means "of lives of". Let's apply that understanding to Genesis 23:1 and 25:7.

Genesis 23:1 (Modified): [1] *And those becoming* (ויהיו) *of lives of* (חיי) Sarah was an hundred and seven and twenty years old: these were the years *of the life* (חיי) of Sarah.

Genesis 25:7 (Modified): [7] And these are the days of the years *of lives of* (חיי) Abraham which he *lived* (חי), an hundred ***threescore*** *(Brits!)* and fifteen years.

The original text says Abraham lived *"an hundred and seventy and five years"* (smile). And each of those numbers in his age participate in the "order of occurrences".

The "lives of Abraham" are the people whose lives Abraham have become from Abraham. That would include his "DNA" children as well as those "grafted in" ***from the covenant.*** Isn't it amazing that the ***DIVINE AND INSPIRED WORD OF GOD*** introduced a new word (חיי) that HE used to denote the life of someone that also included others ***"of lives of"*** them? He introduced this word when He made a covenant with Himself to Abraham. The last occurrence of this word (חיי) occurs in The Dove's Prayer, Jonah 2:6. Is John 17:6 *"the men which thou gavest me out of the world"* the fulfillment of Jonah 2:6? ***DON'T AGREE SO FAST! THERE IS MORE TO COME OF THIS WORD (smile)!***

Let's apply everything we have searched out into our final modified translation of this verse.

Jonah 2:6 KJV: [6] *I went down* (יָרַדְתִּי)[2] *to the bottoms* (לְקִצְבֵי)[1] *of the mountains* (הָרִים)[62]; *the earth* (הָאָרֶץ)[935] *with her bars* (בְּרִחֶיהָ)[1] *was about me* (בַעֲדִי)[10] *for ever* (לְעוֹלָם)[157]: *yet hast thou brought up* (וַתַּעַל)[14] *my life* (חַיַּי)[36] *from corruption* (מִשַּׁחַת)[14], O Lord my God.

===============

Jonah 2:6 (Modified): [6] *I went down* (יָרַדְתִּי)[2] *to the bottoms* (לְקִצְבֵי)[1] *of the mountains* (הָרִים)[62]; *the earth* (הָאָרֶץ)[935] *with her sons and every living thing* (בְּרִחֶיהָ)[1] *saw the door in me* (בַעֲדִי)[10] *for ever* (לְעוֹלָם)[157]: *and you have ascended me up* (וַתַּעַל)[14], *from corruption you anointed* (מִשַּׁחַת)[14] *of lives of* (חַיַּי)[36] the Lord God.

The (ה) Searching out of Verse Seven…

Jonah 2:7 KJV: [7] When *my soul* (נַפְשִׁי)[173] *fainted* (בְּהִתְעַטֵּף)[2] *within me* (עָלַי)[246] *I remembered* (זָכַרְתִּי)[9] the **Lord** (אֶת-יְהוָה): *and my prayer* (תְּפִלָּתִי)[20] *came in* (וַתָּבוֹא)[21] *unto thee* (אֵלֶיךָ)[248], *into thine holy* (קָדְשֶׁךָ)[20] *temple* (אֶל-הֵיכַל)[26].

We underlined the word **Lord** (אֶת-יְהוָה) in this verse, but it's not the last occurrence in the original text. That said, it's important to see that it is preceded by Et (אֵת), *the First and the Last*. The word (אֶת-יְהוָה) means "The Salvation (אֵת) of Yahweh (יְהוָה)". It's another declaration that the experience of Jonah is the womb is a revelation of Salvation and not a period of repentance for sin. How would the church's understanding of the Old Testament be impacted if it knew the significance of the word Et (אֵת) as well as the 7,372 occurrences where it was not translated? Was the decision to not translate the word Et (אֵת) divine and inspired? Salvation was with Jonah during his time in the womb of the fish.

Below is the original text of Jonah 2:7 which reveals the order of the twelve words. Remember that Hebrew is read from right to left.

בהתעטף עלי נפשי את-יהוה זכרתי ותבוא אליך תפלתי אל-היכל קדשך

The word (בְּהִתְעַטֵּף) translated as *"fainted"* occurs twice in the original text and this is the last occurrence. The first occurrence is in Psalm 142:3.

Psalm 142:3 KJV: [3] *When* my spirit *was overwhelmed* (בְּהִתְעַטֵּף) within me, then thou knewest my path. In the way wherein I walked have they privily laid a snare for me.

Yes, the same word (בהתעטף) translated as "fainted" is translated as "When was overwhelmed". Is it clear that this verse does not reveal why he was overwhelmed? It simply declares that when his spirit is overwhelmed. The first letter of this word (בהתעטף) is the letter Bet (ב) which means "In". The second letter is the letter Hey (ה) which means "revelation and/or grace".

Let's review the definition of the letters of this word to determine if it reveals what caused him to be overwhelmed. The definition of the letters of the word (בהתעטף) translated as *"fainted"* is, "In (ב) the Revelation of Grace (ה) of the Covenant (ת) Penned (עט) of My Spoken Words (ף)". Glory to the King!

Jonah 2:7 begins with *"When my soul fainted within me…"*. The next two words (נפשי עלי) from the original text in this verse are quite simple but the depth of understanding can't be shared without contention until after we search out the Book of Malachi.

The word "Malachi" only occurs one time in the KJV in Malachi 1:1. But, the Hebrew word (מלאכי) transliterated as "Malachi" occurs 14 times in the original text. The story of Malachi spans from Moses's visit on Mt Sinai to Him sharing the burden of Yahweh in the Book of Malachi.

Malachi is the only "prophet" that has no genealogy. That said, Dove has a father, Amittai, but Amittai has no genealogy. Note that the word (מלאכי) transliterated as "Malachi" is singular. If it were plural, it would be spelled (מלאכים) which occurs 44 times in the original text. Let's search out the third occurrence of the word (מלאכי) transliterated as "Malachi" in Exodus 23:20-23.

Exodus 23:20-23 KJV: [20] Behold, I send an *Angel* (מלאך) before thee, *to keep thee in the way, and to bring thee into the place which I have prepared.*
[21] Beware of him, and obey his voice, provoke him not; for he will not pardon your transgressions: *for my name is in him.*
[22] But if thou shalt indeed obey his voice, and do all that I speak; then I will be an enemy unto thine enemies, and an adversary unto thine adversaries.
[23] For *mine Angel* (מלאכי) shall go before thee, and bring thee in unto the Amorites, and the Hittites, and the Perizzites, and the Canaanites, the Hivites, and the Jebusites: and I will cut them off.

No, we won't be further diverted but know there is much to be searched out about Malachi. Who is Malachi? Is this passage implying that Malachi is the "cloud by day" and the "fire by night"? Is Malachi the only angel with

God's name in him? Note that the NIV translation capitalizes the word "Name" in the phrase "for my Name is in him".

Likewise, we have searched out nearly two chapters of the Book of Dove and most readers have either reconsidered the traditional passed down story or discarded this book. That said, if you are still reading, then who is Dove? A better question is "Why now?" Well, the next two words are going to require us to accept that Dove has a particular attribute that can only be debated later in Volume 3 after we learn about the birth of Samson and the prophet Malachi. Meanwhile, we will accept the translation as provided for the words (נפשי עלי) translated as "within me" and "my soul".

The word (זכרתי) translated as *"I remembered"* occurs nine times in the original text and this is the last occurrence. The number nine represents "Truth". This occurrence of the word is the fulfillment of the previous eight occurrences. Is our Savior the 10th occurrence of this word? Does he fulfill this word when He says "…do this in remembrance of me…"? Would searching out the previous eight occurrences of this word provide clarity of truth?

Let's apply what we have searched out as well as words we have searched out in previous verses. We will also reposition the words translated in the same order as the original text and view our final modified version.

בהתעטף עלי נפשי את-יהוה זכרתי ותבוא אליך תפלתי אל-היכל קדשך

Jonah 2:7 KJV: [7] When *my soul* (נפשי)[173] *fainted* (בהתעטף)[2] *within me* (עלי)[246] *I remembered* (זכרתי)[9] the ***Lord*** (את-יהוה): *and my prayer* (תפלתי)[20] *came in* (ותבוא)[21] *unto thee* (אליך)[248], into *thine holy* (קדשך)[20] *temple* (אל-היכל)[26].

===============

Jonah 2:7 (Modified): [7] *In the Revelation of Grace of the Covenant Penned of My Spoken Words* (בהתעטף)[2] *within me* (עלי)[246] *my soul* (נפשי)[173]: the *Salvation of **Lord*** (את-יהוה) *I remembered* (זכרתי)[9] *and came in* (ותבוא)[21] *unto thee* (אליך)[248] *my prayer* (תפלתי)[20] ***to the temple*** (אל-[26]היכל) *of thy holiness* (קדשך)[20].

The (ה) Searching out of Verse Eight…

Jonah 2:8 KJV: [8] *They that observe* (משמרים)[2] *lying vanities* (הבלי[3]-שוא[38]) *forsake* (יעזבו)[3] *their own mercy* (חסדם)[1].

This verse only has five words, but the context of this verse is chilling. We will search out each word to validate the depth of meaning. Notice that four of the five words are the last occurrence, and this is the 37th occurrence of the word (שוא) that occurs 38 times.

The word (משמרים) translated as "they that observe" occurs twice in the original text and the first occurrence is Psalm 130:6.

Psalm 130:6 KJV: [6] My soul waiteth for the Lord more than *they that watch* (משמרים)[2] for the morning: I say, more than they that watch for the morning.

The beginning of a day in the Bible is not at midnight, 12:00am. The day begins at sunset which is called twilight in the Bible. Yes, it's difficult to declare that exact second that one day ends and the other begins but a day in scripture is sunset to sunset. So, sunset is morning. That said, the translations are not consistent about which clock they use.

Is Psalm 130:6 referencing someone who is waiting for the Lord's resurrection more than the guards that are assigned to make sure the stone isn't moved? We know that He was buried and resurrected at twilight, the end and beginning of a day.

The word (משמרים) translated as *"They that observe"* is translated as *"they that watch"*. The word (משמרים) is plural, and the singular form of the word (משמר) occurs 10 times in scripture and is means "a guard". The word (משמרים) means *"They that guard" or "The guards"*. Most likely we will find that those who guard lying vanities are far fewer than those who observe them.

There are two words (הבלי-שוא) translated as *"lying vanities"*. These two words (הבלי-שוא) are also translated as *"lying vanities"* in Psalm 31:6.

Psalm 31:5-6 KJV: [5] Into thine hand I commit my spirit: thou hast redeemed me, O Lord God of truth.
[6] I have hated them that regard *lying vanities* (הבלי-שוא): but I trust in the Lord.

That puts an exclamation mark on the topic of *"lying vanities"*!

The word (יעזבו) translated as *"forsake"* occurs three times and this is the last occurrence. It is accurately translated.
The word (חסדם) translated as *"their own mercy"* is unique. The word (חסד) occurs 80 times in the original text and means "mercy". Also, when the letter Mem (ם) is the last letter of a word it means "them". This word is accurately translated.

Jonah 2:8 (Modified): [8] *They that guard (מְשַׁמְּרִים)[2] lying vanities (שָׁוְא[38]-הַבְלֵי[3]) forsake (יַעֲזֹבוּ)[3] their own mercy (חַסְדָּם)[1].*

The (ה) Searching out of Verse Nine…

Jonah 2:9 KJV: [9] *But I (וַאֲנִי)[179] will sacrifice (אֶזְבְּחָה)[2] unto thee (לָךְ)[965] with the voice of (בְּקוֹל)[76] thanksgiving (תּוֹדָה)[15]; I will pay that (אֲשַׁלֵּמָה)[2] that (אֲשֶׁר)[4,838] I have vowed (נָדַרְתִּי)[2]. Salvation (יְשׁוּעָתָה)[2] is of the Lord (לַיהוָה)[577].*

How priceless is it to find our Savior's name in the Old Testament? Those that know Hebrew are aware that His name, Yeshua, is littered throughout the original text of the Old Testament. The word (ישועתה) translated as *"Salvation"* occurs twice in the original text. The first four letters (ישוע) of this word (ישועתה) spells Our Savior's Hebrew name (ישוע), Yeshua (transliterated Jesus). The definition of the letters of this word (ישועתה) is, "Yeshua's (ישוע) Covenant (ת) to be Revealed (ה)". The phrase, *"Salvation is of the Lord (ליהוה)"* is more accurately translated as "Yeshua's (Jesus's) Covenant of Grace to be Revealed (ישועתה) is the Authority/Will (ל) of Yahweh (יהוה)". Jonah 2:9 of the original text provides clarity of the Gospel of our Savior is the will of God!

We have already searched out the word (ואני) translated as "But I". It means "And I AM" (smile).

The word (אזבחה) translated as "will sacrifice" occurs twice in the original text. The last letter of this word is the letter Hey (ה) which means revelation and/or grace. The word (אזבח) without that letter also occurs twice in the original text and is translated as "will I sacrifice" in 2 Chronicles 28:23. The point here is that the letter Hey (ה) is not included in the translation of Jonah 2:9. The word (אזבחה) means "will make a sacrifice (אזבח) of grace (ה)".

Likewise, the word (אשלמה) translated as "I will pay that" occurs twice in the original text and when you remove the letter Hey (ה), the word (אשלמ) occurs six times in the original text and is translated as "I will pay". Once again, if we include the letter Hey (ה), then the word (אשלמה) means "I will pay (אשלמ) the price for grace (ה)".

Once again, the translation has the words out of order. Let's view the original text, and correct their order in the translation, make our changes, and view the final modified version.

ואני בקול תודה אזבחה-לך אשר נדרתי אשלמה ישועתה ליהוה

Jonah 2:9 (Modified): *[9] And I AM (ואני)[179] in the voice of (בקול)[76] thanksgiving (תודה)[15], I shall make a sacrifice of grace (אזבחה)[2] unto thee (לך)[965] which (אשר)[4,838] I have vowed (נדרתי)[2] I will pay the price for grace (אשלמה)[2] Yeshua's Covenant of Grace to be Revealed (ישועתה)[2], the Will of Yahweh (ליהוה)[577].*

The (ה) Searching out of Verse Ten…

Jonah 2:10 KJV: *[10] And the Lord spake unto the fish (לדג)[1], and it vomited (ויקא)[1] out **Jonah** (את-יונה) upon the dry land (היבשה)[5].*

Let's search out the unique word (ויקא) translated as *"vomited"*. The Hebrew pronunciation of the word (ויקא) is "Va-iqa". The word (va-iqa - ויקא) sounds a lot like the word (va-iqra - ויקרא) which is the Hebrew name of the Book of Leviticus. The word (va-iqra - ויקרא) means *"And he called"*. The difference in the spelling is the letter "r" which in Hebrew is the letter Resh (ר) which means "Prince". In Jonah 2:10, Jonah's name (את-יונה) is preceded by Et (את), Salvation, the Prince. Is it possible that (va-iqra - ויקרא) is when the Father (א) and the Prince (ר) are calling but (va-iqa - ויקא) is only when the Father (א) is calling because the Prince is with Jonah?

<u>The Dove's Prayer</u>

Jonah 2:1-10 (Modified): [1] *Then Jonah interceded unto the Lord his God out of the fish's womb,*
[2] *And said, I cried by reason of mine affliction unto the Lord, and he heard me; out of the womb of the unseen (hell) cried I, and thou heardest my voice.*
[3] *For thou hadst cast me from the covering that provides me shade and grace, into the heart of nations; and your lamp is surrounded by those who reject you: all ready to give birth of you, and the revelation of you, you pass on me.*
[4] *And I AM spoke of me; "I cast out the life of Me from in front of your eyes; yea I will add the authority of My grace, My Truth to the temple of thy holiness."*
[5] *Many born of the water compassed me about the Straight Up Man with the Nail who sees the door of the soul: chaos of your virgin birth is surrounded by those who reject you, the end they are bound to the authority of my head.*
[6] *I went down to the bottoms of the mountains; the earth with her sons and every living thing saw the door in me for ever: and you have ascended me up, from corruption you anointed of lives of the Lord God.*
[7] *In the Revelation of Grace of the Covenant Penned of My Spoken Words within me, my soul: Salvation of the Lord I remembered and came in unto thee, my prayer to the temple of thy holiness.*
[8] *They that guard lying vanities forsake their own mercy.*
[9] *And I AM in the voice of thanksgiving, "I shall make a sacrifice of grace unto thee which I have vowed, I will pay the price for grace, Yeshua's Covenant of Grace to be Revealed, the Will of Yahweh."*
[10] *And the Lord spake unto the fish and called out **<u>Salvation-Jonah</u>** upon the dry land.*

Matthew 12:40 KJV: [40] For as Jonas was three days and three nights in the whale's belly; so shall the Son of man be three days and three nights in the heart of the earth.

Did Jonah's conversations with God included him knowing that Jesus would quote Matthew 12:40? Jonah spent three days in the belly of the great fish and prayed … *just as he knew the Son of God would spend three days …* Did he know?

Glory to the King!

Chapter 19 – Jonah Chapter 3

Traditions, Lies from Birth Volume 2, will include more Hebrew word studies and **we** will search out the Lies from Birth about The Power of God. If you are enjoying searching out the truth about the Prophet Dove, then you will enjoy learning the truth about the 12th Judge, Sunshine (Samson).

Volume 2 will hear the Case of Samson verses Sunshine and resolve whether the story is about Samson, the *transliteration* of Samson's Hebrew name, the most famous womanizer in the history of man, or Sunshine, the *translation* of Samson's Hebrew name, the Light of the World and the Power of God. Was Samson, God's appointed 12th Judge, a womanizing muscle man that broke all of God's vows assigned to him from birth or was Sunshine God's Appointed and Righteous Judge who takes us on a journey that reveals the Light of the World and the Power of God from Noah's flood to the outpouring of the Holy Ghost in Acts Chapter 2. The case of Samson verses Sunshine will be heard in Volume 2.

Seriously, you have doubts (smile)?

Let's Search Out Jonah Chapter 3.

Jonah Chapter 3 has ten verses. We know this chapter, right? In the last verse of Chapter 2, Jonah gets vomited onto dry land. In chapter three he goes to Nineveh and preaches. The King of Nineveh called for a forty day fast and they repented for their evil. God then spares them of His wrath. Why search this out? Let's move on to Chapter 4, right? What else is there? Why did it take ten verses to say that? *We could have translated this chapter into two verses (smile).* Let's search out the 3rd Chapter of the Book of Dove.

Jonah 3:1 KJV: And the word of the LORD came unto Jonah the second time, saying,

Once again, let's review the three documented conversations between Jonah and the LORD. The first time the "word of the LORD came unto Jonah" is recorded in Jonah 1:1.

Jonah 1:1 KJV: Now the word of the Lord came unto Jonah the son of Amittai, saying,

So, once again, let's review Jonah's prayer unto the LORD in Jonah 4:2.

Jonah 4:2 KJV: And he prayed unto the Lord, and said, I pray thee, O Lord, was not this my saying, when I was yet in my country? Therefore I fled before unto Tarshish: for I knew that thou art a gracious God, and merciful, slow to anger, and of great kindness, and repentest thee of the evil.

Jonah 3:1 proves that when Jonah said, *"was not this my saying, when I was yet in my country?"* that he is referencing when the word of the LORD came to him the first time. Everything we have searched out in the Book of Jonah, and everything we will search out in this chapter was communicated when the word of the LORD came to Jonah the first time. Again, in Chapter one, Jonah ~~fled~~ *departed* from the LORD with authority and his entire story was ordained by God.

Let's search out the second time the word of the LORD came to Jonah.

We have repeatedly proven that Jonah "fled" from God's presence with the authority of God as well as knowing God's will. Jonah knew about Tarshish, the mariners, the great fish, the vomiting, etc. Jonah Knew! Dove Knew! The spirit knows "all things"!

To further reveal what is concealed in Jonah 3:1 will require that we compare the words of Jonah 3:1 with those of Jonah 1:1 and ALSO, we will need to add Genesis 1:3 to this research.

Jonah 1:1 KJV: Now the word of the Lord came unto Jonah the son of Amittai, saying,

Jonah 3:1 KJV: And the word of the LORD came unto Jonah the second time, saying,

Genesis 1:3 KJV: And God said, Let there be light: and there was light.

Upon review of Jonah 1:1 and Jonah 3:1, there doesn't seem to be anything that stands out or links either of these two verses to Genesis 1:3. Now, let's look at these three verses again while adding a couple words from the original Hebrew text.

Jonah 1:1 KJV: *Now* the word of the Lord *came unto* (ויהי) Jonah the son of Amittai, saying,

Jonah 3:1 KJV: *And* the word of the LORD *came unto* (ויהי) Jonah the second time, saying,

Genesis 1:3 KJV: And God said, *Let there be* (יהי)[50] light: *and there was* (ויהי)[816] light.

__HOW__ did the "word of the Lord came unto" people in the Bible. Most of us never considered it, maybe we just assumed it was like a whisper in the ear. We never expected to find the same Hebrew word (ויהי) translated as "and there was" in Genesis 1:3 to be found in both Jonah 1:3, and 3:1, correct?

In Genesis 1:3 is the first occurrence of the words *Iei* (יהי) and *Viei* (ויהי). Since (יהי) was introduced first, let's search out its meaning first.

The word (יהי) translated as *"Let there be"* occurs 50 times in the original text and it *does not* occur in the Book of Jonah. Before we search out its meaning, let's review its spelling. As you can see there are two Hebrew letter Yod (י). The letter Yod (י) represents the Hand that Does Mighty Deeds. Between the two Yods (יהי) is the letter Hey (ה) which means Revelation and/or grace. Before we start researching, is it possible that this represents our Savior on the Cross Revealing Himself between His two nailed Hands that did a Mighty Deed?

Christians that learn Hebrew are gifted to learn that this word (יהי) occurred fifty times in the original text. Prior to learning Hebrew, many Christians believed these words only occurred in Genesis chapter one. Let's search out a few of the fifty occurrences of this word in the original text.

6th Occurrence - Genesis 49:17 KJV: Dan *shall be a* (יהי) serpent by the way, an adder in the path, that biteth the horse heels, so that his rider shall fall backward.

7th Occurrence - Exodus 7:9 KJV: When Pharaoh shall speak unto you, saying, Shew a miracle for you: then thou shalt say unto Aaron, Take thy rod, and cast it before Pharaoh, and *it shall become* (יהי) a serpent.

10th Occurrence - Deuteronomy 33:24 KJV: And of Asher he said, Let Asher be blessed with children; *let him be* (יהי) acceptable to his brethren, and let him dip his foot in oil.

50th Occurrence - Ezekiel 45:10 KJV: *Ye shall have* (יהי) just balances, and a just ephah, and a just bath.

The multiple English translations of this word could easily introduce a theological study. That said, this book is NOT a theological study. This book provides research of Hebrew words with the intent of searching out the truth of the original text as well as validating the English translations.

As we continue to search out the word "Iei (יהי)" you will see that this Hebrew word references the ***beginning*** of a process of something that does not exist becoming something that does exist. It's the announcement of the beginning of the process of something becoming what it will be. The 6th occurrence reveals that Dan is not a serpent, but he will become a serpent. That 7th occurrence reveals that Aaron's rod is not a serpent, but it will become a serpent.

The story of Aaron's rod becoming a serpent is one of the most known Biblical stories. When did Dan become a serpent? How old were you when you learned that the name Dan means "Judge". That said, there are multiple stories in scripture where Dan and the tribe of Dan participated in "serpent like" behavior. Some of Dan's serpent like behavior is provided in books that used to be part of the translated KJV Bible that were removed by the Catholic Papal in 1684. It wouldn't take much research to learn that Dan was the most responsible for the betrayal of Joseph. The tribes of Dan and Ephraim also built golden images in the lands.

The 10th occurrence of the word "Iei (יהי)" reveals that Asher will become acceptable. The 50th occurrence, also the last occurrence, reveals that the balances of judgement will become just (righteous). The first occurrence of the word (יהי) declares that "something" will become light while the 50th occurrence declares that "the balances of judgement" will become "just or righteous". Is it possible that our Savior is the fulfillment of these two finished processes: the revelation of the first and fiftieth occurrences of this word (יהי)?

Now we can review the Hebrew word Viei (ויהי).

Jonah 1:1 KJV: *Now* the word of the Lord *came unto* (ויהי) Jonah the son of Amittai, saying,

Jonah 3:1 KJV: *And* the word of the LORD *came unto* (ויהי) Jonah the second time, saying,

Genesis 1:3 KJV: And God said, *Let there be* (יהי)[50] light: *and there was* (ויהי)[816] light.

Once again, before reviewing the word Viei (ויהי), let's review the spelling. The only difference in this spelling is that the letter Vav (ו) is added to the beginning of the word Iei (יהי). The definition of the letter Vav (ו) is "The Straight Up Man with the Nail". This word is declaring that Christ is the Revelation between the two Hands that Do Mighty Deeds. The word Viei (ויהי) represents a step or phase within a process. ***It does not represent the completion of the process.***

The phrase "and there was" is used 128 times in the KJV and this Hebrew word (ויהי) occurs 816 times in the original text. It is likely not possible to reconcile the occurrences and translations of this word. That said, is it possible to imagine the increased understanding of scripture that could be attained by searching out these 816 occurrences? This word (ויהי) occurs five times in the Book of Jonah. The number five means Revelation and/or Grace. Coincidence?

Let's apply our understanding of these two words into Genesis 1:3. The phrase "Let there be" refers to the beginning of the process of something that takes place over a set amount of time. In this case the scripture is introducing the process of something becoming LIGHT. That said, below is a proposal of how to apply the definition of these words to Genesis 1:3.

Genesis 1:3 (Modified): And God said, *He shall become*(יהי) light: *and He is becoming*(ויהי) light.

Is it coincidence that the 1st process was the last to be fulfilled? The fulfillment of the first of fifty processes introduced in Genesis 1:3 was fulfilled by our Savior declaring He is the light in John 8:12.

John 8:12 KJV: Then spake Jesus again unto them, saying, I am the light of the world: he that followeth me shall not walk in darkness, but shall have the light of life.

Glory to the King! It's impossible to feel 100% confident about validating the meanings and definitions of Hebrew but it is also easy to know when it's translated wrong.

Now let's do the same with Jonah 3:1.

Jonah 3:1 KJV: *And he is becoming* (ויהי) the *word of the LORD* (דבר־יהוה) *to* Jonah the second time, saying,

Did our Savior, or one of His representatives, make another visit with Jonah and provide the *Word of the LORD* (דבר-יהוה)?

The Hebrew letter Hey (ה) is the 5th letter of the Hebrew alphabet and means Revelation and/or Grace. The word (ויהי) translated as "And" in Jonah 3:1 occurs five times in the Book of Jonah. Coincidence? Hopefully we will get a clearer understanding of this word before we finish Chapter 4.

Let's take another return flight to Jonah 1:4 and review where this word (ויהי) was previously used in the Book of Jonah.

Jonah 1:4 (Modified): But the Lord _sent out_ (הטיל)[1] ~~great~~ _greatness to be revealed_ (גדולה)[72] ~~wind~~ _spirit of Him_ (רוח)[214] into *the sea* (הים), and ~~there was a~~ _He is becoming_ (ויהי)[816] ~~mighty~~ _great_ (גדול)[179] *tempest* (סער)[2] in the sea, *so that the ship* (והאניה)[1] ~~was like~~ _meant it_ (חשבה)[2] *to be broken* (להשבר)[1].

The Lord sent out His Great Spirit to be revealed and _it is becoming_ a great tempest, rushing mighty wind that was seen from those on the _ship_.

Let's skip ahead and review the next occurrence of the word "Viei (ויהי)" in the Book of Jonah while recalling that Genesis 1:3 translates this word (ויהי) as "and there was".

Jonah 1:17 KJV: Now the Lord had prepared a great fish to swallow up Jonah. And (ויהי) Jonah was in the belly of the fish three days and three nights.

The first time we discussed this verse, we shared that the Hebrew word translated as belly is also translated as "womb" in Ruth 1:11. Notice that the word (ויהי) was not translated in Jonah 1:17 or Jonah 3:1. Yes, many times this word is skipped in the translations. Let's apply our research and propose a modified translation of Jonah 1:17.

Jonah 1:17 (Modified) Now the Lord had prepared a great fish to swallow up Jonah *and he is becoming* (ויהי) Jonah while in the belly (womb) of the fish three days and three nights.

When we are "reborn", we begin the process of becoming what our Savior desires us to be. We become light! Remember the song *This Little Light of Mine*? We go through a process of becoming just as our Savior revealed the process of Him being the Light in John 8:12 which began in Genesis 1:3.

In Jonah 3:1, it proclaims that the word of the Lord came to Jonah. This verse is not properly translated but it is awesome to know that it will become even more evident as we continue.

Similar to how Jonah 3:1 resembles Jonah 1:1, Jonah 3:2 resembles Jonah 1:2.

Jonah 1:2 KJV: "Arise, go to Nineveh, *that great* (הגדולה)[31] city, *and cry out* (וקרא)[13] against it; for their wickedness has come up before Me."

Jonah 3:2 KJV: Arise, go unto Nineveh (נינוה)[11], *that great* (הגדולה)[31] city, *and preach* (וקרא)[13] unto it *the preaching* (את-הקריאה)[1] that I bid thee.

God's second request for Jonah to go to Nineveh is worded different than the first request in Chapter 1. The Hebrew word (וקרא) translated as *"and cry out"* in Jonah 1:2, is translated as "and preach" in Jonah 3:1.

The Hebrew word (את-הקריאה) translated as "preaching" in Jonah 3:2 is unique, only once in the original text. It is also preceded by the word Et (את) which means the First and the Last, Jesus's signet. This verse is declaring that Jonah is to preach the message that God "bids him" to preach. We know that Jonah spoke five words which would be more like "Crying Out" rather than "Preaching" (smile). The Hebrew word translated as preaching also has the Hebrew letter Hey (הַקריאה) at the beginning and ending of the word. So, whatever this noun means, the two letters at the start and end of the word are emphasizing "Behold What You See".

The Hebrew word (קרי) occurs five times in the original text and means "To Read Something Contrary". If you add the letter Alef (א), the get the unique word (קריא) translated as "city" and references a "rebellious city" in Ezra 4:15. Jonah is to "Read Something Contrary of God" to a rebellious city. Considering Jonah is about to do something that is only done once in the original text, it's difficult to associate this with preaching. That said, if Jonah isn't preaching, then what is he doing?

Let's continue…

Jonah 3:3 KJV: So Jonah *arose* (ויקם)[128], *and went unto* (וילך)[224] Nineveh, ***according to*** the *word* (כדבר)[58] of the Lord. Now Nineveh *was* (היתה)[116] ***an*** *exceeding* great city (עיר-גדולה) of three days' *journey* (מהלך)[6].

The word (ויקם) translated as "arose" occurs 128 times in the original text and the last three occurrences are in the Book of Dove. This is the second occurrence of this word (ויקם) in the Book of Dove.

The word (וילך) translated as "and went unto" occurs 224 times and this is the last occurrence. This is also the only occurrence of this word (וילך) in the Book of Dove.

Note that the words "according to" and the words "an exceedingly" are added by the translators and not translated from the original text.

The word (כדבר) translated as "word" occurs 58 times in the original text and this is the last occurrence and the only occurrence of this word in the Book of Dove. The first letter (כ) of the word (כדבר) is the letter Kaph (כ) which means a covering. The remaining three letters (דבר) is the word pronounced "Debar" which means "Word". The word (כדבר) means "The Covering (כ) of the Word (דבר)".

The word (היתה) translated as "was" occurs 116 times in the original text and only once in the Book of Dove. This word (היתה) means "became".

In Jonah 3:3, the NKJV declares that the exact meaning of the Hebrew word (מהלך) that occurs six times in the original text and translated as "journey" is not known. That said, the other five occurrences of this word were translated into the NKJV without any notes. Is this another translation anomaly? Let's search it out!

Many of the English translations translate this word (מהלך) as some form of the word "walking". What is *CRAZY INTERESTING* is that if you remove the letter Hey (מַהֲלַך) from the word, it spells the word (מלך) which means "King" and occurs 1,030 times in the original text. Recall that the letter Hey (ה) is the Revelation/Grace letter. The spelling of the word (מַהֲלַך) is declaring that somehow a "King will be Revealed", but the translations are consistently translating this as either journey, or walking three days, or walking. Nothing in the translations hint this word is related to a King.

Here is the big moment. Jonah is finally going to "preach". The sermon is a total of five Hebrew words in the original text. Further research of each word in these verses doesn't reveal anything unique about Jonah's appearance that would explain how only five words would have such an impact on the entire city. There is no mention of anything he's wearing, does he glow like Moses, or seaweed around his neck. There is no hint of anything that would impact people other than just five words.

Jonah 3:4 KJV: *And* Jonah *began* (ויחל)[14] *to enter into* (לבוא)[81] *the city* (בעיר)[100] *a* (אחד)[500] *day's journey* (מהלך)[6], *and he cried* (ויקרא)[211], *and said* (ויאמר)[2,084], Yet *forty* (ארבעים)[93] *days, and Nineveh* (ונינוה)[3] *shall be overthrown* (נהפכת)[2].

The underlined words from the original text denote that they are the last occurrence of the word.

There is only one more occurrence of the word (בעיר) translated as "city", and it occurs later in the Book of Dove.

The word (אחד) translated as "a" occurs 500 times in the original text and only once in the Book of Dove. There are only eleven more occurrences, and this word is almost always translated as "one". The number eleven denotes a covering. After Dove, there are eleven (a covering) more occurrences of the word (אחד) translated as "one", then the Word becomes flesh.

After Dove, there are forty more occurrences of the word (ויאמר) translated as "and said", then the Word becomes flesh.

The word (ונינוה) translated as "and Nineveh" occurs three times in the original text and this is the second occurrence. The third and last occurrence is in the Book of Nahum (נחום). That said, the word (נחום) translated as Nahum only occurs twice in the original text and means "Comforter". The word Nineveh (נינוה) means "fish town" and the last occurrence of Fish Town occurs in the Book of the Comforter. Coincidence?

> ***Dove (Jonah) is going to Fish Town (Nineveh)***
> ***which is the burden of Comforter (Nahum 1:1)***
> ***and our Savior (Salvation) is teaching the disciples***
> ***to become fishers of men.***
> **** Matthew 4:4 ****

The Hebrew word (נהפכת) translated as "shall be overthrown" occurs twice in the original text. The other verse is Jeremiah 2:21.

Jeremiah 2:21 KJV: Yet I had planted thee a noble vine, wholly a right seed: how then art *thou turned* (נהפכת) into the degenerate plant of a strange vine unto me?

The Hebrew word (נהפכת) translated as "shall be overthrown" is also translated as "thou turned". What is Jonah preaching? We need more clarity. Let's continue.

Jonah 3:5 KJV: So the people of Nineveh *believed* (ויאמינו)[3] *God* (באלהים)[31], and proclaimed a fast, *and put on* (וילבשו)[1] *sackcloth* (שקים)[12], *from the greatest of them* (מגדולם)[1] even to the *least of them* (קטנם)[1].

Again, the underlined words from the original text denote that they are the last occurrence of the word. Notice that there are three unique words.

The word "believed" is in the KJV Old Testament 22 times, but the Hebrew word (ויאמינו) translated as "believed" only occurs three times in the original text. Yes, there are several words from the original text that are translated as "believed". Let's review another story in scripture where this Hebrew word is used.

Exodus 14:29-31 KJV: [29] But the children of Israel walked upon dry land in the midst of the sea; and the waters were a wall unto *them on their right hand* (מימינם)[2], *and on their left* (ומשמאלם)[2]. (*NOTE: the word HAND is not in the* _original text!_ **_Remember that the word HAND was added!_**)
[30] Thus the LORD saved Israel that day out of the hand of the Egyptians; and Israel saw the Egyptians dead upon the sea shore.
[31] And Israel saw that great work which the LORD did upon the Egyptians: and the people feared the LORD, *and believed* (ויאמינו)[3] the LORD, and his servant Moses.

Isn't it remarkable that the people of Nineveh are as impacted by five words from Jonah as the children of Israel were impacted when they witnessed the dead Egyptian soldiers on the seashore of the Red Sea. Is there anything concealed in the Nineveh story that compares to the parting of the sea? The word (ויאמינו) translated as "believed" that only occurs three times implies that there is. We must find it! That said, are we searching out something that God concealed for His glory (Proverbs 25:2) or something that is mistranslated? Surely the translators couldn't miss an event as big as the parting of the Red Sea, right? Let's look again.

Jonah 3:5 KJV: So the people of Nineveh *believed* (ויאמינו)[3] *God* (באלהים)[31], and proclaimed a fast, *and put on* (וילבשו)[1] *sackcloth* (שקים)[12], *from the greatest of them* (מגדולם)[1] even to the *least of them* (קטנם)[1].

The Hebrew word translated as "and put on" (וַיִּלְבְּשׁוּ) is a unique word only used one time in the original Hebrew text. This doesn't make sense, right? How or what is so important about the Hebrew word (וַיִּלְבְּשׁוּ) that describes how they put on sackcloth?

All other occurrences of "putting on" sackcloth use the word (ילבש) translated as "girded" and not the word (וַיִּלְבְּשׁוּ) translated as "and put on". Yes, the answer is in the spelling of the Hebrew word. The Hebrew root word for "and put on" is spelled (ילבש). The *First and the Last* letters of the word (וַיִּלְבְּשׁוּ) are added which make this word unique. Both of those letters are the Hebrew letter Vav (ו) which means "The Straight Up Man with the Nail". Six times in the original Hebrew text the priest (ילבש) "girded" their holy linens in accordance with the instructions. All six times they use this Hebrew root word (ילבש) without the *First and the Last* Vav (ו) letters. According to the spelling of the Hebrew word (ילבש) "and put on", the people of Nineveh are putting on sackcloth in the same manner as the priest put on linens. How is that possible? How did these evil people whose sins are so great that God would send Dove to warn them, know that they should gird themselves in sackcloth?

Now would be a good time to review that *the definition of the letters that spell Jonah*, "The Hand That Does Mighty Deeds (י) is the Straight Up Man with the Nail (ו) whose Life (נ) will be revealed (ה)." Isn't that beautiful! Is this starting to make sense? The definition of Dove is to reveal the life of our Savior whose hands do mighty deeds, and we know from Jesus's baptism that this is exactly what the Dove did.

We aren't near done with this story and surely you agree that it is far different than the passed-down traditions before we were born, correct? Okay, we still must find this event, equivalent to parting of the Red Sea, that made the people of Nineveh believe like Israel believed. Whatever this is, it has to be HUGE, right?

Jonah 3:5 KJV: So the people of Nineveh *believed* (וַיַּאֲמִינוּ)[3] *God* (בֵּאלֹהִים)[31], and proclaimed a fast, *and put on* (וַיִּלְבְּשׁוּ)[1] *sackcloth* (שַׂקִּים)[12], *from the greatest of them* (מִגְּדוֹלָם)[1] even to the *least of them* (קְטַנָּם)[1].

The Hebrew word (מִגְּדוֹלָם) translated as "from the greatest of them" is another unique Hebrew word only used once and the root noun is the word (גָּדוֹל) translated as "great" which occurs 179 times in the original text. It is not an accident that the Hebrew letter that means "from" is added as the *First and the Last* letter to the root Hebrew noun "great". Here we go again, right? Again, the original text adds the same letter to the beginning and end of a word to make it unique. What's the letter and what's the message?

The Hebrew letter that means from is the Mem (ם, מ) which is spelled differently if it is the last letter of a word. The letter Mem means a woman's womb. All Hebrew letters have a numeric value, the Mem has a value of 40 which is also the number of weeks a woman is pregnant. Nineveh fasted 40 days. When the letter Mem (ם, מ) is the last letter of the word it translates to a Closed Womb (ם), otherwise it's an Open Womb (מ). So, the definition of the letters that spell the word (מגדולם) is, "At his Birth (מ), Wealth (ג) comes through the Door (ד) and He is the Straight Up Man with the Nail (ו) that has all Authority (ל) and Born of a Virgin (ם)".

In Hebrew this word (מגדולם) is translated as "the great **one** of them" which means that it is referring to a single person that is viewed by the people of Nineveh as the greatest. If you know Hebrew spelling, then you know that this word is NOT plural. It is absolutely referring to a single person that is the greatest of them and that person is born of a virgin. Is Jonah's sermon becoming clearer?

Jonah 3:5 KJV: So the people of Nineveh *believed* (ויאמינו)[3] *God* (באלהים)[31], and proclaimed a fast, *and put on* (וילבשו)[1] *sackcloth* (שקים)[12], *from the greatest of them* (מגדולם)[1] even to the *least of them* (קטנם)[1].

The same is true for the unique word (קטנם) translated as "least one of them". That said, when you remove the last letter from this word it translates to "Small". Once again, the last letter is the Mem (ם), the Closed Womb. We are our smallest while in the womb and our Savior was born in a Closed Womb.

Is it possible that the uniqueness and last occurrence of so many words in the Book of Jonah is our Creator using the Prophet Dove to teach us all things. That said, notice that sometimes Nineveh is described as great and other times it isn't and yet other times it is simply called a city. Why?

Jonah 3:5 KJV: So the people of Nineveh *believed* (ויאמינו)[3] *God* (באלהים)[31], and proclaimed a fast, *and put on* (וילבשו)[1] *sackcloth* (שקים)[12], *from the greatest of them* (מגדולם)[1] even to the *least of them* (קטנם)[1].

Jonah 3:6 KJV: *For* (ויגע)[14] *word* (הדבר)[237] came unto the *king* (מלך)[1,022] of Nineveh, *and he arose* (ויקם)[128] *from his throne* (מכסאו)[1], and *he laid* (ויעבר)[52] *his* *robe* (אדרתו)[3] *from him* (מעליו)[26], *and covered him* (ויכס)[5] *with sackcloth* (שק)[17], and sat in *ashes* (האפר)[3].

Just when you thought it was unexplainable. Let's review the Hebrew word (ויגע) that occurs 14 times in the original text and *seems* to be translated as "For" in verse six. It is also used in Genesis 32:25.

Genesis 32:25 KJV: And when he saw that he prevailed not against him, *he touched* (ויגע) the hollow of his thigh; and the hollow of Jacob's thigh was out of joint, as he wrestled with him.

In Genesis 32:25, the same word (ויגע) translated as "For" in Jonah 3:6 is translated as "he touched". WHAT?!?

Jonah 3:6 reveals that somebody in the previous verse (Jonah 3:5) brought word to the King of Nineveh. In Jonah 3:5, the previous verse, the only person identified is the greatest "one" or the least "one" in Nineveh. According to the spelling of those two Hebrew words that would be the person born of the Closed Womb. These Hebrew words are implying that our Savior or a representative of our Savior, physically touched the King. Does that sound impossible? Does he "touch" us? Well, the Dove just visited Nineveh and now the King is being "touched".

Are we convinced? Let's search out how this word is used in 2 Kings 13:21.

2 Kings 13:21 KJV: And it came to pass, as they were burying a man, that, behold, they spied a band of men; and they cast the man into the sepulchre of Elisha: and when the man was let down, *and touched* (ויגע) the bones of Elisha, he revived, and stood up on his feet.

Yes, the Hebrew word (ויגע) translated as "and touched" is the same word (ויגע) used in Jonah 3:6 and translated as "For". This Hebrew word (ויגע) is used fourteen times in the original Hebrew text and Jonah 3:6 is the last time it occurs. Coincidence?

The King of Nineveh is the last person in the Old Testament that is physically touched by God until our Savior shows up. The number fourteen in Hebrew represents "Life". The King of Ninevah is being touched just like Jacob was touched by the angel he wrestled and just like the person raised from the dead was touched by the bones of Elisha, and the King of Nineveh is the fourteenth occurrence.

Jonah 3:6 KJV: *For* (וַיִּגַּע)[14] *word* (הדבר)[237] came unto the *king* (מלך)[1,022] of Nineveh, *and he arose* (וַיָּקָם)[128] *from his throne* (מכסאו)[1], and *he laid* (ויעבר)[52] *his robe* (אדרתו)[3] *from him* (מעליו)[26], *and covered him* (ויכס)[5] *with sackcloth* (שק)[17], and sat in *ashes* (האפר)[3].

How many of us have always wondered why Nineveh reacted so overwhelmingly to Jonah. No, Jonah's face didn't glow, and he didn't have seaweed around his neck. When Dove talks, you will be touched! Wait, that's not all! The Hebrew word (הדבר) translated as "word" is the same word used in Genesis 16:13.

Genesis 16:13 KJV: And she called the name of the Lord *that spake* (הדבר)[237] unto her, Thou God seest me: for she said, Have I also here looked after him that seeth me?

Hagar, mother of Ishmael, called the name of the Lord *that spake* unto her. The King of Nineveh was physically touched, and he heard an audible voice speaking to him. Wait! Does this mean that every time we see this word translated as "that spake" that the words spoken can be heard?

The translations would have us visualize that a messenger from town notified the King about Jonah's message, like some form of a sticky note. NO! ***The King had a visit from the Lord who both touched him and spoke to him.***

Let's apply our efforts to a modified version of Jonah 3:6.

Jonah 3:6 (Modified): ~~For~~ The Lord touched (וַיִּגַּע)[14] ~~word came~~ and spake His Word (הדבר)[237] unto the *king* (מלך)[1,022] of Nineveh, *and he arose* (וַיָּקָם)[128] *from his throne* (מכסאו)[1], *and he laid* (ויעבר)[52] *his robe* (אדרתו)[3] *from him* (מעליו)[26], *and covered him* (ויכס)[5] *with sackcloth* (שק)[17], and sat in *ashes* (האפר)[3].

Is it becoming clearer? The prophet Dove never spoke to anyone in Israel and neither did he perform deeds/works in Israel. In fact, when he got on the boat in Joppa, he had to pay a fare. Nobody in Israel knew who he was. He is a prophet to the gentiles. Is that possible? Prophets are just for Israel, right? God doesn't send prophets to the gentiles, right? Is this why there are so many unique words in this book? Is this why we are finding the last occurrence of so many words? Does the phrase "the first shall be last and the last shall be first" apply here? The gentiles are the last to receive a prophet but the first to receive "The Dove". Coincidence?

Jonah spoke to the people of Nineveh, who are not descendants of Abraham, the Lord supported the words of the prophet and now He is talking and visiting with these people just like He does with Israel after they hear from a prophet. The Lord's behavior with the gentiles is exactly like His behavior with Israel after they hear from a prophet. The scriptures are using the exact Hebrew words that are used in prior books of the Bible.

This is the fourteenth and last time that the Lord "touched" but nonetheless, the last time He "touched" it was a gentile. Coincidence? Are you seeing a trend? Jesus is the same to EVERYBODY! Glory to the King!

After the King is touched and hears from the Lord, he arises. For many of us, the phrase "he arose" is unremarkable. That said, this Hebrew word (ויקם) occurs 128 times in the original text, and this is the last occurrence. This word (ויקם) is used to describe when Cain rose against Able, when Abraham rose to take Isaac to be sacrificed, and when Abraham rose to purchase land to bury Sarah. There are 128 events in scripture that begin with someone rising and this is the last time anyone "arises" in the Old Testament. The King of Nineveh rose like the other 127 times that the Word of God deemed it necessary for us to know that someone arose. Could "arise" also mean that the person acted without wavering?

In Jonah 3:6, the unique Hebrew word (מכסאו) translated as "from his throne" is only in the Hebrew text one time. Where does this end (smile)? How many times do we find unique words in the Book of Dove?

Jonah 3:6 KJV: ~~For~~ *The Lord touched* (ויגע)[14] ~~word came~~ *and spake* (הדבר)[237] unto the king of Nineveh, and *he arose* (ויקם)[128] *from his throne* (מכסאו)[1], and *he laid* (ויעבר)[52] *his robe* (אדרתו)[3] *from him* (מעליו)[26], *and covered him* (ויכס)[5] *with sackcloth* (שק)[17], and sat in *ashes* (האפר)[3].

The Hebrew word (אדרתו) translated as "his robe" occurs three times and the other two refer to Elijah's mantle. This is the same word used in 1 Kings 19:19 when Elijah "flung" his **mantle** over Elisha and in 2 Kings 2:8 when Elijah folded his **mantle** and smote the river Jordan so that he and Elisha crossed the Jordan on dry land. This gentile King is using the same Hebrew words used in the story of Elijah, one of the greatest stories of Israel. Again, our God is the same God for all! Let's continue and look at Jonah 3:7.

Jonah 3:7 KJV: And he caused it to be proclaimed and published *through Nineveh* (בנינוה)[3] *by the decree* (מטעם)[1] of the king and his nobles (וגדליו)[1], saying, Let neither man nor beast, herd *nor flock* (והצאן)[3], taste *any thing* (מאומה)[28]: let them not feed, nor drink *water* (ומים)[25]:

The word "decree" occurs 55 times in the KJV 55, but the Hebrew word (מטעם) translated as "decree" in Jonah 3:7 is unique. Surprised? Of course not. The word (וגדליו) translated as nobles is also unique.

Jonah 3:8 KJV: But let man *and beast* (והבהמה)[5] *be covered* (ויתכסו)[1] *with sackcloth* (שקים)[12], *and cry* (ויקראו)[32] *mightily* (בחזקה)[4] unto God: *yea*, let them turn every one *from his* evil *way* (מדרכו)[14], and from *the violence* (החמס)[2] *that is in their hands* (בכפיהם)[2].

Yes, all the underlined words are the last occurrence. Coincidence?

The Hebrew word (ויתכסו) translated as "be covered" is a unique word only used once in the original text. Are they providing a covering for themselves?

Jonah 3:9 KJV: Who can tell if God will turn and repent, and turn away from his *fierce* (מחרון)[8] *anger* (אפו), *that we perish* (מחרון)[2] not?

The words "anger or angry" are in the KJV Book of Jonah five times but the Hebrew words translated as "anger (אף) or angry (אפו)" only occur once in this book. "Anger" is behavior, an outward expression. "Angry" is a condition of your spirit, an inward expression.

Jonah 3:10 KJV: *And God saw* (וירא)[166] *their works* (את-מעשיהם)[8], *that they turned* (שבו)[35] *from their* evil *way* (מדרכם)[3]; and God *repented* (וינחם)[19] of the evil, that he had said that he would do unto them; and he did it not.

Yes, there is much more to share in these last three verses but let's skip forward to verse ten and see that we have the word Et (את) included in the

Hebrew word (את-מעשיהם) translated as "their works". Again, the word Et represents Jesus's stamp, and this is the first occurrence since the prophet Dove preached in Jonah 3:2. God turned away from His wrath and Nineveh was spared.

Are we shocked about what was hidden in the original Hebrew text of Jonah Chapter 3?

Let's do the Honor of Kings and search out Jonah Chapter 4.

Glory to the King!

Chapter 20 – Jonah Chapter 4

Sorry, quick personal note to my kids!

Long before this page of the book my kids are likely asking, "Ok dad, what are you saying? What do you want us to do? If you are right, then you are revealing page after page of poor translations. Can we use our translations or not?

Yes, absolutely use your translations but know that they are translations! Know they are simply incomplete. I would not be able to provide this research without the translations. I am exceedingly grateful for our translations. I am not a Hebrew translator but rather a Hebrew validator. Without a translation I would not know the Gospel that turned me from my wretched ways. That said, everything you see in English is a translation. *That includes EVERYTHING IN ENGLISH, including me.*

What do I want you to do? Dad wants you to learn the Hebrew letters and how to research Hebrew words. Download Interlinear Scripture Analyzer 3 Basic and learn how to research the original Hebrew text for yourself. This tool is something that has only been available in our generation. It's truly cheating (smile)! The research in this book could not be provided without this tool or one similar.

Again, I have successfully taught a one-day eight-hour class where students leave able to read and research the Hebrew text. Yes, it is difficult to speak Hebrew, but it is very easy to read and research. The advantage of knowing Hebrew and researching as demonstrated in this book is that I get to know my Savior so much better. That said, my efforts to write this book have not been without insults and persecution. Learn our Father's alphabet, the Alef-Tav (את)!

Back to the research of Jonah, thank you!

When we began this journey, we didn't know we were going to find so many variations between the translations and the searching out of the original Hebrew text. At first, we were timid about entertaining the idea that anything was translated incorrectly. Now we can take what we have searched out and realized that there are approximately 100 English translations of the Bible. It's as though the only requirement for anyone to accept each translation as *divine and inspired* is that it says "Holy Bible" on the cover. Humorously, it seems that if the words "Holy Bible" are embossed with gold print on leather canvas then that translation is even more qualified.

We can all respect the struggle to consider that any translation is not accurately translating the original Hebrew text. That said, it only takes 50 hours to learn Hebrew and prove it yourself. Learn that it takes a pure heart to learn Hebrew and not a brain, 1 Corinthians 1:22-27.

1 Corinthians 1:22-27 KJV: [22] For the Jews require a sign, and the Greeks seek after wisdom:
[23] But we preach Christ crucified, unto the Jews a stumblingblock, and unto the Greeks foolishness;
[24] But unto them which are called, both Jews and Greeks, Christ the power of God, and the wisdom of God. [25] Because the foolishness of God is wiser than men; and the weakness of God is stronger than men.
[26] For ye see your calling, brethren, how that not many wise men after the flesh, not many mighty, not many noble, are called:
[27] But God hath chosen the foolish things of the world to confound the wise; and God hath chosen the weak things of the world to confound the things which are mighty;

Learning how to read and understand a Hebrew word is easy! Most of us have been told and conceded that learning how to research the Hebrew text is impossible. That is another lie that was passed down from birth. Those that have taken this journey can confirm that this is VERY EASY! Prove us wrong!

If our Heavenly Father openly declares that He conceals things, then He cannot require that we possess the mental capability to have it revealed. He only requires that we want to know. If we seek then we shall find. Understanding scripture is revealed to the heart that seeks. Prove it and know this book is true, otherwise you are simply trusting this book as you have trusted others your entire life. Hey kids, don't trust this book! Learn Hebrew and teach it to your kids when they are young!

<u>Let's search out the last chapter of the Book of Jonah.</u>

Oh, how wonderful it would have been to share the efforts of searching out Dove chapter four. Let's search out Jonah 4:1.

Jonah 4:1 KJV: *But it displeased* (וירע)[14] Jonah *exceedingly* (רעה גדולה), *and he was very angry* (ויחר)[50].

How do we explain Jonah is displeased? We have an entire chapter devoted to searching out Jonah 4:2, but we did not discuss Jonah 4:1. The Hebrew word (וירע) translated as "displeased" occurs 14 times in the original and this is the last occurrence. The first occurrence is Genesis 21:11.

Genesis 21:11 KJV: And the thing was very grievous (וירע) in Abraham's sight because of his son.

So, this Hebrew word (וירע) used in these two stories shows that Jonah and Abraham had the same reaction to what God was asking of them. Hebrews 11:17-19 tells us that Abraham had faith to believe God would save his son and Jonah 4:2 shows that before he left the presence of God, that Jonah told God he knew God would spare Nineveh.

Hebrew 11:17-19 KJV: [17] By faith Abraham, when he was tried, offered up Isaac: and he that had received the promises offered up his only begotten son, [18] Of whom it was said, That in Isaac shall thy seed be called: [19] Accounting that God was able to raise him up, even from the dead; from whence also he received him in a figure.

Understand that Jonah and Abraham had the same reaction to very diverse situations. Abraham's displeasure is due to a test of faith while it seems that Jonah's displeasure is due to an act of mercy.

Now we will search out the Hebrew words (רעה גדולה) translated as "exceedingly".

Jonah 4:1 KJV: *But it displeased* (וירע)[14] *Jonah exceedingly* (רעה גדולה), *and he was very angry* (ויחר)[50].

The traditional story of this verse varies because of the translations. This chapter is ***littered*** with poor translation which supports the traditional dialog of the passed down traditional teaching. Searching out the original text of Jonah 4:1 will be the initiation that leads us to truth and away from traditional lies. The true translation of these words combined with the documentation of the many ***ERRORS*** of translation reveals a glorious truth about Dove. But first, let's take a path of added confusion to help make this more clear.

Let's begin our path of added confusion (smile)…

We have already searched out one of the two words (גדולה) translated as "exceedingly". Earlier we revealed that the word (גדולה) means "Great (גדול) to be Revealed (ה)". What is not revealed in the translations is the second word from the original text that was included in the translation of the word "exceedingly" (רעה גדולה). This word (רעה) that was *not* translated.

The word (רעה) that is not translated occurs 164 times in the original text and is commonly translated as "Evil". So, it seems that Jonah was displeased and exceeding evil (smile). The extreme always reveals the truth. How is it possible for Dove to view the events of God with the people of Nineveh with displeasure and reference it as exceedingly evil. Surely, we understand and agree that this is impossible! That said, this is *LITERALLY* what is says in the original text!

This seems to be progressing further from any similarity to Abraham's use of the word (וירע) translated as displeased. *It is blatantly clear that we are missing something, right! Are we missing the correct translation of a word from the original text or are we unknowingly applying the words from the original text to the traditional story that doesn't reveal truth!*

Are we capable of abandoning the passed down traditional story and conceive a narrative that would explain Dove being displeased about a great evil to be revealed. Though it doesn't make sense, it appears as though this great evil is something good. How can a "great evil" be good? Are there any examples in the Bible of great evils that were later revealed to be good? Let's look at Genesis 50:19-21.

Genesis 50:19-21 KJV: [19] And Joseph said unto them, Fear not: for am I in the place of God?
[20] But as for you, ye thought evil against me; but God meant it unto good, to bring to pass, as it is this day, to save much people alive.
[21] Now therefore fear ye not: I will nourish you, and your little ones. And he comforted them, and spake kindly unto them.

Wouldn't it be fun to search out the original text of those three verses?

Yes, we have at least one precedent of a great evil that God meant for good and many of us are aware of at least two more stories with this plot.

Now, we have the dilemma of trying to forget what we know so that we can SEE what DOVE is trying to teach. Are we allowed to consider that the prophet Dove, who has repeated conversations with God, is God's spokesperson to teach us what we would otherwise never know? Yes, had to walk the tight-rope on that question (smile).

Let's continue…

Jonah 4:1 KJV: *But it displeased* (וירע)[14] Jonah *exceedingly* (רעה גדולה), *and he was very angry* (ויחר)[50].

Earlier in this book we searched out the Hebrew word translated as fled and proved Jonah did not sin. We searched out Chapter 2 and proved that Jonah did not repent because he didn't sin, rather we learned that Dove interceded for us. Now we can search out the rest of Jonah 4:2 and bring clarity to Jonah 4:1 while preparing ourselves to ***FINALLY SEE DOVE REVEALED! DON'T BLASPHEME DOVE (smile)!***

Jonah 4:2 KJV: *And he prayed* (ויתפלל)[19] unto the LORD, and said, I pray thee, O LORD, was not this *my saying* (דברי)[300], *when I was yet* (הייתי)[1] in *my country* (אדמתי)[3]? ***Therefore I*** (קדמתי)[2] *fled* (לברח)[4] ***before*** (קדמתי)[2] *unto Tarshish* (תרשישה)[4]: for I knew that thou art a *gracious* (חנון)[60] God, and *merciful* (ורחום)[8], *slow to* (ארך)[60] *anger* (אפים)[28], *and of great* (ורב)[37] kindness, and repentest thee of the evil.

Jonah is praying again! Yes, the Hebrew word (ויתפלל) translated as "And he prayed" occurs 19 times in the original text. This is the same Hebrew word (ויתפלל) used in Jonah 2:1 and these are the last two occurrences. Once again, the word (ויתפלל) is the word for intercessory prayer. Who is Jonah praying for? Is he praying for the people of Nineveh who have already received God mercy? Does anything in these first two verses directly state that they are related to the story of God's mercy to the people of Nineveh or is that part of the passed down tradition? Let's continue and search out whether Dove is praying for the people of Nineveh because of their evil past or because of the evil of their future not yet revealed. Will God once again make their evil result in something good?

How can Jonah be displeased about God's mercy on Nineveh and even be angry, yet in the next verse it reveals that he is interceding for them? This doesn't reconcile!

The word (אפים) translated as "anger" in Jonah 4:2 occurs 28 times in the original text, and this is the 27th occurrence. The last occurrence is in the

Book of Comforter (Nahum). Notice that this word (אפים) has no resemblance to the word (וייחר) translated as "anger" in Jonah 4:1. This word (אפים) is also the plural form of the word (אף) which means anger. The two letters (ים) at the end of the word (אפים) denote plurality in Hebrew.

The word (וייחר) translated as "anger" in Jonah 4:1 occurs 50 times in the original text, and this is the last occurrence. This word ***DOES NOT*** mean anger. The number fifty represents a Jubilee of Jubilees. The next occurrence, which is not in the Old Testament, will be the beginning of a new Jubilee. Let's look at Genesis 30:2.

Genesis 30:2 KJV: And Jacob's *anger* (אף)[28] *was kindled* (וייחר)[50] against Rachel: and he said, Am I in God's stead, who hath withheld from thee the fruit of the womb?

This verse provides the singular form of the word (אפים) translated as "anger" in Jonah 4:2 as well as the word (וייחר) that is incorrectly translated as "anger" in Jonah 4:1. The word (וייחר) translated as "anger" in Jonah 4:1 literally means "hot". Jonah was hot, like you would experience from sitting in the sun.

Ok, so if Jonah is not angry then how do we explain the remainder of the translation of Jonah 4:1? Well, first, if Jonah is not angry then the tone or spirit of Jonah 4:2 is not a continuation of anger! Rather, it's an expression of adoration. Adoration based on knowledge. Let's apply all that we have searched out of the words in Jonah 4:1.

Jonah 4:1 (Modified): *And it displeased* (וירע)[14] Jonah *a great* (גדולה) *evil* (רעה) *to be revealed, and he was very hot* (וייחר)[50].

Jonah 4:1 reveals that Dove is displeased; he is displeased about a great evil that has not yet happened. An evil to be revealed. Oh, and he is evidently sitting in the sun because he is hot (smile). What is the revelation of the 50th occurrence of "being hot"? What is this?!? Can you see it yet (smile)?

Ok, it's time to reveal Dove! Prepare yourself for an amazing timeline of events. Prepare to search out the original text that will reveal a chronological calendar of events. Know that Dove will clearly express when referencing the past and he is not the author of confusion! The only confusion in this story is the huge chasm between the truth of the original text and the traditional passed down story from many generations ago.

After searching out the original text of Jonah 4:1, let's introduce ourselves to the idea that Jonah is not displeased with God's mercy on Nineveh in the past but rather Jonah is displeased about a great evil in the future which will also receive God's great mercy.

<u>STOP!</u>
Take a minute to do your best to forget all you know about Dove!
For Dove to teach us about our Savior,
we must forget the traditional story from the past
that taught us about God's mercy to forgive Jonah.
We must not mix these two stories.
This story is about Dove teaching us!

In an attempt to assist in forgetting the story of the past, let's consider the last words of the Book of Dove from Jonah 4:11, *"...persons that cannot discern between their right hand and their left hand; and also much cattle?"*

Back home we have several slang comments that include the phrase "don't know your left hand from your right hand" (smile). We have a journey to take but know that the original text will reveal *a huge chasm* between the truth and the translation about what's on the left and what's on the right portrayed in this verse.

Let's continue searching out what Dove is trying to teach. Dove, the teacher that teaches all *things*. That said, did you know that the word "thing" or "things" occurs 784 times in the KJV? Did you also know that there is no Hebrew word for "thing"? Did you know that many times the word translated as "things" is the same word that was translated into Greek as "Deuteronomy"? The Hebrew word that was translated into Greek as "Deuteronomy" occurs 134 times in the original text and is never translated as Deuteronomy except for the title of the book. Again, often this word is translated as "things" or "things". Can you imagine the preacher saying, "Turn with me to the Book of Things" or "The Holy Ghost will teach you all Deuteronomy"? Isn't it awesome that the New Testament was written in Greek, because in Hebrew it is impossible to teach "all *things*". Traditions, Lies from Birth Volume 2 will search out <u>***ALL***</u> *those things* (smile).

If you think that's bad, let's continue searching out Jonah Chapter 4.

Jonah 4:2 KJV: *And he prayed* (<u>ויתפלל</u>)[19] unto the LORD, and said, I pray thee, O LORD, was not this *my saying* (<u>דברי</u>)[300], *when I was yet* (<u>הירותי</u>)[1] in *my country* (<u>אדמתי</u>)[3]? ***Therefore I*** (<u>קדמתי</u>)[2] *fled* (<u>לברח</u>)[4] ***before*** (<u>קדמתי</u>)[2] *unto Tarshish*

(תרשישה)[4]: for I knew that thou art a *gracious* (חנון)[60] God, and *merciful* (ורחום)[8], *slow to* (ארך)[60] *anger* (אפים)[28], *and of great* (ורב)[37] kindness, and repentest thee of the evil.

The Hebrew word (הייתי) translated as "when I was yet" is a unique word only in the Hebrew text one time. The definition of the Hebrew letters is, "Behold (ה) The Straight Up Man with the Nail (ו) on the Cross (ת) is between the Hands of God (י י)." Again, this is the only time this word is used in the original Hebrew text. Those that know Hebrew understand the significance of a word that has the Hands of God (י י) in the spelling. Is Jonah declaring that he was in the hands of God just like Jesus was in His hands on the cross?

So, while Jonah was still in his country, he had a conversation with Yahweh. The Hebrew word (אדמתי) translated as "in my country" occurs three times in the original text. We know that Jonah is Galilean so let's review the first occurrence of this Hebrew word (אדמתי) in the original text.

2 Chronicles 7:19-20 KJV: [19] But if ye turn away, and forsake my statutes and my commandments, which I have set before you, and shall go and serve other gods, and worship them;
[20] Then will I pluck them up by the roots out of *my land* (אדמתי) which I have given them; and this house, which I have sanctified for my name, will I cast out of my sight, and will make it to be a proverb and a byword among all nations.

The word (אדמתי) translated in Jonah 4:2 as "my country" is referred to as God's Land which He has given Israel. In the NKJV it's "My land". Jonah and God visited in their land which He allows Israel to dwell if they follow His statutes and commandments. Jonah is ***NOT*** referring to Israel's land, he is referring to God's land as "my country". How is that possible? Is Jonah simply claiming to be a resident of Yahweh's land or is he implying that he has a deed?

Jonah 4:2 KJV: *And he prayed* (ויתפלל)[19] unto the LORD, and said, I pray thee, O LORD, was not this *my saying* (דברי)[300], *when I was yet* (הייתי)[1] in *my country* (אדמתי)[3]? ***Therefore I*** (קדמתי)[2] *fled* (לברח)[4] ***before*** (קדמתי)[2] *unto Tarshish* (תרשישה)[4]: for I knew that thou art a *gracious* (חנון)[60] God, and *merciful* (ורחום)[8], *slow to* (ארך)[60] *anger* (אפים)[28], *and of great* (ורב)[37] kindness, and repentest thee of the evil.

Okay, it's time to explain "***Therefore I*** (קדמתי)[2] *fled* (לברח)[4] ***before*** (קדמתי)[2] ". The problem is that the translators translated the word (לברח) as "fled" and inserted it in the middle of the translation of word (קדמתי) which is "Therefore I before" which doesn't make sense. But, thankfully, the word (קדמתי) translated as "Therefore I before" occurs twice in the original text and the other occurrence is Psalm 119:147.

Psalm 119:147 KJV: *I prevented* (קדמתי) the dawning of the morning, and cried: I hoped in thy word.

The word (קדמתי) is translated as "I prevented" but "The dawning of the morning", the morning our Savior was beaten, wasn't prevented but maybe it was forestalled. A better translation would be "I forestalled".

Because of Nineveh's wickedness, God sent Jonah with His authority on a boat ride and a fishing trip before Jonah prophesied to Nineveh. Now it seems as though this trip had another purpose, it seems that Nineveh's wickedness must be judged so that something will be forestalled into the future. What event is being forestalled?

Jonah 4:3 KJV: Therefore now, O LORD, *take* (קח)[6], *I beseech thee* (נא)[407], *my life* (את-נפשי)[173] *from me* (ממני)[87]; for it is *better* (טוב)[300] *for me to die* (מותי)[2] *than to live* (מחיי)[2].

Dove is still grieving about something. His displeasure has been expressed for three verses and now he is expressing that he would rather be dead. Something is very wrong, but it has not yet been revealed…or has it?

We only have eight more verses in the story of Jonah. ***Who is ~~Jonah~~ Dove?*** We know his father is Amittai and we know that Amittai means "My Truth". We don't know Amittai's genealogy! Go research and see that nobody knows My Truth's genealogy. That's interesting, Jesus's real Father doesn't have a genealogy either. No, we couldn't include that while comparing the boat story, right?

Before searching out the words of this verse, let's propose an alternative view to the passed down traditions and see if what we are searching out validates that view. Let's openly declare that this is an effort to condition and influence our thoughts before presenting the facts, just like the traditional teaching since before we were born!

Is it possible that Dove is far more aware of God's Will, our Father's Will, than indicated by the translations? Is it possible that Dove is *NOT* whining about his plight but rather trying to teach us about our Father? Is it possible that the translation and traditional narrative of Jonah 4:1-3 is the building of the chasm that separates translation and tradition from the truth?

The traditional passed down narrative that influences how we view the Old Testament is quite different than the narrative of how we view the New. We have already searched out an alternative view to our Father forsaking His only Son. If we had been raised with that view, we would have never considered our Good Father to one to forsake His son. Is there more evidence that our Father is truly greater than His Son, John 14:28?

How many times do Christians tell each other "He knows, He hears us talking right now. He's with us this very moment". It's true! That said, He knows the troubles many of us have trying to teach John 14:28, "…My Father is greater than I…" He knows, He knows, He knows! The fact that we have any hesitation acknowledging that the Father is greater than the son proves the error of translation and the traditional passed down stories. Our God, our Good Father loves proving who He is to us and Our Savior loves revealing His Father who is greater than Him.

One way to prove the Father is greater than the Son is to prove that the Father would never ask His Son to do anything that He wouldn't do Himself. It's the golden rule, right? Let's consider Jesus's words to Cleopas on the walk to Emmaus.

Luke 24:25-27 KJV: [25] Then he said unto them, O fools, and slow of heart to believe all that the prophets have spoken:
[26] Ought not Christ to have suffered these things, and to enter into his glory?
[27] And beginning at Moses and all the prophets, he expounded unto them in all the scriptures the things concerning himself.

Jesus taught Cleopas the Gospel by only using Moses and the prophets of the Old Testament. Could we do that? Is our Father's work in the Old Testament so perfect that His Son can tell the Gospel story without any New Testament scripture? Yes, it is!

Exposing, correcting, and revealing the truth from the original text of the four chapters of Dove cannot compete with the errors of translation of the remaining chapters of the Old Testament, but it's a start. Jesus can only be as loving as His Father. The Son cannot inherit character that doesn't exist. The house of Our Father and His Son is not a 21st Century Hollywood dysfunctional drama. Our Father's house is pure, virtuous, and sinless; perfect love.

Just a few verses ago we learned about how our Father had grace and mercy on Nineveh. Wait! We read that sentence far too fast. The traditional narrative doesn't teach that God is void of grace and mercy in the Old Testament, but it hints and adds to the narrative and many of us perceive that it can be measured. How long were you a Christian before considering our Father was more merciful and graceful than His Son? The narrative is all about us judging His character while ignoring the character of His corrupted creation, us! The implied and unspoken narrative of the Gospel is that our Savior provided us grace and mercy that was unattainable prior to the His resurrection and occasionally we include that it was the Will of the Father. The Good Father who resurrected His Son.

Now we are ready to search out Jonah 4:3.

Jonah 4:3 KJV: Therefore now, O LORD, *take* (קח)[6], *I beseech thee* (נא)[407], *my life* (את-נפשי)[173] *from me* (ממני)[87]; for it is *better* (טוב)[300] *for me to die* (מותי)[8] *than to live* (מחיי)[2].

The grotesque mistranslation and misinterpretation of this verse is screaming the 21st Century narrative that our sin can lead us to depression and suicide.

The word (את-נפשי) translated as *"my life"* has Et (את) preceding the noun. Jonah is asking for the LORD to take his soul, the Salvation (את) of his life (נפשי), from him.

The word (טוב) translated as "better" means "good". The first occurrence of this word is Day One in Genesis when God says, "It is good."

The word (מחיי) translated as *"than to live"* occurs twice in the original text and both occurrences are in this chapter! This word is unique to the story of Dove! What if the truth about the word (מחיי) is so far from *"than to live"* that you can't see it with a telescope?

Can we recall the searching out of the ***amazing word*** (חיי) that occurs 36 times in the original text and the last occurrence was The Dove's Prayer in Jonah 2:6? Can we recall that it referenced God's covenant to Abraham and those "of lives of" Abraham? This is the same word but has the letter Mem (מ) added as the first letter. The letter Mem (מ) is a woman's womb and if it's the last letter of a word then it represents a closed womb, a virgin. When the letter Mem (מ) is the first letter of a word it is translated as "from". That said, the letters of Hebrew also include a depth of understanding called "the mystery of the letter". The word (מחיי) means *"from lives of"* or it could mean *"born of the life of"* (smile).

What is Jonah declaring? What is God's purpose of the Prophet Jonah? Who is Jonah?

If Jonah isn't teaching that suicide is an alternative, then what is he teaching? Is it possible that we will witness Jonah repeatedly revealing the Gospel story? No! This book isn't hinting or leading to a conclusion that Jonah is Yeshua, but isn't the truth about Jonah getting further and further from the traditional passed down story? The chasm between truth and the traditions passed down before we were born is getting wider and wider.

Is it possible to read Jonah 4:3 and see a hint that Dove is trying to reveal that the Spirit calls us to redemption? Is Dove interceding for us again, and again? Does the Spirit lead us to Salvation, to the promised land?

Let's apply our efforts to the modified version of Jonah 4:3.

Jonah 4:3 (Modified): And now (ועתה), LORD, *take You please* (קח[66]-נא[407]) *Salvation-soul of me* (את[173]-נפשי) *from me* (ממני)[87], *that it is* (כי) *good* (טוב)[300] *from the death of me* (מותי)[8] *from of lives of* (מחיי)[2].

The death of Dove was good for the lives of Dove. Does that sound familiar?

Let's search out Jonah 4:4.

Jonah 4:4 KJV: *Then said the* (ויאמר)[2,084] LORD, *Doest thou well* (ההיטב)[2] *to be angry* (חרה)[18]?

The word (ויאמר) translated as *"Then said the"* is correctly translated. Note that the original Hebrew text does not have the question mark, "?". A question is denoted by using other words like (וישאל) which means "and he is asking". The word (ויאמר) denotes that this verse is *NOT* a question. Yahweh is making a comment. Yahweh and Jonah are having another conversation. We truly must pay attention when these two have a conversation (smile).

The Hebrew word (חרה) translated as "angry" occurs 18 times in the original text, three times in the Book of Dove and this is the first occurrence in the Book of Dove. Let's look at the first occurrence.

Genesis 4:6 KJV: And the Lord *said* (ויאמר) unto Cain, Why art thou wroth (חרה)? and why is thy countenance fallen?

At first glance, it would seem that "wroth" and "angry" are synonyms and the word (חרה) is accurately translated. That said, we are also seeing the word (ויאמר) which means that the Lord is speaking but not asking questions. *THIS IS HUGE!* Let's look at the second occurrence of the word (חרה) translated as "angry" and "wroth".

Numbers 11:33 KJV: And while the flesh was yet between their teeth, ere it was chewed, *the wrath* (ואף)[29] of the Lord *was kindled* (חרה) against the people, and the Lord smote the people with a very great plague.

Jonah 4:4 translated the word (חרה) as "angry" but in this verse it is translated as "kindled" which means "set on fire".

To further prove that Jonah was hot and not angry let's search out the word (ואף) which occurs 29 times in the original text and has a wide range of translations in the KJV. The first five occurrences of the word (ואף) translated as *"the wrath"* occur in Leviticus 26:39-44.

Leviticus 26:39-44 KJV: [39] And they that are left of you shall pine away in their iniquity in your enemies' lands; *and also* (ואף) in the iniquities of their fathers shall they pine away with them.
[40] If they shall confess their iniquity, and the iniquity of their fathers, with their trespass which they trespassed against me, *and* that *also* (ואף) they have walked contrary unto me;
[41] And that I also have walked contrary unto them, and have brought them into the land of their enemies; if then their uncircumcised hearts be humbled, and they then accept of the punishment of their iniquity:
[42] Then will I remember my covenant with Jacob, *and also* (ואף) my covenant with Isaac, *and also* (ואף) my covenant with Abraham will I remember; and I will remember the land.
[43] The land also shall be left of them, and shall enjoy her sabbaths, while she lieth desolate without them: and they shall accept of the punishment of their iniquity: because, even because they despised my judgments, and because their soul abhorred my statutes.
[44] *And yet* (ואף) for all that, when they be in the land of their enemies, I will not

cast them away, neither will I abhor them, to destroy them utterly, and to break my covenant with them: for I am the Lord their God.

In Deuteronomy 31:27, the word (ואף) is translated as *"and how much more"*. In 1 Samuel 21:5 as *"yea"*. In 2 Samuel 16:11 it isn't translated.

When the letter Vav (ו) is the first letter of a word, it is translated as "and". The remaining letters of the word (ואף) is the word (אף) which occurs 177 times in the original text. The second occurrence is Genesis 27:45.

Genesis 27:45 KJV: Until thy brother's *anger* (אף) turn away from thee, and he forget that which thou hast done to him: then I will send, and fetch thee from thence: why should I be deprived also of you both in one day?

The word (אף) means "anger"! The word (ואף) means "and anger". Reread the Leviticus 26:39-44 and see that the Lord is speaking, and He is angry about their iniquities. See that the people walked with anger against Him. Israel didn't accidentally establish a generational culture that strayed from the ways of God, they angrily rebelled against His ways.

The translators translated the word (חרה) as "angry" but once again Jonah is hot. The LORD told Jonah that he does well to be **hot**. Why are there so many references to Jonah being hot? Also, why did the translators translated the word (יהוה) as "LORD" when they translated it as "Lord" many other times?

The word (ההיטב) translated as *"Doest thou well"* occurs twice in the original text and both occurrences are in the Book of Dove. The traditional story has us thinking that the conversation is related to God having mercy on Nineveh in chapter three. The word (ההיטב) begins with (הה). The letter Hey (ה) means grace and/or revelation. If these two letters (הה) are removed, the remaining word (יטב) is unique and found in 1 Samuel 24:4.

1 Samuel 24:4 KJV: And the men of David said unto him, Behold the day of which the Lord said unto thee, Behold, I will deliver thine enemy into thine hand, that thou mayest do to him as it **shall seem good** (יטב)[1] *unto thee* (בעיניך)[67]. Then David arose (ויקם), and cut off the skirt of Saul's robe privily.

The unique word (יטב) is translated as *"shall seem good"* which is somewhat consistent with the word (ההיטב) translated as *"Doest thou well"* in Jonah 4:4. The letter Hey (ה) means revelation and/or grace and when it's the first letter of a word it is most often translated as "the", but it could also be represented by the words "behold" or "grace". The word has two Hey letters (הה) which could imply "Behold, behold…" or "Grace, grace…" *It all depends on how you see it* (smile).

To bring clarity to the word (ההיטב) that only occurs twice and both occurrences are in the Book of Dove, let's divert and search out a couple of words that will assist in this effort. That said, yes, it all depends on how you see it (smile). For example, in the verse above, 1 Samuel 24:4, the word (בעיניך) translated as "unto thee" occurs 67 times in the original text. Let's look at the second occurrence of this word (בעיניך) in Exodus 23:22-23.

Exodus 23:22-23 KJV: [22] But if thou shalt indeed obey his voice, and do all that I speak; then I will be an enemy *unto thine enemies* (את-בעיניך)[67], and an adversary unto thine adversaries.
[23] For *mine Angel* (מלאכי)[14] shall go before thee, and bring thee in unto the Amorites, and the Hittites, and the Perizzites, and the Canaanites, the Hivites, and the Jebusites: and I will cut them off.

The word (בעיניך) translated as *"unto thee"* in 1 Samuel 24:4 is translated as *"unto thine enemies"* in Exodus 22:22. And it also has Et (את) preceding the word. Wow, that's a big difference. David is given permission to do *"as he shall seem good unto Salvation* (את) *of thine enemy"* and David, whose name means Beloved, decides to simply cut a piece of material from the hem of his enemy's garment.

Oh, but wait, there is more! The word (מלאכי) translated as "mine Angel" in Exodus 23:23 is also translated as "Malachi". Yes, "Malachi" as in the Book of Malachi. The word "Malachi" only occurs once in the KJV, but it occurs 14 times in the original text. The word "angel" occurs 108 times in the KJV and is rarely capitalized as it is in this verse. Why is it capitalized? Wow, translating this word as "mine Angel" without additional information is far different than "Malachi"!

Traditions, Lies from Birth Volume 3 will search out the Book of Malachi.

So, why did we divert? Because we needed to see that word (ההיטב) translated as *"Doeth thou well"* is from the root noun (יטב) translated as *"shall seem good"*. Now we can add the meaning of the first two letters (הה). The word (ההיטב) means "Behold, behold shall seem good" or "Grace, grace shall seem good". Let's apply this to the modified verse.

Jonah 4:4 KJV: *Then said the* (ויאמר)[2,084] LORD, *Doest thou well* (ההיטב)[2] *to be angry* (חרה)[18]?

===============

Jonah 4:4 (Modified): *Then said the* (ויאמר)[2,084] LORD, *Grace, grace shall seem good* (ההיטב)[2] *to be* (לך)[965] *hot* (חרה)[18].

There is no doubt that the word (חרה) means hot. The past down tradition would have us believe that this verse was another expression of Jonah's disappointed that God had mercy on Nineveh. Jonah is not angry, he is hot! How do we explain that Dove is hot? How can grace seem good to be hot?

Let's search out Jonah 4:5

Jonah 4:5 KJV: So Jonah *went out of* (ויצא)[194] the city (מן-העיר), *and sat* (וישב)[240] *on the east* (מקדם)[22] side of the city, *and there made* (ויעש)[239] him a booth (סכה)[1], *and sat* (וישב)[240] *under it* (תחתיה)[17] *in the shadow* (בצל)[13], till he might see *what would become* (יהיה)[423] *of the city* (בעיר)[100].

Wait! So, Jonah was hot while he was in the city, right? And now, he goes out of the *city* and is sitting on the east side of the *city* and there made a sukkah or booth.

Nineveh, Fish Town, is referenced three times in this verse but not called by name and it's not called great. Why not? Do we really think it's a grammar issue (smile).

Again, he was hot and not angry, so he built a booth, a covering. The unique word (סכה) translated as "booth" is a HUGE TOPIC. Below are a few references to the word "booth".

- When the mixed multitude left Egypt, they camped at Sukkot which means booth and built booths (sukkahs) to shelter. That was the first time in the history of man that God tabernacled with man.
- There is a feast named Sukkot and it will be searched out in Volume 2.
- Mary and Joseph had to go to a booth (sukkah) during the birth of Christ.

What is more revealing is that this spelling of the Hebrew word (סכה) translated as booth is unique. Is it unique because it's Dove's Sukkah? How would you know from the English translations that this spelling of booth is unique in the original text? ***THIS WORD*** (סכה) ***IS A ONE HOUR LESSON!***

There are several variations of how "Booth" is referenced in the original Hebrew. The definition of the letters of the word (סכה) is, "Lean (ס) on the Covering (כ) to be Revealed (ה)." That said, does "to be Revealed" imply that there will be another covering in this story (smile)?

The Hebrew word (בצל) translated as "in the shadow" occurs 13 times in the original text and this is the last occurrence. This is the last shadow that will come from a covering built with hands. Think about that! This is the thirteenth covering and the thirteenth letter of the Hebrew AlefBet is the Mem (מ or ם) which represents a woman's womb. Is Jonah about to reveal a fourteenth covering, a covering made without hands? No way, right?

Jonah went to the east side to see "what becomes of the city". The east side is where our Savior was crucified and where our Savior will return. The city has already been judged and received God's mercy. Let's search out these words translated as "what becomes of the city" to determine what Jonah is waiting to see.

The word (בעיר) translated as "of the city" occurs 100 times in the original text and this is the last occurrence. Wait! The number 100 reminds us of "100 fold". Is Nineveh, Fish Town, an example of Matthew 13:8, the seed that brought forth "an hundredfold"?

The first letter of this word (בעיר) is the letter Mem (ב) and when it's the first letter it is translated as "in". Jonah is waiting to see something ***IN THE CITY***.

The Dove preached ***IN THE CITY***. The people listened and God repented of His wrath. Now Dove, the Spirit, is waiting to see what will become of HIM in the city. Will the next generation follow the ways of God? Will the next? Will the… What did Dove become in your city?

In Matthew 27:35-36 we gave people sitting down on the east side of the city watching… What became of our Savior in the city?

Matthew 27:35-36 KJV: [35] And they crucified him, and parted his garments, casting lots: that it might be fulfilled which was spoken by the prophet, They parted my garments among them, and upon my vesture did they cast lots. **[36] And sitting down they watched him there;**

Is it possible? Is the prophet Dove prophesying about the crucifixion?

In Chapter 1 the men on Jonah's boat didn't know Jonah. They were amazed that after they lifted Jonah up and hurled him into the sea that the wind

and waves calmed *and they were saved by doing what Dove told them to do*.
Likewise, the disciples didn't know Jesus when He calmed the waters. They
were amazed that they were saved when He said unto the sea, "Peace, be still."
Mark 35:39.

In Chapter 2 we have Jonah's intercessory prayer. Likewise, Jesus
prayed for His disciples. John 17:9-23. If Jonah Chapter 4 represents
prophesying of the crucifixion, then what was Chapter 3? It feels like we are
missing something (smile)!

What was Chapter 3's Nineveh story about? In Jonah Chapter 1 we
mentioned that the prophet Nahum's name translates to "Comforter". Surely
you knew we were going to revisit that, right? Let's look at the Book of
Comforter 1:1.

Nahum 1:1 KJV: The burden of Nineveh. The book of the vision of Nahum the
Elkoshite (האלקשי)[1].

Nineveh is also the burden of the prophet Comforter. Isn't this
beautiful!

Nahum is an Elkoshite. What is an Elkoshite? Well, good luck
retrieving understanding from our recently AI managed internet. The Hebrew
word translated as Elkoshite (האלקשי) is unique, only once in the original text.
Well, that doesn't help. Let's research the spelling of the Hebrew letters. The
first letter is the Hey (ה) which means "behold". The next two letters are El (אל)
which means "God". So, the first three letters mean "Behold the God of". The
last three letters of this word "קשי" occur two times in the original text,
Deuteronomy 9:27 and Ezekiel 2:4. In Deuteronomy 9:27 it is translated as
"stubbornness" and in Ezekiel 2:4 it is translated as "impudent". Let's pick the
synonym "obstinate" to represent both of those descriptions.

An obstinate person is someone that stubbornly refuses to change their
opinion despite attempts to persuade them. Comforter, the Elkoshite, the
prophet that God sent to those that are obstinate. Well, that describes our world
and evidently it described Nineveh. It says that Comforter has the "burden of
Fish Town".

What kind of a burden is this? The first time the word burden is used is
with the sons of Kohath who were burdened to physically carry the tabernacle
from one location to the next. That represents a physical burden. They were
physically burdened to transport the House where God dwelled with His people.

Hmm… Christ told his disciples to cast their nets, and they became full of fish, and they were burdened to get all the fish in the boat. Ok, how are those two stories related? Consider that Nineveh translated to English is "Fish Town". Glory! The AI powered internet would have you believe Nineveh's name is based on paganism. Now you know that the burden of Comforter (Nahum) was to save all the fish of the world. Glory!

God sent Dove to Fish Town. Does Jonah Chapter 3 resemble what we call The Great Commission, Matthew 28:19?

Glory to the King!

Don't get dizzy, we are about to do the "Jonah thing" again. Seems we are constantly having something new revealed about something we had already researched.

Notice that Jonah went out of the city. The word city is in the verse three times and the name Nineveh isn't mentioned. It seems that Nineveh is only great if Dove or God are coming or occupying.

Let's search out Jonah 4:6. Wow! Much is concealed in this verse.

Jonah 4:6 KJV: And the *Lord God* (יהוה-אלהים) *prepared* (וימן)[5] *a gourd* (קיקיון)[1], *and made it to come up* (ויעל)[118] **over** Jonah, *that it might be* (להיות)[67] a *shadow* (צל)[6] over his head, *to deliver* (להציל)[11] him *from his grief* (מרעתו)[3]. *So* (וישמח)[10] Jonah was *exceeding* (גדולה)[72] *glad* (שמחה)[35] *of the gourd* (על-הקיקיון)[4].

Because there is so much concealed, we will search out each word of the original text and after every 4-5 words we will apply the changes to our modified version of this verse. We will continue until the entire verse is revealed. That said, the chasm between the KJV translation and the original text continues to grow.

To assist in revealing the chasm and overcoming our objection to these changes, the first word we will search out is the Hebrew word (וישמח) translated as "So". If you search the interlinear section of the Blue Letter Bible, you will find that it translates this word as "So was glad" but in the verse it translates it as "So". Craziness! We are talking about the Word of God! How can they justify doing that?

The word "so" is in the KJV Old Testament 2,720 times, but this Hebrew word (וישמח) occurs 10 times in the original text. ***How do we reconcile this?***

Most of the Hebrew words translated in the last five verses of Jonah have significant variance with the original text. Luckily the error of translation becomes more and more obvious as we continue. That said, we will further expose and ***DEFEND*** the translators in Volume 2 of this book series.

Wait! Are we declaring that the Hebrew word (וישמח) translated as "So" only occurs ten times in the original text? Yes, the Hebrew word most commonly translated as "so" is the word (כן) and is first used in Genesis 1:7 and the word (כן) occurs 878 times in the original Hebrew text. Again, the Hebrew word (וישמח) translated as "So" in this verse occurs 10 times in the original text and this is the last occurrence! ***THIS IS CRAZINESS!*** Let's look at 1 Kings 5:7.

1 Kings 5:7 KJV: And it came to pass, when Hiram heard the words of Solomon, *that he rejoiced* (וישמח) greatly, and said, Blessed be the Lord this day, which hath given unto David a wise son over this great people.

The word (וישמח) means "He is rejoicing". This is a big deal!!! What is happening here? Is this an act of God concealing or is this another example of incomplete translation? Bottom line is that "He is rejoicing" is a huge chasm from "So".

Jonah 4:6 KJV: And the *Lord God* (יהוה-אלהים) *prepared* (וימן)[5] *a gourd* (קיקיון)[1], *and made it to come up* (ויעל)[118] **over** Jonah, *that it might be* (להיות)[67] a *shadow* (צל)[6] over his head, *to deliver* (להציל)[11] him *from his grief* (מרעתו)[3]. ~~So~~ ***And he is rejoicing*** (וישמח)[10] Jonah was *exceeding* (גדולה)[72] *glad* (שמחה)[35] *of the gourd* (על-הקיקיון)[4].

The word (וימן) translated as *"prepared"* occurs 5 times in the original text and is also translated as appointed in several translations. A meal is ***prepared*** but a cook is appointed or assigned. We will learn that the "gourd" was appointed but for now we will change prepared to appointed.

The Hebrew word (ויעל) translated as *"and made it to come up"* is in the original text 118 times and this is the last occurrence. It is translated in many ways, and they all resemble what is translated in this verse. We will go with what was translated.

We have emphasized the word (מעל) translated as "over" because it plays such a ***pivotal role*** in understanding this verse that we will search out later. Below is the current status of our work.

Jonah 4:6 KJV: And ***the Lord God*** (יהוה-אלהים) ~~*prepared*~~ *assigned* (וימן)[5] *a gourd* (קיקיון)[1], ***and made it to come up*** (ויעל)[118] **over** (מעל)[216] ***Jonah*** (ליונה)[1], *that it might be* (להיות)[67] *a shadow* (צל)[6] *over his head, to deliver* (להציל)[11] *him from his grief* (מרעתו)[3]. ~~*So*~~ ***And he is rejoicing*** (וישמח)[10], *Jonah was exceeding* (גדולה)[72] *glad* (שמחה)[35] *of the gourd* (על-הקיקיון)[4].

The uniqueness of the spelling of Jonah's (ליונה) name is because the Hebrew letter that represents authority (ל) has been added as the first letter of his name. Coincidence? Jonah is being given authority. Let's put that in memory and see if that authority reveals itself. That said, after reviewing 32 different English translations, none of them acknowledged that Jonah's name is spelled differently with the authority letter added to the beginning of his name. Below is the current status of our work.

Jonah 4:6 KJV: And ***the Lord God*** (יהוה-אלהים) ~~*prepared*~~ *assigned* (וימן)[5] *a gourd* (קיקיון)[1], ***and made it to come up*** (ויעל)[118] **over** (מעל)[216] ***Jonah to give him authority*** (ליונה)[1], *that it might be* (להיות)[67] *a shadow* (צל)[6] *over his head, to deliver* (להציל)[11] *him from his grief* (מרעתו)[3]. ~~*So*~~ ***And he is rejoicing*** (וישמח)[10], *Jonah was exceeding* (גדולה)[72] *glad* (שמחה)[35] *of the gourd* (על-הקיקיון)[4].

The Hebrew word (להיות) translated as "that it might be" is in the original text 67 times and is almost always translated as "to become to". Yes, that is a bit strange in English. The first example of "to become to" is Nimrod, the founder of Nineveh, "to become to" the people as a master. The next example is Elohim (God) "to become to" Abraham as Elohim. The next is Sarah "to become to" Abraham as pregnant. So, the "gourd" is going "to become to" Jonah as a shadow. This phrase "to become to" will be more friendly to read as we continue searching out the words of this verse.

The Hebrew word (צל) translated as "a shadow" occurs 6 times in the original text and this is the last occurrence. The word "shadow" occurs 77 times in the KJV 77. The real issue is that Jonah built a booth in the previous verse to provide himself with shade. What is the "gourd" doing? Where did the booth go? Let's look again.

Jonah 4:5 KJV: So Jonah went out of the city, and sat on the east side of the city, and there made him a **booth**, and sat under it in the **shadow** (בצל), till he might see what would become of (יהיה) the city (בעיר).

It says that he sat under the booth in the shadow until he might see what would become of the city. That said, after he witnesses what would become of the city, then he moved on from the booth. Right?

The two Hebrew words "become of (יהיה) the city (בעיר)" actually translate to "till he might see what would become of the shadow in the city". Yes, the Hebrew word (עיר) means "city" and the Hebrew word (בעיר) means "in the city". The Hebrew word (יהיה) is in the original text 423 times. This (יהיה) word means "he shall become" but a bit different. Is Jonah watching to see what "he shall become" in Fish Town? What has Dove become of in your town? In most towns Dove has become a sinner that rebelliously fled from God. In most towns, Dove repented in Chapter 2.

Did Dove sit under the booth to see what might become of the shadow? Let's search this out. Once again, we are going backwards in the Book of Jonah (smile). Let's look at Psalm 91:1.

Psalm 91:1 KJV: He that dwelleth in the secret place of the most High shall abide *under the shadow* (בצל) of the Almighty.

Isn't this beautiful? The Hebrew word (בצל) translated as "shadow" is the same word (בצל) in both verses. Since Jonah is "in the shade" under the booth he built with his own hands, does this add understanding to the mixed multitude that departed from Egypt and built booths with their own hands on the 3ʳᵈ day after leaving Egypt. Is Dove's booth in Jonah 4:5 a reference to the mixed multitude living under the shadow of the Almighty?

Yes, consider that in Jonah 4:5, he is in the shadow of something built with his own hands and in Jonah 4:6 he is in the shadow of something built without hands. Glory!

Now let's update verse six.

Jonah 4:6 (MODIFIED): And *the Lord God* (יהוה-אלהים) *assigned* (וימן)⁵ *a gourd* (קיקיון)¹, *and made it to come up* (ויעל)¹¹⁸ *over* (מעל)²¹⁶ *Jonah to give him authority* (ליונה)¹, *to become* (להיות)⁶⁷ *a shadow* (צל)⁶ *over* (על) *his head* (ראשו), *to deliver* (להציל)¹¹ *him from his grief* (מרעתו)³. ~~So~~ *And he is rejoicing* (וישמח)¹⁰, Jonah was *exceeding* (גדולה)⁷² *glad* (שמחה)³⁵ *of the gourd* (על-הקיקיון)⁴.

Yes, as we search out words, our modified version becomes confusion. Let's continue searching out more words and watch as it becomes clear.

Now we are ready to search out the two instances of the word "over" in this verse. Notice that the first instance is referencing when the "gourd" was assigned and at that moment of time it is ascending over Jonah. The first word (מעל) translated as "over" is different than the second occurrence (על). The word (מעל) occurs 216 times in the original text and is usually translated as "from over". The next occurrence of the word "over" reveals that the "gourd" has finished ascending and it is completely over his head. More evidence that this is true is that the last Hebrew spelling of the word translated as "gourd" begins with the letter Hey (ה) which means "behold" and that it can be seen because it is no longer ascending/coming up.

Let's update the verse and continue.

Jonah 4:6 (MODIFIED): And *the Lord God* (יהוה-אלהים) *assigned* (וימן)[5] *a gourd* (קיקיון)[1], *and made it to come up* (ויעל)[118] *from over* (מעל)[216] *Jonah to give him authority* (ליונה)[1], *to become* (להיות)[67] *a shadow* (צל)[6] *over* (על) *his head* (ראשו), *to deliver* (להציל)[11] him *from his grief* (מרעתו)[3]. ~~So~~ And he is rejoicing (וישמח)[10], Jonah was *exceeding* (גדולה)[72] *glad* (שמחה)[35] *of the gourd* (על-הקיקיון)[4].

Let's remove some the original text to make this easier to read.

Jonah 4:6 (MODIFIED): And *the Lord God assigned* a gourd (קיקיון)[1], *and made it to come up from over Jonah to give him authority*, *to become* a shadow over his head (ראשו), *to deliver* (להציל)[11] him (לו)[1,150] from his grief (מרעתו)[3]. And he is rejoicing (וישמח)[10], Jonah was *exceeding* (גדולה)[72] glad (שמחה)[35] of the gourd (על-הקיקיון)[4].

There are 594 variations of the phrase "to deliver" in the KJV, but the Hebrew word (להציל) translated as "to deliver" only occurs 11 times in the original text and this is the last occurrence. The first letter of this word is the letter Lamed (ל) which means authority but when it's the first letter it is translated as "to". The remaining letters spell the word (הציל) which occurs 10 times in the original text and in 1 Samuel 30:18 it is translated as "rescued". The said, the word (להציל) is translated as "to deliver" in the KJV, but several translations including the NKJV translate this word as "to rescue" which is more applicable. The word (להציל) could also mean "Authority (ל) to Rescue (הציל)".

This is not insignificant. The Hebrew word (לו) translated as "him" is in the original Hebrew text 1,150 times and almost always translated as "to him" as though something is given "to him". The word "him" is in the KJV 5,343 times. That said, the Hebrew word (אתו) is translated as "him" in Genesis 1:27 is not the same Hebrew word (לו) in Jonah 4:6. At the time this book was published, the latest version of the Blue Letter Bible says that the translation of this word (לו) is not available. Coincidence? The phrase "to him" means that something is being given to Dove. ***This is critical because*** when you combine "to him" with the word searched out that means "to rescue" then it reveals what authority Dove is given. The authority to rescue was given TO HIM.

The Hebrew word (מרעתו) translated as "from his grief" occurs three times in the original text (Jonah 4:6, Jeremiah 18:8, and Jeremiah 23:14).

Jeremiah 18:8: If that nation, against whom I have pronounced, turn *from their evil* (מרעתו), I will repent of the evil that I thought to do unto them.

Jeremiah 23:14: I have seen also in the prophets of Jerusalem an horrible thing: they commit adultery, and walk in lies: they strengthen also the hands of evildoers, that none doth return *from his wickedness* (מרעתו); they are all of them unto me as Sodom, and the inhabitants thereof as Gomorrah.

Do you see it? Jeremiah 18:8 is exactly what Jonah and Nineveh are demonstrating. Jonah is not a man being delivered of an evil sin. Jonah is a righteous prophet, revealing that "the gourd" has given him the authority to rescue others from their evil. Let's update the verse.

Jonah 4:6 (MODIFIED): And *the Lord God assigned* a gourd (קיקיון)[1], *and made it to come up from over Jonah to give him authority, to become* a *shadow over his head, to give him authority to rescue others from their evil. And he is rejoicing*, Jonah was *exceeding* (גדולה)[72] *glad* (שמחה)[35] *of the gourd* (על-הקיקיון)[4].

We only have three more words to search out before we search out the unique Hebrew word (קיקיון) translated as "gourd".

We have already searched out the Hebrew word (גדולה) translated as "exceeding". This the word "great to be revealed".

The word (שמחה) translated as "glad" occurs 35 times in the original text and the first occurrence is 1 Kings 1:40 where it is translated as "rejoiced". When you combine these two words, Jonah is not "exceedingly glad" but rather he is "greatly rejoicing". What's confusing about these two words is that the last letter of each word is the letter Hey (ה) which means that Jonah is greatly rejoicing about something yet to be revealed.

The Hebrew word (על) translated as "of" occurs 3,568 times in the original text and is almost always translated as "on" or "over".

Now, let's review the original KJV translation and compare it to the updated and modified version and see how these words might apply.

Jonah 4:6 KJV: And the Lord God prepared a gourd, and made it to come up **over** Jonah, that it might be a shadow over his head, to deliver him from his grief. So (וישמח) Jonah was exceeding glad of the gourd.

Jonah 4:6 (MODIFIED): And the Lord God assigned a *gourd* (קיקיון)[1], and it is ascending from over Jonah to become a shadow over his head, and to give him authority to rescue others from their evil. Jonah is rejoicing, and in the future, he will greatly rejoice over *the gourd* (הקיקיון)[4].

Before we search out the Hebrew word (קיקיון) translated as "gourd", is it obvious that it is a reference to our Savior? That said, we know that the spirit descends "like a dove" upon (over or on) Christ after His Baptism (in the future). ***Is this beautiful or is this wonderfully beautiful!***

So, imagine you are Jonah, and you are sitting on a hill on the east side of the city. You are in the sunshine and facing the sun. You see somebody walking up to you, but you can't tell who it is because the sun is blocking your vision. As they walk closer and their shadow ascends over you to block out the sun, you begin rejoicing because you think you know who it is. When you finally find yourself completely under their shadow, you recognize it's "the gourd" and now you are rejoicing greatly!

This is the story told many times in the Gospels. It's a common occurrence of Jesus in the gospels as he walked from town-to-town, and He was being revealed. He was constantly healing and loving, right? This is another Jonah and Jesus moment, right?

Below is Jonah 4:6 with all the Hebrew words used to translate the verse.

Now let's determine who/what is a gourd?

- The NIV has a footnote that says "The precise identification of this plant is uncertain; also in verses 7, 9 and 10."
- The NKJV has a footnote that says "Heb. kikayon, exact identity unknown."
- The NASB1995 translates this word as "a plant" and has a footnote that says "Probably a castor oil plant, and so in vv 7, 9 and 10"

The translations are simply incomplete. Yet another excuse to learn Hebrew (smile)! Do it! It's easy!

Jonah rejoiced greatly when he beheld the gourd. Wow, don't we wish we knew what this was (smile)! The Hebrew word (הקיקיון) translated as "the Gourd" occurs four times in the Book of Jonah. The spelling of the unique Hebrew word translated as gourd is (קיקיון). Notice that the last three letters (יון) of this word (קיקיון) are the first three letters of Jonah's (יונה) name.

Wait! The last letter of Jonah's name is the letter Hey (ה). Jonah is Dove to be Revealed. Jesus revealed Jonah! The Pharisees who were supposed to identify the Messiah when he came, didn't recognize Christ, and didn't know about Jonah. Jonah is revealing our Savior (the gourd), and our Savior revealed Jonah. Glory to the King!

The definition of the letters that spell the word (קיקיון) translated as "the gourd", pronounced KiKaYon is, "My Holiness(קי) is the Holiness (ק) of The Hand That Does Mighty Deeds (י) and The Straight Man with the Nail (ו) who brings Life (ן)" or "My Holiness is the Holiness of Yon (the dove)". Glory!

We are ready to search out Jonah 4:7...

Jonah 4:7 KJV: But God (האלהים) *prepared* (וימן)[5] *a worm* (תולעת)[11] when *the morning* (השחר)[11] *rose* (בעלות)[8] *the next day* (למחרת)[2], *and it smote* (ותך)[3] *the gourd* (את-הקיקיון)[4] *that it withered* (וייבש)[2].

The word (תולעת) translated as *"worm"* occurs 11 times in the original text and this is the last occurrence. Note that this worm smote the *"gourd"*, and it withered. The word (תולעת) is commonly translated as "worm" or "crimson".

Consider that the 12th occurrence of the word (תולעת) is our Savior covered in crimson during the crucifixion.

Again, the Hebrew word (וימן) translated as "prepared" is better translated as "appointed" or "assigned" and is translated as all three options in many translations.

The word "morning" occurs 214 times in the KJV, but the Hebrew word (השחר) translated as morning only occurs 11 times in the original text and this is the last occurrence. Coincidence? No way, right?

Again, in Hebrew the number eleven represents a covering and is considered "one short" of the number twelve which that represents authority or a government. Our Savior was beaten, and His body destroyed the morning of the day He was crucified. His body was covered with both crimson-colored dry blood and new flowing scarlet blood. These two colors represent the scarlet material of the tabernacle inner curtain that was double-dipped scarlet. Consider that the 12th occurrence, the fulfillment of these eleven occurrences of the word (השחר) translated as "morning", was the morning that our Savior established His government while being mocked, falsely accused, crucified, and not recognized by those who were appointed to make us aware of His coming.

To further prove the Hebrew Rule of Occurrences, let's search out the 10th occurrence of the word (השחר) translated as morning. As mentioned, several times, the tenth occurrence means "completion", it's the "It is Finished" occurrence. The 10th occurrence of this word (השחר) is in Psalm **22:0**. Before we explain verse **22:0**, let's recall that this the chapter that Jesus quoted while on the cross when He quoted, "My God, My God, …". We searched this out earlier in the Donkey Chapter. ***Check this out!***

Psalm 22:1 KJV: My God, my God, why hast thou forsaken me? why art thou so far from helping me, and from the words of my roaring?

Do you see it? Do you see the word "morning"? No, I don't see it either. Let's check another translation. Let's see if it is visible in the NKJV.

Psalm 22:1 NKJV: To the Chief Musician. Set to "The Deer of the **Dawn** (השחר)." A Psalm of David.
[1] My God, My God, why have You forsaken Me?
Why are You so far from helping Me,

Yes, the header of Psalm 22, we chose to call it **22:0** (smile) because it precedes the first verse and is translated from the original Hebrew text. It is skipped in the KJV and several other translations. The KJV omitted the translation of 55 headers in the Book of Psalms that exist in the original text. Literally, the header in the NKJV is translated from the original Hebrew text and is not included in the KJV. Within the header is the 10th occurrence of the Hebrew word (השחר) translated as "dawn" which is the same word translated as "morning" in Jonah 4:7. Does that matter? Remember, this is the same chapter of Psalm that proved our Father did not forsake his Son.

What's the significance about this word "dawn" being in the header? The number ten in Hebrew means completion which is synonymous with it being finished. Psalm 22:1 is the 10th time this word (השחר) occurs in the original text and the entire chapter is prophesying about the crucifixion. Psalm 22:1 is the 10th occurrence and Jonah 4:7 is the 11th occurrence where we witnessed a covering. Could our Savior's crucifixion be the 12th occurrence and represents Jesus declaring His Kingdom (government), John 18:35-36?

John 18:35-36 KJV: [35] Pilate answered, Am I a Jew? Thine own nation and the chief priests have delivered thee unto me: what hast thou done?
[36] Jesus answered, My kingdom is not of this world: if my kingdom were of this world, then would my servants fight, that I should not be delivered to the Jews: but now is my kingdom not from hence.

Jonah 4:7 KJV: But God (האלהים) *prepared* (וימן)[5] *a worm* (תולעת)[11] when *the morning* (השחר)[11] *rose* (בעלות)[8] *the next day* (למחרת)[2], *and it smote* (ותך)[3] *the gourd* (את-הקיקיון)[4] *that it withered* (וייבש)[2].

Notice this is the only time that the Hebrew word for gourd is preceded by Alef-Tav (את). Why? Could it be because the gourd is smitten? The Hebrew word (ותך) translated as "smote" is in the original text three times, two of those in the Book of Jonah. The third time is in Psalm 10:7.

Psalm 10:7 KJV: His mouth is full of cursing and deceit and fraud (ותך): under his tongue is mischief and vanity.

We know that Jesus was smitten during the night of the mock trial. Is this Hebrew word another link of "the gourd" with Jesus?

We know that after the mock trial, Christ was "smote" the morning of the ***next day*** (למחרת), the day that He gave himself by His own hands. He was not sacrificed, rather by His own hand He gave himself. The word (למחרת) translated as "next day" only occurs twice in the original text. The other occurrence is 1 Chronicles 29:21.

1 Chronicles 29:21 KJV: And they sacrificed sacrifices unto the Lord, and offered burnt offerings unto the Lord, ***on the morrow*** (למחרת) after that day, even a thousand bullocks, a thousand rams, and a thousand lambs, with their drink offerings, and sacrifices in abundance for all Israel:

We have now navigated more than 100 pages of coincidences, right (smile)? Now we see more of the omniscience of our creator. He has so many threads of revelation. He is using occurrences of the same word eleven times, twelve times, and now two times. This occurrence is not simply referring to a sacrifice, but it includes sacrificing exactly 1,000 Bulls, 1,000 Rams, and 1,000 Lambs. Could the three thousand sacrifices represent three thousand years after the crucifixion which begins the great eighth day, the beginning of eternity? Coincidence?

In defense of all translators that provided translations prior to having the electronic research tools available today, how would they provide the research we are searching out? They didn't have these tools. It's practically impossible to provide these analytics. How would they know how they had previously translated a particular word?

But what about the new translations being published? Should they include it? Are they just supposed to translate without sharing these understandings? When the next new translation is published, should we expect to find more clarity about Dove, or Donkey or Psalm 22 or Lamb? Should we expect the nouns to be translated, and the Book of Jonah be named the Book of Dove? Should we expect to learn that "Behold the KikaYon" conceals "Behold Christ"? How much of what we are learning should we expect "a translation" to be accountable to provide? Yes, the questions are limitless!

A child reads the KJV Bible three times before he/she was 13 years old because the KJV is all that was available. They learned that Simon Barjona is Simon Son of Dove almost four decades later. Was it the child's fault or the translators? ***Only judgment will answer that question AND THAT CHILD IS SCREAMING INJUSTUCE!***

Oh my! How much do we search out before we begin seeing Dove without considering the traditional lies passed down before we were born? Many have witnessed that the embedded lies hinder revelation even after researching the original text of the Book of Dove many times. It is nearly impossible to rid our minds of the embedded false teaching. It's as though the divine space in our soul for truth was willfully invaded by our loyalty to family and church tradition. No, that doesn't get "cleaned up" without deliberate effort.

We have all heard teaching about the Holy Ghost or Holy Spirit depending on your denomination. Thankfully all denominations teach of the meekness and beauty of the Spirit. The Book of Dove is not about Dove, it's about the lives that Dove impacts, the lives that Dove loves, the lives that Dove willfully gives his life to save, the lives that Dove "fled" from God knowing he would impact. Again, Dove is not Yeshua, Dove is sent to teach us about the works of the Spirit.

The chasm between the translations and the truth doesn't get any wider than it gets in the last three verses of this Book of Dove. Glory to the King!

Let's search out Jonah 4:8.

Jonah 4:8 KJV: [8] *And it came to pass* (ויהי)[816], when *the sun* (השמש)[91] *did arise* (כזרח)[2], that God *prepared* (וימן)[5] a *vehement* (חרישית)[1] *east* (קדים)[28] wind; and *the sun* (השמש)[91] *beat* (ותך)[3] upon the head of Jonah, that he *fainted* (ויתעלף)[1], *and wished* (וישאל)[23] *in himself* (את-נפשו)[87] *to die* (למות)[35], and said (ויאמר)[2,084], *It is better* (טוב)[300] *for me to die* (מותי)[8] *than to live* (מחיי)[2].

This verse seems familiar...

The sun rose that morning when our Savior was beaten. There was a mighty east wind as the sun beat upon the head of our Savior as He believed it was good for Him to die for those He loved.

If we remove the first and the last letter from the unique word (ויתעלף) translated as *"fainted"*, the remaining letters (יתעל) is a unique word translated as *"lifted himself up"* in Jeremiah 51:3. The two letters removed (וף) do not spell a valid word but the definition of the letters is, "The Straight Up Man with the Nail (ו) is Speaking (ף)". Dove lifted himself up and wished himself to die while speaking and said, *"It's better for me to die than the **lives of me**"*. Coincidence? Is Dove becoming clearer? Is Dove being hot becoming clearer?

There are several ways to relate Jonah's three declarations wishing he were dead to the crucifixion story. In Matthew 26:39-44, Jesus is praying in the Garden with His disciples. Is our Savior's prayer for the cup to pass from Him three times similar to Jonah's request? In Luke 22:44, the second time Jesus prayed for the cup to pass from him, his sweat was as it were great drops of blood falling to the ground. The second time Jonah declares he is better dead than alive, he "fainted".

Once again, we have the word (חרה) translated as "angry". Let's find out why Jonah is hot and why it is good that he is hot. That just doesn't make sense!

The Hebrew word translated as "vehement (חרישית)" is unique, only once in the Hebrew text. The key here is that since this word is unique, then the east wind is unlike any in the history of the Bible. The definition of the letters that spell the Hebrew word translated as "vehement" is, "The Protected (ח) Prince (ר) Whose Hand Does Mighty Deeds (י) was Destroyed (ש) By His Own Hand (י) on the Cross (ת)". Wow! The definition of the letters that spell this wind suggest it occurred during the crucifixion and it's from the east.

The phrase "*It is better (טוב) for me to die (מותי) than to live (מחיי)*" is identical to Jonah 4:3. Recall it means "*it is good (טוב) from the death of me (מותי) from of lives of (מחיי)*".

Let's search out Jonah 4:9.

Jonah 4:9 KJV: [9] And God said (ויאמר)[2,084] to Jonah, *Doest thou well (ההיטב)*[2] to be *angry* (חרה)[18] *for* (על) the *gourd* (הקיקיון)[4]? And he said, *I do well* (היטב)[9] *to be angry* (חרה)[18], even unto *death* (מות)[125].

Once again, the Lord is speaking and not asking a question.

We have two occurrences of the word (חרה) translated as "angry" which means "hot". Is there any resemblance to our Dove being hot, our Savior being hot, and the red heifer burning in the fire?

Jonah 4:9 (Modified): [9] And God said (ויאמר)[2,084] to Jonah, *Grace, grace shall seem good (ההיטב)*[2] *to be hot* (חרה)[18] *for* (על) *grace is my holiness, the holiness of Dove* (הקיקיון)[4]? And he said, *grace is good* (היטב) *to be hot* (חרה)[18] *unto those from the death of me* (עד-מות)[125].

Let's search out Jonah 4:10.

Jonah 4:10 KJV: Then said the LORD, _Thou hast had pity_ (חסת)[1] on the _gourd_ (הקיקיון), for the which thou hast _not - laboured_ (לא-עמלת)[1] (בו)[365], _neither_ (ולא) _madest it grow_ (גדלתו)[1]; _which came_ (היה)[345] _up in - a night_ (שבן-לילה[83])[1], _and perished_ (אבד)[30] _in a night_ (ובן-לילה[83])[35]:

The word (בו) occurs 365 times and is not translated. The word (בו) means "in him".

Earlier we searched out the word (אבן) which means "Stone" and we learned how the first two letters (אב) spell the word that means "Father" while the last two letters (בן) spell the word that means son. The unique word (שבן) is translated as "up in". The first two letters (שב) spell the word that means "return" and the last two letters (בן) spell the word that means "son". The word (שבן) means "The return of the son". Yes, He did ascend forty days after the resurrection so "up in" is applicable but the translators have us believing this is a plant or a vine that came up and there is no reference that this is the **return of the Son**.

Look and see that the word (ובן) is not translated. The word (ובן) occurs 35 times and means "and son of".

Isn't it awesome that the word (אבד) translated as perished occurs 30 times in the original text? The number thirty represents betrayal. The first two letters (אב) spell the word "father", and the last two letters (בד) spell the word "linen". The word translated as perished also means "Father's linen".

Also, notice that the word (היה) is translated _"which came"_. Some interlinear apps declare that the word (היה) means "came up" or "came in". The word (היה) occurs 345 times and is mostly translated as "he became" or "is become". Let's look at Genesis 3:22.

Genesis 3:22 KJV: And the Lord God said, Behold, the man _is become_ (היה) as one of us, to know good and evil: and now, lest he put forth his hand, and take also of the tree of life, and eat, and live for ever:

The word (גדלתו) translated as "madest it grow" is unique. If we remove the last letter the remaining word (גדלת) occurs seven times and the seventh occurrence is Psalms 104:1.

Psalm 104:1 KJV: Bless the Lord, O my soul. O Lord my God, *thou art* very *great* (גדלת); thou art clothed with honour and majesty.

Let's apply our research as well as relocate the words into the order from the original text into the modified version.

Jonah 4:10 KJV: Then said the LORD, <u>*You protect and lean on the covenant*</u>, (חסת)[1], *grace is My holiness, the holiness of Dove* (הקיקיון), for the which thou hast *not* - <u>*laboured*</u> (לא-עמלת)[1] *in Him* (בו), <u>*neither madest Him a great*</u> (גדלתו)[1] <u>*Son that returned in*</u> - *a night* (שבן-לילה[83])[1] which <u>*He became*</u> (היה)[345] *Son of night* (ובן-לילה[83])[35] *and perished* (אבד)[30].

The Last Verse of the Book of Dove!
This is where it all comes together!
Take your time! Enjoy this! Enjoy each revelation!
Don't try to memorize,
enjoy it one understanding at a time!

Jonah 4:11 KJV: And should not I spare (אחוס)[3] Nineveh, that great (הגדולה)[31] city, wherein are more than sixscore thousand persons that cannot discern between their right hand (ימינו)[30] and their left hand (לשמאלו)[2]; and also much cattle (ובהמה)[17].

This verse has words that are screaming for attention. The Hebrew words translated in the phrase, "*more than sixscore thousand persons that cannot discern between their right hand and their left hand; and also much cattle*" must be searched out. This phrase just doesn't sound right and truly doesn't make sense. It's worded as though God is making a joke about the Nineveh's lack of intelligence. That can't be true, right? Surely this book doesn't end on that note. So much has been revealed! Let's finish searching out the Book of Dove.

WE MUST SEARCH THIS OUT!

The Hebrew word (ימינו) translated as *"their right hand"* is in the original text 30 times. The Hebrew words for "Right (ימינו) Hand (יד)" is two words (יד ימינו). In Hebrew it reads *"hand (יד) to the right of him (ימינו)"*. So, the phrase "their right hand" and "their left hand" should be "to the right of him" and to the left of him". Let's update the verse...

210

Jonah 4:11 (Modified): And should not I spare (אחוס)[3] Nineveh, that great (הגדולה)[31] city, wherein are more than sixscore thousand (משתים עשרה רבו) persons that cannot discern between <u>the one to the right of him and the one on the left of him</u>; and also much cattle (ובהמה)[17].

Now let's search out "sixscore thousand". My apologies but Hebrew does not measure by scores (20's), that is definitely influenced by the British translators. Ok, so here is the number in Hebrew:

(משתים עשרה רבו)

The Hebrew words are translated as Two (משתים), Ten (עשרה), and Ten Thousand (רבו). So, to get 120,000, they added (2 + 10) and then multiply that by 10,000 to get 120,000.

The first word (רבו) we will search out is translated as "Ten Thousand". This word (רבו) occurs 23 times in the original text and the first occurrence is Genesis 26:22.

Genesis 26:22 KJV: And he removed from thence, and digged another well; and for that *they strove* (רבו) not: and he called the name of it Rehoboth; and he said, For now the LORD hath made room for us, and we shall be fruitful in the land.

Wait! The Hebrew word (רבו) translated as the number "10,000" is translated as *"they strove"*?

The 2nd occurrence is Numbers 20:13 and it's translated as "strove".

The 3rd occurrence 1 Samuel 25:10 … "there be many".

We can research each occurrence, but when done we will know that this is not how you spell the number 10,000 in Hebrew. Below are the numbers 5,000 to 10,000.

5,000	חמשת אלפים	kha-me-shet a-la-fim
6,000	ששת אלפים	she-shet a-la-fim
7,000	שבעת אלפים	shi-vat a-la-fim
8,000	שמונת אלפים	shmo-nat a-la-fim
9,000	תשעת אלפים	tshat a-la-fim
10,000	עשרת אלפים	a-<u>se</u>-ret a-la-fim

Let's look at Judges 1:4.

Judges 1:4 KJV: And Judah went up; and the Lord delivered the Canaanites and the Perizzites into their hand: and they slew of them in Bezek *ten thousand* (עשרת אלפים) men.

The word (רבו) translated as "10,000" is also translated as quarrel, strove, many, contend, and… and… Let's agree on "contended". Let's continue and see how this plays out. So, now we must remove the "10,000" number from this verse. Now, instead of 120,000, the number is twelve. Coincidence? Let's make the change and see where it leads us.

Jonah 4:11 (Modified): *And should not I* (ואני)[179] *spare* (אחוס)[3] Nineveh, that great (הגדולה)[31] city, *wherein are* (בה[288]-יש[90]) *more than* (הרבה) *twelve* (עשרה[191]-משתים[1]) *contending* (רבו)[23] *for persons* (אדם)[367] *that* (אשר)[367] *cannot discern* (ידע[30]-לא[3,323]) **between the one to the right of him** (בין[30]-ימינו[172]) **and the one on the left of him** (לשמאלו)[2]; *and also much* (רבה)[48] *cattle* (ובהמה)[17].

Are you seeing this? What is more enlightening is that the number two (משתים) in this verse is unique in the original text. How is that possible? It's unique because the first letter which is a Mem (מ) was added. The Mem (מ) adds the preposition "from" to the noun that it precedes. So, the "two and ten" in this verse is more accurately translated as "from the twelve". More proof that this is true is that the first occurrence of the numbers two and ten is in Genesis 5:8 where it tells us that Shem lived 9*12* years. Let's update the verse again.

Jonah 4:11 (Modified): *And should not I* (ואני)[179] *spare* (אחוס)[3] Nineveh, that great (הגדולה)[31] city, *wherein are* (בה[288]-יש[90]) *more than* (הרבה) **from the twelve** (עשרה[191]-משתים[1]) *contending* (רבו)[23] *for persons* (אדם)[367] *that* (אשר)[367] *cannot discern* (ידע[30]-לא[3,323]) **between the one to the right of him** (בין[30]-ימינו[172]) **and the one on the left of him** (לשמאלו)[2]; *and also much* (רבה)[48] *cattle* (ובהמה)[17].

We have already searched out the word (ואני) translated as "And I". It means "And I AM" (smile).

Now let's search out the word (ובהמה) translated as "cattle". Understand that "to the right of him" and "to the left of him" are both singular but "cattle" is plural. After searching out all 17 occurrences in the original text we found that all of them translate as "beast" not cattle. Let's look at the first occurrence of this word in the original text, Leviticus 27:25.

Leviticus 27:28 KJV: Notwithstanding no devoted thing, that a man shall devote unto the Lord of all that he hath, both of man *and beast* (ובהמה), and of the field of his possession, shall be sold or redeemed: *every devoted thing is most holy unto the Lord*.

First, notice that anything devoted to the Lord is MOST HOLY unto the Lord. Some translations call these devoted things the "holy of holies" to the Lord. Notice that the <u>last</u> letter of this Hebrew word (ובהמה) translated as "beast" is the letter Hey (ה). Whatever this word means, it also means that its true meaning *has not yet been revealed*. What is even more special is that this word without the letter Hey (ה) is the unique word (ובהמ) and only occurs in Malachi 2:17 where it is translated as *"he delighteth in them"*.

Visualize your Savior on the Cross. Visualize the man to the right of him and the man to the left of him. Now visualize one of the apostles explaining the many sacrifices made by the man in the middle and how He delights in anything that we devote to Him (smile).

Let's close our study of the Book of Jonah with one last update of Jonah 4:11.

Jonah 4:11 (Modified): *And should not I AM spare* **Fish Town** *(Nineveh), that great city, wherein are many from the twelve contending for those that cannot discern between the one to the right of him and the one on the left of him; and the one that is delighted in those devoted to Him that will be revealed.*

Glory to the King!

Chapter 21 Ruth - Friend

Can you imagine the Word of God declaring you to be His friend? Unfathomable! Well, there are several examples of God's friends. So many that we will not attempt naming all of them.

For many, the most boldly declared friends of God are the twelve disciples. In addition to having the title "The Twelve Disciples" they are also eternally memorialized in the wall of New Jerusalem.

Revelation 21:14 KJV: And the wall of the city had twelve foundations, and in them the names of the twelve apostles of the Lamb.

There are some friends of God that come as a surprise when we learn of the closeness of their friendship. There should be no debate that if your name is written on the gates of New Jerusalem, then you are one of God's closest friends.

Revelation 21:12 KJV: And had a wall great and high, and had twelve gates, and at the gates twelve angels, and names written thereon, which are the names of the twelve tribes of the children of Israel:

The stories of the twelve sons of Jacob range from brotherly love to extreme family dysfunctionality. The Bible tells of the mischief of these men. We can quickly recall the sinful stories of Rueben, Simeon, Levi, Judah, and Benjamin. That said, we can also recall the amazing story of Joseph. The sons of Israel don't require an introduction, many of the books that share their most amazing stories are no longer in the Canon, our Bible. We can easily search the Bible and read the embarrassment of Rueben but what we don't know is the amazing stories of Rueben. Those stories are shared in what is now called historical, non-Biblical text. Many of us have read those stories. Stories equally as amazing as those of the twelve apostles and provide understanding to their names being memorialized in Revelation 21:12.

There are many Biblical references to friends of God.

James 2:23 KJV: And the scripture was fulfilled which saith, Abraham believed God (יהוה), and it was imputed unto him for righteousness: and he was called the Friend of God (יהוה).

Isaiah 41:8 KJV: But thou, Israel, art my servant, Jacob whom I have chosen, the seed of Abraham my friend (אהבי).

Ruth 4:10 KJV: Moreover Ruth (את-רות) the Moabitess, the wife of Mahlon, have I purchased to be my wife, to raise up the name of the dead upon his inheritance, that the name of the dead be not cut off from among his brethren, and from the gate of his place: ye are witnesses this day.

Once again we have more than one Hebrew word translated into the same English word. Notice that the Hebrew word referenced with Abraham is not the same as Ruth whose name means Friend.

Note to my kids that will hopefully read this one day. *Come on kids, your dad simply did not know this while you were in the house. Whatever version of this movie you have watched during my life, simply add these 15 seconds to the movie and purchase another ticket.* My apologies for the personal insertion.

Ruth's name in Ruth 4:10 (את-רות) provides another intro to the Hebrew word Et (את). Imagine yourself at church, the worship has just ended, and the Pastor gets behind the pulpit and says, *"If you will turn with me into the Word of God (יהוה) to the Book of Friend chapter four. We will begin reading in verse ten. This is the first time that Friend's name is preceded with the First and the Last (את) stamp of our Savior. Prior to this verse, Friend's name was not preceded with His stamp. Notice also that this is the verse where Boaz declares that he has redeemed her."* Though it is 100% accurate, it's not likely that it has ever been shared behind a pulpit.

So, we have two people in the Bible referred to as a friend of God (יהוה). One is Abraham whom we know well, and the other is Ruth (רות), the Moabitess. Most Christians are not aware of the origin of a Moabitess. A Moabitess is a woman from Moab which is a city named after the incestual relationship between Lot and his oldest daughter. Moab is synonymous for Sin. Ruth is not from the tribes of Israel but was married to Mahlon whose mother and father were both from Bethlehem. Now let's research the definition of the Hebrew letters of these two Hebrew words translated as Friend.

The word translated as friend in the Abraham story is *Aebi* (אהבי). The definition of the word derived from the Hebrew letters is "God (א) Reveals (ה) His House (ב) Where His Hands do Mighty Deeds (י)."

Isn't that exactly what Yahweh (God יהוה) used Abraham for? God will bless them that bless Abraham and curse them that curse Abraham. Pretty sure that was a personal promise to Abraham and his seed. Christians are grafted into the seed of Abraham; therefore, those promises are for Christians as well. Glory to the King!

Ruth's name translated to English is the word, Friend. The definition derived from the Hebrew letters is, "The Prince of Heaven (ר) is the Straight-up Man with the Nail (ו) that fulfilled His Covenant (ת)." There are many acceptable variations of the revelation sentence for the word Friend.

Ruth the Moabitess is a gentile woman from the land of sin. She is the Great Grandmother of King Beloved (David).

Chapter 22 Tower

There is a town named Migdol (מגדל) which is where Moses stood when God (יהוה) parted the waters and the mixed multitude (all nations) crossed over on dry land. We are very familiar with the Crossing of the Red Sea story, but few are familiar with the name of the town where Moses stood and even fewer are familiar with its significance.

There is another very familiar New Testament story about a lady named Mary who was the first to witness that Jesus was not in the tomb. Until learning Hebrew and the significance of the town named Migdol (מגדל), it's not likely that you would consider the extent of the privilege of being the first to witness our Savior's Resurrection granted to Mary. Because there are so many women in the New Testament named Mary, rarely is this Mary's name mentioned without including the town she is from. She is commonly referenced as Mary Magdalene. Many Christians attend church for decades believing Magdalene to be her last name. Mary Magdalene is Mary from Magdala. People from Magdala are called Magdalene's. Hebrew studies will reveal that Magdala is the Aramaic name of the town and the Hebrew word for Magdala is Migdol (מגדל).

Now we have two of the most well-known people of scripture that are both associated with a town by the same name, Migdol. One is in the Old Testament, and one is in the New Testament. By now we know that the link is concealed within the revelations of the Hebrew letters that spell Migdol. But before revealing that understanding let's consider something very special when comparing these two people.

Moses's name in Hebrew is Moshe (משה) which means "To Draw Out". His name spelled backwards is Hashem (השמ) which means "The (ה) Name (שמ)". Mary Magdalene on the other hand is described as a woman with seven devils. Because seven is the number that represents perfection, let's view her description as being the perfect sinner. Mary had the perfect number of devils. Could you possibly choose two people further apart on the spectrum of holiness?

God (יהוה) chose Moses (משה) to lead the people out of Egypt which is commonly referred to as "The World". And He chose the perfect sinner to be the first to observe that His son had left this world.

The definition of the Hebrew letters that spell Migdol (מגדל) is,

Those Born of Flesh (Womb) (מ) Receive Wealth (ג)
From the Door (ד) of Him who has Authority(ל)

The Moses, Mary, and Migdol story could make a great sermon. The stories of Migdol provide more proof that Jesus is the same yesterday, today, and forever.

This story has additional revelations when you research the two Hebrew words spelled by the first two letters and the last two letters. The first two letters spell Mig (מג) which occurs twice in the original text and seems to be related to great wealth. The last two letters spell Dol (דל) which occurs twenty-one times and is translated as poor. An alternative definition of the Hebrew letters is, "For those born (מ) of the flesh to become rich (ג), they must walk through a door (ד) that leads to becoming poor in spirit, giving authority (ל) of life to the Savior (ישוע)."

Numbers 33:1-7 reveals that Moses encamped at Migdol in Egypt on the 3rd Day after leaving Rameses. Mary from Migdol in the promised land visited the tomb on the 3rd Day. These two events took place on the exact same date on the calendar. Coincidence?

Chapter 23 Yahweh

The original Hebrew holds amazing revelation about the name of God, Yahweh (יהוה). The word Yahweh (יהוה) is in the Hebrew Old Testament 6,007 times. The Hebrew word Elohim (אלהים) is in Hebrew scriptures 680 times and is also translated as God or Lord, including in Genesis 1:1.

The definition of the Hebrew letters that spell Yahweh is,

"The Hand(י) Reveals(ה), the Nail(ו) Reveals (ה)"

Is there an undisputable link between His name and Jesus on the cross? Many of us recall watching the movie "The Greatest Story Ever Told". Remember the scene where they hung the sign over his head? Were you aware that it was in three languages? The sign read "Jesus the Nazarene King of the Jews". Only the Gospel of John provides any evidence that there was contention between the chief priest trying to get the wording of the sign changed. Both the scriptures and the movie draw your attention away from what is hidden in the Hebrew letters of that sign. Bring your focus only to what the sign says. Below is that sign in Hebrew.

ישוע הנצרי ומלך היהודים

Do you see it? God (יהוה) conceals his glory in many ways within the original Hebrew words and letters. One of those is hiding a word within the first letters of words within a phrase. Let's look at the words of the sign again and as you can see, we have emphasized what the chief priest saw that created the contention in the Gospel of John.

יׁשוע הנצרי וׁמלך היהודים

Now it is more obvious (smile). Yet another instance where Jesus, his Hebrew name being Yeshua's (ישוע) and the first word of the sign, is identified and revealed for everyone that looked upon Him. The sign reads "Yeshua King of the Jews". The Father, who never forsakes His Son, has his name concealed within the first Hebrew letter of each word of the sign above Jesus's head. This form of concealing understanding is commonly known within the Hebrew community. The chief priests were not offended by Jesus being called "King of the Jews" but rather they didn't want the name Yahweh (יהוה) revealed on the cross.

Chapter 24 Yeshua

Yeshua (ישוע) - The Hebrew name of Jesus

The last Hebrew word we will search out in Volume 1 is Yeshua (ישוע), Jesus's name in Hebrew. Is it possible to teach on The Name Above All Names and do it justice? Probably not.

Before searching out the name Yeshua, let's first understand from where the name Jesus was derived. Jesus is ***derived*** from the Roman Catholic Latin[1] Iesus. The Roman Catholic Latin Iesus is ***derived*** from the Ancient Greek[2] Ιεσους. The Ancient Greek Ιεσους is the ***derived*** Hellenized[3] version of the Aramaicized[4] Hebrew[5] name Yeshua. The English name Jesus is ***derived*** from five languages. Decide for yourself if ***derived*** implies it was ***translation or transliteration***.

Jesus's Hebrew name is Yeshua. Yeshua translated into English is Salvation. Imagine substituting the word Salvation everywhere you see the word Jesus in scripture. Initially it would be very difficult but likely after repetitive reading it would become easier and likely even more understandable. Now, understand that the disciples and everyone in the Bible that knew Hebrew **new that they were calling Him by the name "Salvation"**.

Before continuing, let's once again review the sign that was placed above Yeshua while He was on the cross.

יֵשׁוּעַ הַנָּצְרִי וַמֶלֶךְ הַיְהוּדִים

This time Yeshua's name is in bold and larger font. The sign was translated earlier as "Yeshua King of the Jews". When His name is translated to English as we have done the other words, the sign reads "Salvation King of the Jews". Our Salvation was lifted up on a cross made from a Cedar Tree. Cedar means the Father (God א) and His Son (ר) are Perfect (ז). Tree means See (ע) Righteousness (צ). Our Salvation was lifted up on Cedar Tree cross that reveals the Father and the Son are Perfect and Righteous. Glory to the King!

Let's review the Hebrew letters that spell Yeshua. The first letter of Yeshua (ישוע) is the Hebrew letter Yod (י), and this letter represents the hand of God (יהוה) that does mighty deeds. As you can see, it is also the first letter of God's name, Yahweh. The second letter of Yeshua (ישוע) is the Shin (ש), and this letter represents destruction. The third letter of Yeshua (ישוע) is the Vav (ו),

and this letter represents a straight-up man with a nail. The fourth and last letter of Yeshua (ישוע) is the Ayin (ע), and this letter represents an eye. The definition of the letters that spell the word (ישוע) Yeshua is, "By His own hand that does mighty deeds (י) He was destroyed (ש) and is the straight-up man with the nail (ו) for everyone to see (ע)". This is Salvation. This is a good time to restate the definition of His Father's name, Yahweh, "The Hand (י) Reveals (ה), the Nail (ו) Reveals (ה)". What a message!

Earlier we learned that the Resurrection story is concealed within the Old Testament Gilgal story. No surprise that story includes Joshua (יהושע - Yehoshua), which sounds and is spelled very similar to Yeshua. In the teaching about Gilgal we learned how the Resurrection story is concealed in this story of Joshua taking God's people into the promised land. In Hebrew there are many words that translate to English as Salvation. The name Joshua and Hosea are two examples that we will search out later. That said, Salvation spelled with the exact spelling as Yeshua is only in the Hebrew scriptures nineteen times and only in the Book of Ezra (עזרא) whose name means Help and the Book of Nehemiah (נחמיה) whose name means God Comforts.

The original Hebrew text validates the Salvation of the Gospels!

Glory to the King!

Gal – Reveal (Documentation)

This will seem like documentation and education, but it is a privilege and to share *"The Honor of Kings"*. God knows how much joy it was having this revealed and then packaging it for your pleasure. That said, it is the analytical documentation proving the results of the research. Enjoy! Read and enjoy as you would a church service. Do your best not to impose memorizing or learning but rather enjoy it as though you are fellowshipping with the Word.

If you recall from Chapter One, we shared that the word "formed" is in the KJV thirty-one times. We didn't go through the exercise of providing a count of how many different Hebrew words were translated as "formed". That said, because we are revealing the concealed story of the resurrection in the Old Testament, it is necessary to provide all the documentation that got us here.

Many describe learning each letter in Hebrew as milk, and each word as meat. As mentioned earlier, each Hebrew letter has 1) a definition which provides a depth of meaning, 2) a word (generally three letters) that is enunciated exactly like the letter and adds further clarity of understanding, and 3) a numeric value. The 1st letter of Hebrew is the Alef and the 2nd is the Bet, so when you combine the first two letters of the Hebrew you get the word "Alef Bet" which is where English gets the word Alphabet.

There are amazing internet videos that provide an awesome study of each Hebrew letter. There are 22 letters so in less than 50 hours you can learn the Hebrew AlefBet. It is truly that easy. And, like English, once you know the letters, you can immediately read the language. But what is amazing is that the definition of the Hebrew word is within the combined definition of the letters. The Creator's language is BEYOND GENIUS. Now let's review the meaning of the two Hebrew letters in the spelling of Gal (גל) and the concealed revelations of this word.

One of the internet search engines translates Gal being the word "wave". Many of us utilize various search engines to get a quick translation of a particular word from English to Hebrew or visa-versa. Realize that the information provided from a search engine is nothing more or less than another translator using technology to provide yet another translation. Today, one of these search engines openly declares that it accesses the latest AI (Artificial Intelligence) tools which again, is nothing but another translation. It's a struggle forcing the interpretation of Gal to be Wave. Well, thank you God for your heavenly language which provides us the definition of a word by researching the definition of the letters that spell the Word. Yes, Hebrew sounds like a difficult language but as we continue, you will see that it is truly a language of the heart and requires minimal cerebral assistance.

Hebrew is read right to left so the first letter of the word Gal (גל) is Gimel (ג) which means Camel or Wealth. The last letter is the Lamed (ל) which means Authority or Shepherd's hook. The Hebrew letters that spell the word Gal (גל) define it as "The Wealth (ג) of Authority (ל)".

Can we explain this clearly? There is no wealth more valuable than the wealth of God. He ordained a letter within His language to assist us to understand that. That letter Gimel (ג) represents a Camel or Great Wealth. The letter looks like a camel. Remember Abraham sent his unnamed faithful servant with ten camels of wealth to go find his son a bride. Those camels carried some of Abraham's wealth. Is it surprising that we are learning that His wealth is concealed in His revelations? Only God has the authority to reveal His wealth.

We have chosen to document the research of the variations of the word "reveal" that are used in scripture. We won't do this in the future but felt it necessary to "show our work" this time. Let's see if we can search out some of His wealth. Enjoy the journey and prepare for amazing revelation as we reveal the revelations of the many Hebrew words translated as "reveal", "revealeth" and "revealed" in the KJV translation of the divine and inspired Word of God.

The word "**revealed**" is found in the Old Testament of the KJV 13 times. There are nine different Hebrew words translated as "revealed". Those nine Hebrew words are in the Hebrew Old Testament (called Tanakh) 27 times. Below are the nine Hebrew words and how many times each Hebrew word occurs in the Hebrew Old Testament (Tanakh). When the word is found one time, then the verse is also provided. Note that the common letters found in each word are (גל) and have a bold font.

ונהגלת One time (Deuteronomy 29:29)

יגלה Seven times

נגלה Four times

גליתה One time (2 Samuel 7:27)

ונגלה Six times

נגלתה One time (Isaiah 53:1)

להגלות One time (Isaiah 56:1)

גליתי Three times

גלי Three times

Above are the words translated as "**revealed**". Likewise, below are the three Hebrew words that were translated as "**reveal**" in the KJV. These three Hebrew words are found in the Tanakh 9 times.

יגלו Three time

וגליתי Five times

למגלא One time (Daniel 2:47)

One more time, below are the five Hebrew words translated as "**revealeth**". These five Hebrew words are in the Tanakh 44 times.

מגלה Nine times

גלה Twenty-Three times

גולה Nine times -- eight of nine refer to deportation of some sort

גלא Two times (Daniel 2:22, 2:28 revealer of secrets)

וגלא One Time (Daniel 2:29 revealer of secrets)

Summarizing, there are a total of 17 different Hebrew words that are translated as either "Reveal", "Revealeth" or "Revealed" and six of them are unique, only used one time in scripture. These 17 Hebrew words are found in the Hebrew Old Testament (Tanakh) 79 times. These three forms of the word reveal are in the KJV 51 times which means that there are 28 occurrences in the original text where these same Hebrew words are translated as something other than "Reveal", "Revealeth" or "Revealed" in the KJV. All but one of these seventeen Hebrew words contains the word Gal (גל) within their spelling.

To eliminate even the slightest amount of conjecture, let's review the ten verses where the Hebrew word Gal (גל) is used within the Old Testament.

Genesis 31:46 is the first time that both words Gal (גל) and Stones (אבנים) are in the Hebrew text. Note that the first time the word "stones" is in the KJV is Genesis 28:11 and it is not the same Hebrew word nor the same spelling.

Genesis 31:46 KJV: And Jacob said unto his brethren, Gather stones (אבנים); and they *took stones* (אבנים)*, and made an heap* (גל)[1]: and they did eat there upon the heap (הגל)[0].

Note that in verse 45, Jacob (Israel) erects a stone as a pillar (monument). Now his brethren Gather stones and make a *heap (mound) of stones*, and they eat. Also notice that the last word heap in Genesis 31:46 is not the root word spelling of reveal, so it has a superscript value of zero.

Joshua 7:26 KJV: Then they raised over him *a great heap* (גל)[2] *of stones* (אבנים), still there to this day. So the Lord turned from the fierceness of His anger. Therefore the name of that place has been called the Valley of Achor to this day

Joshua 8:29 KJV: And the king of **Ai** (העי) he <u>hanged</u> on a tree until evening. And as soon as the sun was down, Joshua commanded that they should take his corpse down from the tree, cast it at the entrance of the gate of the city, and raise over it *a great heap* (גל)[3] *of stones* (אבנים) that remains to this day.

Hilarious, the King of (AI – artificial intelligence) is "<u>hanged</u>" from a tree. Is it revealing that Joshua whose name means "God is Salvation" hung AI from a tree and then at evening piled a great heap of stones (Father and Son) over him?

2 Samuel 18:17 KJV: And they took Absalom and cast him into a large pit in the woods, and laid *a very large heap* (גל)[4] *of stones* (אבנים) over him. Then all Israel fled, everyone to his tent.

Job 8:17 KJV: His roots are wrapped *about the heap* (גל)[5], and seeth the place of *stones* (אבנים).

So, the first five occurrences of the word Gal (גל) is translated as HEAP and related to a Heap of Stones. Let's continue.

Psalm 22:8 KJV: He *trusted* (גל)[6] *on the LORD* that he would deliver (יפלטהו) him: let him deliver (יצילהו) him, seeing he delighted in him.

Note that several translations (NASB 1995, Living Bible, etc.) translate this as literally meaning "To Roll" by the LORD. And the two words translated as deliver are both unique words only used once in the Bible. And the last one has two Yods (י) similar to the word "formed" we searched out earlier. This verse ***PLAYS A HUGE ROLE*** later in our research.

Psalm 119:18 KJV: *Open thou* (גל)[7] mine eyes (עיני), that I may behold wondrous things out of thy law.

Also translated as "Expose or Reveal Yourself" to my eyes. Two Yods (יי) in a word seems to be common but it's not. The fact that it is common in these verses is not surprising.

Psalm 119:22 KJV: Remove (גל)[8] from me reproach and contempt; for I have kept thy testimonies.

Proverbs 16:3 KJV: Commit (גל)[9] thy works unto the LORD (יהוה), and thy thoughts shall be established (מחשבתיך).

Again, other translations (NASB 1995, Legacy Standard Bible, etc.) translate this as literally meaning To Roll thy works unto the LORD. The word "established: is in the KJV 72 times but the Hebrew word translated as "established" is only in the Hebrew Old Testament twice.

So, the previous four verses show the occurrences of something being rolled or something done to expose something. Now it's time to see His wealth, the "thing" He chose to conceal and requires us to search out. The **last** occurrence of Gal is located in the book of the Song of Solomon. Hilarious, right? A book so difficult to understand and seldom researched. What a GREAT PLACE to conceal something!

Song of Solomon 4:12 KJV: "My *darling bride is like a private garden* (גל)[10], a spring (נעול) that no one else can have, a fountain (נעול) of my own.

The final, tenth occurrence of the word is translated as a private garden in the King James and is compared to "My darling bride". The Hebrew word (נעול) is only in the Old Testament twice and both times are in this verse. Coincidence?

Glory to the King!

9 798224 851423